SECOND EDITION

LEARNING IN TWO WORLDS

An Integrated Spanish/English Biliteracy Approach

BERTHA PÉREZ
THE UNIVERSITY OF TEXAS, SAN ANTONIO

MARÍA E. TORRES-GUZMÁN
TEACHERS COLLEGE, COLUMBIA UNIVERSITY

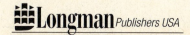
Longman *Publishers USA*

Learning in Two Worlds:
An Integrated Spanish/English Biliteracy Approach, Second Edition

Copyright© 1996, 1992, by Longman Publishers USA.

Longman, 10 Bank Street, White Plains, N. Y. 10606

Associated companies:
Longman Group Ltd., London
Longman Cheshire Pty., Melbourne
Longman Paul Pty., Auckland
Copp Clark Longman Ltd., Toronto

to Nydia, Analisa, Justin,
and all the children in our lives

Production editor: Ann P. Kearns
Editorial Assistant: Matt Baker
Cover Design: Dorothy Wachtenheim
Text art: Fine Line Inc.
Production supervisor: Winston Sukhnanand
Compositor: University Graphics

Library of Congress Cataloging-in-Publication Data

Pérez, Bertha, Date.
    Learning in two worlds : an integrated Spanish/English biliteracy
approach / Bertha Pérez, María Torres-Guzmán. — 2nd ed.
        p.   cm.
    Includes bibliographical references (p.) and index.
    ISBN 0–8013–1572–7
    1. Education, Bilingual—United States. 2. Spanish language-
Study and teaching (Elementary)—United States. 3. English
language—Study and teaching (Elementary)—United States.
I. Torres-Guzmán, María E. II. Title
LC3731.P465 1996
371.97 00973—dc20   95–4930
                                          CIP

1 2 3 4 5 6 7 8 9 10-MA-9998979695

Credits

We give special thanks to the students and teachers at the Pájaro Unified School District, the Freedom School, and the San José Unified School District, the Olinder School, for their contributions to this text and to José B. Morales for his gracious contribution of photographs.

Excerpt, pp. 24–25: Reprinted by permission of the publisher from Ana Huerta-Macías, "Child Bilingualism: To Switch or Not to Switch?" in Theresa H. Escobedo, ed., *Early Childhood Bilingual Education; A Hispanic Perspective* (New York: Teachers College Press, © 1983 by Teachers College, Columbia University. All rights reserved.), pp. 23–25.

Figure 2.1: A. B. Anderson and W. H. Teale, "La lecto-escritura como práctica cultural." *Nuevas perspectivas sobre los procesos de lectura y escritura* by E. Ferreiro amd M. Gomez Palacio (eds.). México City: Siglo Veintiuno Editores, 1982. Reprinted by permission.

Figure 2.2: María Alzugaray's class, the Olinder School, San José Unified School District, San José, CA. Reprinted by permission.

Figure 3.2: Mafalda by Quino, in *Los sistemas de escritura en el desarrollo del niño,* by Ferreiro/Teberosky. Buenos Aires, Argentina. Reprinted by permission of Joaquin Salvador Lavado—Quino.

Figure 3.4: Nydia M. Zamorano-Torres, P. S. 84, Community School District 3, New York City.

Excerpt, p.76: Max Velthuys, *El Gentil Dragón Rojo*. Valladolid, Spain: Editorial Miñón.

Figure 4.1: Damian Campos, Freedom School, Pájaro Unified School District, Watsonville, CA. Reprinted by permission.

Figure 4.2: María Alzugaray's class, the Olinder School, San José Unified School District, San José, CA. Reprinted by permission.

Figure 4.3: Carlos Acosta's class, Olinder School, San José Unified School District, San José, CA. Reprinted by permission.

Figure 4.4: Carlos Acosta's class, Olinder School, San José Unified School District, San José, CA. Reprinted by permission.

Figure 4.5: Vivian Baltrusis, *Voy a Leer Escribiendo*. Hato Rey, Puerto Rico. Story by Roberto Torres, University Lab School, San Juan, Puerto Rico. Reprinted by permission.

Poem, p.105, "Desfile del Circo," E. Feliciano Mendoza, *Ilán-Ilán*. Rio Piedras: Editorial de la Universidad de Puerto Rico, 1985, pp. 25–26.

Figure 5.1: Ester Hernandez, Pájaro Unified School District, Watsonville, CA. Reprinted by permission.

Figure 5.2: "Vamos a" from Mrs. Ordonez's class, P. S. 84, Community School District 3, New York City. Reprinted by permission, "Pelea" from Mrs. Foster's class, P. S. 84, Community School District 3, New York City. Reprinted by permission.

Figure 5.4: María Alzugaray's class, the Olinder School, San José Unified School District, San José, CA. Reprinted by permission.

Figure 5.5: María Alzugaray's class, the Olinder School, San José Unified School District, San José, CA. Reprinted by permission.

Figure 6.2: M. Osorio, *La Mariposa Dorada*. Valladolid, Spain: Editorial Miñón, 1985.

Figure 6.3: Nydia María Zamorano-Torres, "Development of a Chick," Reprinted by permission.

Figure 7.3: Taken from: Barrera Rosalinda, "Reading in Spanish: Insights from Children's Miscues" and Sarah Hudelson's "An Investigation of the Oral Reading Behavior of Native

Spanish Speakers Reading in Spanish." In: Hudelson, Sarah (ed.) *Learning to Read in Different Languages.* Washington, D.C.: Center for Applied Linguistics, 1981.

Figure 7.5: J. Flores et al., "La Pájara pinta." New York: Macmillan, 1987.

Figure 7.7: Reproduced with permission from K. S. Goodman, Y. M. Goodman, and W. J. Hood: *The Whole Language Evaluation Book* (Heinmann: Portsmouth NH, 1989).

Figure 7.8: I. M. Tiedt et al., *Reading/Thinking/Writing*. Boston: Allyn & Bacon, 1989. Reprinted by permission.

Figure 8.2: M. Torres-Guzmán and the parents of the San Antonio Independent School District, *Incidental Teaching Techniques*.

Contents

Foreword

Biliteracy for Personal Growth and Social Participation

Alma Flor Ada

Language is among humankind's highest achievements, one that might even be called a defining characteristic of humanness. All civilizations, whether in the Amazonian jungles, the Arctic Circle, the Pacific islands, or the lofty peaks of Tibet, have developed symbolic systems that allow people to share feelings and emotions, generate and express ideas, recount the past, and plan the future. But although all cultures develop a central language, and all languages fulfill their particular culture's communicative needs, cultural approaches to literacy vary.

As diverse as their origins, the materials for recording language may take the form of Incan knots on wool threads, delicately drawn Egyptian hieroglyphic or Aztec pictographs, Babylonian imprints on bricks, or Slavic marks on birch bark. Systems of writing, whether ideographic, syllabic, or phonetic, also vary. The purpose and social function of writing itself differ significantly in different times and different lands.

Often tied to sacred rites and religion control or political rulers, the knowledge of encoding and decoding language has traditionally been the province of a few and has carried with it privileges and power.

In a highly literate society such as the present-day United States, the ability to read and write restricts or opens possibilities for work and survival and influences people's daily lives in innumerable ways.

Children from homes in which the spoken language is other than English are faced with complex contradictions as their schooling and the process of becoming literate begin. In most instances parents see education as their children's only avenue to a future life better than their own. These parents, who frequently have had very limited schooling, trust that educators will know what their children need and will provide them with the tools for academic and societal success. Often their traditional upbringing makes them regard the school with a deep respect, perhaps deriving from an earlier linking of school with church. It is very common for Hispanic parents to tell their children to behave in school as in a temple and that teachers deserve their respect and should be looked upon as their second father or mother.

Consider, then, the contradiction facing such children, who have looked up to their parents as teachers, mediators with reality, and transmitters of value, when they enter school and are presented with a curriculum that ignores or devalues the home language and culture.

Since the early 1970s, enlightened educators in the United States have recognized that acquisition of reading and writing requires that beginning readers be able to glean meaning from the text, be rewarded with immediate understanding of the meaning of written words, and find validation of their predictions. These educators have proposed or implemented various forms of bilingual education in which children have learned to read in their home language.

But the use of the mother tongue at school, necessary as it is if children's linguistic rights are to be respected and their learning potentials are not to be hindered, is far from sufficient. The schooling process can be restrictive, domesticating, and oppressive in two languages as well as in one.

If schools make bilingual education an optional practice—in contrast to the required teaching of mathematics, science, or social studies, for example—parents receive the message that the school is not as committed to the bilingual program as it is to the rest of the curriculum.

A double standard exists in practice in our school system. High school and college credits are granted to native English speakers who learn some rudiments of another language, but advanced standing and recognition through credits are not given to children who come to school with a knowledge of a language equal or superior to that acquired through "foreign" language instruction. This double standard sends the message to students whose first language is not English that their home language is not worth maintaining.

By failing to bridge the gap between a highly literate school, with its book-driven curriculum, and homes where literacy is not prevalent, the school system disempowers parents in the eyes of their children. For these children, accepting the school curriculum often results in a sense of shame about their own language and family, yet maintaining cultural identification may bring a sense of alienation from the school, a feeling that they do not belong in the kind of classrooms that ignore or devalue their culture.

Bertha Pérez and María Torres-Guzmán, conscientious educators and responsible scholars, have brought a significant contribution to the dialogue concerning the education of Hispanic children. They have developed a text that combines theory and practice, recognizing the teacher's potential for intellectual discourse and the need for all classroom practice to be supported by analysis of the theories behind the practice as well as the social implications. Thus, they begin their book with a discussion of the role that cultural identity plays in the definition of the total person and the need to look carefully at the culture, as embodied in the students, that is present in the classroom. They then look beyond the walls of the classroom to the relationship of culture to power.

The authors present basic sociolinguistic principles that will help clarify why children in our schools who speak a language other than English have a valuable resource that deserves recognition. Drawing on cognitive theories and the current literature on the development of reading and writing skills, the authors provide clear explanation of the underlying theories that support their methodological premises, following up with a direct and specific orientation to setting an integrated biliteracy process in motion.

For those of us who value and love books, who believe that an adequately developed ability to read and write will enable our youth to open doors to the richness of printed words and gain a better understanding of the world, this book is a valued contribution.

All children have the right to have their language and cultural identity recognized by the school. They all deserve to be encouraged to carry on a dialogue with the books they read, in order to recognize that protagonists live not only on printed pages, but in daily life and that all children are indeed the valued protagonists of their own life stories. All children also deserve to be invited to become authors— of the stories born of their fantasy and experiences and of the stories conveyed to them by their parents and relatives.

María Torres-Guzmán and Bertha Pérez have much to say that will contribute to bring about this awareness. May you, the reader, be rewarded with the excitement of helping children enter with joy into the world of books while realizing their potential as authors and their existence as protagonists.

Prefacio

El bialfabetismo para el desarrollo personal y la participation social

Alma Flor Ada

El lenguaje es uno de los logros más importantes del ser humano, de tal forma que se puede llegar a pensar que es uno de los rasgos definitorios de la condición humana. Todas las civilizaciones, desde las selvas Amazónicas hasta el círculo Artico, desde las islas del Pacífico hasta las más altas elevaciones del Tíbet, han desarrollado sistemas simbólicos que permiten que se compartan sentimientos y emociones, que se generen y expresen ideas, que se narre el pasado y que se planee el futuro. Pero, aún cuando todas las culturas evolucionan alrededor de un lenguaje, y todos los lenguajes son intrínsecamente autosuficientes para cumplir las necesidades comunicativas, las culturas han diferido en cuanto a sus enfoques respecto al alfabetismo.

Los materiales para registrar el lenguaje son tan diversos como los lugares en los que se han originado—nudos incas en cordeles de lana, jeroglíficos egipcios o pictogramas aztecas delicadamente trazados, impresiones babilónicas sobre ladrillos, marcas eslavas en cortezas de abedules—y los sistemas de escritura, ya sean ideográficos, silábicos o fonéticos también varían. El propósito y la función social de la misma escritura ha sido significativamente diferente en distintas épocas y en tierras distintas.

A menudo, ligado a ritos sagrados y al control religioso, o a fuerzas del estado o de la nobleza, el conocimiento necesario para codificar y descodificar el lenguaje ha estado tradicionalmente en manos de unos pocos y se ha acompañado de privilegios y poder.

En una sociedad altamente literaria, como es la del día de hoy en los Estados Unidos, la habilidad de leer y escribir no sólo limita o amplia las posibilidades de trabajo y de sobrevivencia sino que también afecta la vida diaria de las personas de numerosas maneras.

Los niños provenientes de hogares donde se habla una lengua distinta al inglés se enfrentan a complejas contradicciones cuando comienzan la vida escolar y su proceso de alfabetización. En la mayoría de los casos los padres que los envían a la escuela ven la educación como la única vía posible para que sus hijos se labren un futuro mejor que el que ellos han tenido. Estos padres, que frecuentemente cuentan con una escolaridad muy limitada, confían en que los educadores sepan con certeza lo que sus hijos necesitan y provean a los estudiantes de los medios necesarios para obtener éxito académico y social. A menudo su educación tradicional los lleva a considerar la escuela con profundo respeto, lo que está probablemente conectado con una previa identificación de la escuela con la iglesia. En las familias hispánicas es bastante común decir a los niños que deben comportarse en la escuela como en un templo, que los maestros y maestras merecen respeto y que se los debe considerar como un segundo padre o una segunda madre.

Es necesario pensar por un momento en la contradicción que se provoca en los niños que han estado viendo a sus padres como a maestros, mediadores con la realidad, transmisores de valores, y que, cuando comienzan la escuela se ven enfrentados con un programa que ignora o desvaloriza la lengua y la cultura de sus hogares.

Desde principios de la década de los setenta, en los Estados Unidos, educadores esclarecidos han reconocido que la adquisición de la lectura y la escritura requiere que los lectores incipientes sean capaces de extraer significado del texto, se vean recompensados con una comprensión inmediata del significado de la palabra escrita y encuentren en ella una confirmación de sus predicciones. Estos educadores han propuesto o implementado varias formas de educación bilingüe gracias a lo cual los niños han podido aprender a leer en la lengua de sus hogares.

Pero el uso de la lengua materna en la escuela, por más necesario que sea si se respeta el derecho linguístico de los niños y si su potencial para el aprendizaje no se restringe, está lejos de ser suficiente. El proceso de escolarización puede ser restrictivo, subyugador y opresivo en dos lenguas tanto como en una sola.

Si las escuelas hacen de la educación bilingüe una práctica electiva—al contrario de la enseñanza de las matemáticas, las ciencias o los estudios sociales, por ejemplo—se les da a los padres un mensaje muy claro de que la escuela no apoya el programa bilingüe con la misma intensidad que dedica al resto del currículum.

Un criterio doble se lleva a la práctica en nuestro sistema escolar en la actualidad. Se otorga reconocimiento a los estudiantes secundarios y universitarios cuya lengua nativa es el inglés que aprenden los rudimentos de otra lengua, pero el sistema rehusa reconocer y dar una posición de ventaja a los niños que llegan a la escuela con conocimientos de una lengua iguales o superiores a los que se adquieren a través de la enseñanza de una lengua «extranjera». Debido a ese criterio doble, los estudiantes cuya primera lengua no es el inglés reciben el mensaje de que no vale la pena mantener la lengua que hablan en casa.

En su fracaso para llenar el vacío entre una escuela altamente literaria con un currículum guiado por libros y los hogares donde no se practican ni la lectura ni la escritura, el sistema escolar disminuye a los padres ante los ojos de sus hijos. Para estos niños, la aceptación del currículum escolar resulta a menudo en un sentimiento de vergüenza de su propia lengua y de su propia familia, mientras que el hecho de mantener su identificación cultural puede resultar en un sentimiento de alienación respecto a la escuela, una sensación de ser ajeno en una sala de clase que ignora o desvaloriza su cultura.

Bertha Pérez y María Torres-Guzmán, educadoras conscientes y estudiosas responsables, han aportado una contribución significativa al diálogo sobre la educación de los niños hispánicos. Han desarrollado un texto donde se incluye tanto la teoría como la práctica. Reconociendo el potencial de los maestros para la disertación intelectual así como la necesidad de que toda la práctica hecha en la sala de clase esté apoyada en un análisis de las teorías en las que se basa y en las implicaciones sociales de dichas teorías, las autoras comienzan el libro con una discusión del papel que la identidad cultural tiene en la definición de la persona como un todo y en la necesidad de observar cuidadosamente la presencia de la cultura tal como se personifica in los estudiantes y en la clase. Ellas trascienden los límites de las paredes de la sala de clase al examinar la relación que existe entre cultura y poder.

Las autoras proveen al lector con un entendimiento de los principios sociolingüísticos básicos que servirán de ayuda para poner en claro la idea de que los niños de nuestras escuelas que hablan una lengua diferente al inglés poseen, por cierto, un valioso recurso que merece ser reconocido.

Basándose en su familiaridad con las teorías cognitivas y con la bibliografía actual sobre el desarrollo de las habilidades para la lectura y la escritura, las autoras ofrecen una comprensión clara de las teorías subyacentes que fundamentan sus premisas metodológicas, y le proporcionan también al lector una orientación directa y específica para llevar a cabo un proceso integral de bialfabetismo.

Para aquéllos de nosotros que valoramos y amamos los libros, que creemos que la habilidad para leer y escribir, si se desarrolla en forma adecuada, podrá capacitar a nuestra juventud para abrirse las puertas a la riqueza de la palabra impresa, y al mismo tiempo para obtener una mejor comprensión del mundo, esta obra es una colaboración sumamente valiosa.

Todos los niños tienen el derecho de que la escuela reconozca su lengua y su identidad cultural. Todos ellos merecen que se los aliente a establecer un diálogo con los libros que leen, para poder reconocer así que los protagonistas no sólo viven en la página impresa, sino también en la vida diaria—ya que todos los niños son protagonistas valiosos, los protagonistas de las escenas de su propia vida—. Todos los niños merecen que se los invite a ser autores—de las historias nacidas de su propia fantasía y de sus experiencias propias, de las historias que les transmiten sus padres y sus parientes—.

María Torres-Guzmán y Bertha Pérez tienen muchas cosas que decir que contribuyen para que surja la conciencia de todo lo aquí expresado. Ojalá usted, el lector o lectora, se vea recompensado con el entusiasmo de ayudar a que los niños penetren con alegría en el mundo de los libros al mismo tiempo que hacen realidad su potencial como autores y protagonistas de su existencia.

Acknowledgments

Our knowledge about biliteracy has mushroomed during the last two decades, with numerous textbooks, articles, workshops, and courses on the art and science of teaching and learning in bilingual contexts now available. Never before have we had such a variety of resources! Nonetheless, we are a long, long way from finding ultimate answers to the many difficult questions we have been asking about first and second language learning and teaching. We have grown accustomed to the absence of definitive solutions, as we have become used to the vicissitudes of sociopolitical opinion that affect us as bilingual educators. However, through many small, determined steps we have made great progress toward our goal of educating Latino, Spanish-speaking children in the United States. It is our hope that this book will be another small, determined step toward that goal.

The idea of this book grew out of courses in the areas of theoretical foundations and methods of language arts, Spanish reading, and second language teaching that I have taught at San José State University in California, the University of Texas at El Paso, and the University of Texas at San Antonio. My first debt of gratitude is therefore to my students—for their insight, enthusiasm, and support. During the last several years, my students have offered invaluable comments on many of the concepts developed in this book, and I have attempted to incorporate those insights and ideas.

Thanks are also due to the teachers and staff of Olinder Elementary School, San José Unified School District, who have allowed me to observe, study, teach, and learn from them and the children. In particular, the second and fourth graders have given me many of their ideas and writing samples and have patiently tried out many of my ideas—some of which did not make it into this book. I am also very appreciative of Alma Flor Ada's generous interest and critique.

I feel a deep sense of gratitude to María, who throughout the development and writing of this book kept us focused on the "big questions" and theoretical issues. My appreciation of her as a colleague and friend has grown as a result of our collaboration on this project.

Finally, I owe a very special thanks to my husband, Xavier, not only for his help and assistance in reading and editing numerous drafts, but mostly for being there and being supportive throughout.

Bertha Pérez

To Bertha's acknowledgment of veteran and novice teachers and their students, I would like to add a special thanks to the teachers and students of P.S. 84 for their work and the photos and to their district coordinator, Ruth Swinney. Ruth and I are engaged in continuous dialogue and constantly share our thoughts about culture, language, learning, and literacy—about knowing life in Latin America, experiencing the joys of reading Spanish literature, and appreciating the richness of our linguistic and cultural heritages. All of this has come into play in the preparation of this book.

And to Xavier, I would like to add my appreciation for his active yet nonintrusive support. I did not see a lot of his unselfish giving, but learned to appreciate it.

I want to add a few names of people who, for me, were instrumental in the early stages of this book: Ellen Clark, for helping me to put the project in perspective; Frederick Erickson, for encouraging me and helping me to demystify the process of book writing; and James Crawford, for teaching me about the pride of authorship and writing. And special thanks are due to Alma Flor Ada for her critical perspective throughout the process and to Rosalma Zubizarreta for her help with the section on children's literature.

My own daughter, Nydia, has been the inspiration for much of what I have become in the last decade, and she contributed with her writings and illustrations. Needless to say, I am appreciative of her patience and acceptance.

But the most important person was Bertha. She was the force, and her friendship, the inspiration. She challenged me to think and write about many ideas that flowed from my insistence on making connections between culture, language, and instruction in bilingual/bicultural settings.

One day as I sat there writing, I finally realized that what I was seeing in print was the result of different voices in collaboration. The concept of integration was constantly on my mind because it was central to our project. Yet, I began to understand that in our own attempt to present an integrated methodology, we were confronted with the struggle *for* and *of* voices in the process of collaboration and felt a sense of incompleteness as we approached our deadline. We were, in essence, a living example of Vygotskian thinking: in the cooperative mode we were reaching potentials beyond those we had been able to achieve individually. Although I felt comfortable and safe in this cooperative mode, I was confronted with surfacing tensions between my individual voice and our collective voice. What were *my* views about literacy? What could I compromise? How could I do this with a dear friend and colleague?

I was relieved when reminded that this had been faced by many others who had also had the experience of coauthoring. Putting aside future possibilities, I undertook the rewriting and editing with a sense of acceptance. I saw my task as making ideas, connections, and concepts more explicit. In doing so, and by engaging in dialogue with Bertha, I found out that our voices coincided at many more levels than I had initially thought. We were both growing, together and separately, and we both saw the need to struggle to integrate ideas that teachers are faced with day after day.

Bilingual/bicultural teachers face an awesome task of integration in their classrooms and our struggle was no different. We were struggling to find a voice in the direction of integration at multiple levels, to create legitimate intellectual spaces for the emergence of multiple classroom voices, and as two people in the process of "becoming." What eventually came through was a humbling and liberating feeling of incompleteness. The more I rewrote, the more I realized what "becoming" was about. The process is a lifelong companion. The more I realized this, the stronger my conviction became that one way of helping teachers is to emphasize the incompleteness of our ideas.

Contained in this book are but a few ideas. Although many of them are based on the integration of theory and practice, we, as teacher educators, can never be expected to do the work teachers must do for themselves in their classrooms. The tension between theory and practice continues as teachers try out, adapt, and change some of the ideas contained in this book. The most I felt we could do was to encode bilingual/bicultural classroom literacy practices in ways that novice and veteran teachers could understand and by which they could challenge.

I was privileged to have Bertha's healthy, competitive, and supportive friendship. Through mutual respect, it was possible to stamp this book with some of the voices within me.

María Torres-Guzmán

We would like to thank Naomi Silverman, the senior editor and valued guide of the first edition, and Laura McKenna for her patience and assistance in the preparation of this second edition. We would like to acknowledge the following reviewers of the first and second editions:

- Alma Flor Ada, University of San Francisco
- Lisa Baldonado, St. Thomas Aquinas College
- Carmen L. Canales, California State University–Hayward
- Ines Marquez Chisholm, Arizona State University West
- Ellen R. Clark, University of Texas–San Antonio
- Jesus Cortez, California State University–Chico
- Marcos Guerrero, University of San Francisco
- Patricia Alba Mulligan, Cal Poly San Luis Obispo
- Irma Josefina O'Neill, State University of New York–College at Old Westbury
- Suzanne Peregoy, San Francisco State University
- Betty Sunday, Western Illinois University

Introduction

Like the first edition, this second edition of *Learning in Two Worlds: An Integrated Spanish/English Biliteracy Approach* proposes to address how teachers can organize the curriculum and the learning environment to enhance growth in literacy in both Spanish and English, with particular emphasis on the Spanish-speaking student's needs. Although the focus is on Spanish and English, we believe that others can benefit from the principles on which we base the book. For children who come to our schools speaking a language other than English, developing literacy in the language for which they have oral forms is essential. Children who use their first language to solve problems and discuss abstract ideas also learn to use a second language in similar ways. A substantial amount of research (among others, Cummins, 1981; Hakuta, 1986; Krashen, 1985b; Mace-Matluck, 1982; Ramirez, 1991) has shown that the most effective route to English language literacy for language minority students is through a strong foundation in their first language. Whether both languages are introduced simultaneously or consecutively is not as critical. As Hornberger (1989:287) so aptly states, the determining factor is that "the first language must not be abandoned before it is fully developed."

The content and organization of this text once again reflect our belief that integration of the children's language and cultural knowledge becomes the key principle for literacy instruction and organizing literacy environments. Speaking, listening, writing, and reading activities are integrated and organized as natural happenings in the context of exploring the world of things, events, ideas, and experiences in schools and communities. An integrated biliteracy approach allows for the development of literacy skills around children's interests, strengths, and needs. The children use all of their language tools for both literacy and cognitive development.

The goals of our integrated biliteracy program emanate from the unique characteristics and needs of the bilingual child whose first or home language is Spanish. These goals are:

- to attach significant meaning to literacy by using the child's sociocultural, situational, and Spanish/English linguistic background;
- to create teaching/learning classroom rules that enhance and expand literacy;
- to assist students in developing linguistic and cultural repertoires;
- to develop the essentials in the four cue systems (graphophonic, syntactic, semantic, and pragmatic) in the child's first language;
- to enhance the interest and appreciation basic to the independent pursuit of literacy as a source of pleasure, information, intellectual development, and creativity; and
- to encourage teacher observation, planning, and organization around children's strengths and needs and with a vision of the future.

As in the first edition, this rationale served as the foundation for the chapters that follow. In Chapter 1, we discuss social and cultural perspectives of literacy.

After examining the role of culture in literacy learning in general, we suggest that the culture of the various Latino Spanish-speaking communities is a powerful resource that could be used for achieving literacy. In Chapter 2, we examine the developmental characteristics of the child learner. The nature of language, the Spanish/English language system, and biliteracy contexts are presented in Chapter 3. In Chapters 4, 5, and 6, we share teaching ideas that engage the student in relating thinking, reading, and writing processes through meaningful lessons and learning experiences that are based on the child's cultural and linguistic systems. In those chapters, we present the elements of an integrated biliteracy approach and how to create and organize social interactions to facilitate the development and use of literacy. We present activities that incorporate oral language to support growth in working with the written language, and we stress the importance of showing students how all of the literacy skills connect and how their own thinking processes work. We suggest ways of assessing student progress in an integrated biliteracy program in Chapter 7. In Chapter 8, we suggest how to organize the literacy environment and how to make parents and community resources part of the learning experience. We also provide a list of children's Spanish literature.

The notions in this book that serve to organize the presentation of an integrated biliteracy approach in bilingual/multicultural education settings emerge from theories of learning and culture, theories and research on literacy and bilingualism, classroom experiences, and work with many teachers. The intent, however, is not to be prescriptive, but to provide current information that will help you make sound educational decisions about your biliteracy program. We ask that you focus on the meaning conveyed by the examples of the approach. But rather than focus on getting the lesson right from the perspective of transposing what we provide to your classroom, we ask that you alter, change, or implement the organization of instruction and the lessons by taking into account your community, school, and classroom. Our goal is to guide you on the road to enabling your students to name their world, understand the world of others, examine these worlds critically, and engage in transforming both themselves and others in the process.

NEW TO THIS EDITION

Each chapter contains expanded and updated information. New end of chapter activities will assist the student in understanding and integrating the concepts and content. The end of chapter activities from the previous edition are included, but have been divided into discussion and field-based activities with new and modified activities added where needed. New, reflective journal activities are also included. The purpose of these activities is to model the types of student/teacher activities suggested throughout the book.

The discussion on the role of culture in literacy development in Chapter 1 has been clarified and strengthened. The discussion on the development of writing in Chapter 2 has been updated to include new research on principles of writing development and on children's construction of theories of writing. The discussion on code-switching in Chapter 3 has also been updated to include information we overlooked in the first edition as well as new studies and examples that strengthen the case for viewing code-switching as the creative communicative process that it is. The instructional activities in Chapter 4 and Chapter 5 have been updated and a new section on authors that highlights Latino writers has been added to Chapter 5.

The literacy in the content areas in Chapter 6 includes new discussion of the constructivist teaching approach and authentic instruction in the content areas. The classroom activities in this chapter have been revised within the context of the new information.

The discussion of assessment in Chapter 7 has been reorganized around the purposes of assessment and the use of portfolios for organizing the assessment process. Information found in the previous edition has been revised and included in the section on an array of classroom assessment strategies.

Resources in Chapter 8 have been updated to include information on how to access developing technologies. The children's literature annotated books include selected titles published since the previous edition; it constitutes an updated and comprehensive, but not all-inclusive, recommended list. This chapter also includes end of chapter activities that are new to this edition.

PART I

Pensamiento y cultura: La integracion de nuestras ideas

CHAPTER 1

Society, Culture, and Literacy

Chapter Overview

Multiculturalism: A Matter of Definition?
Culture and Schooling
Cultural Repertoire or Culture and Power

INTRODUCTION

Literacy is a set of cultural practices that includes the encoding and decoding of print and is used to convey a message that has specific shared meaning for a group of individuals in a particular context (Conklin, 1949; Basso & Anderson, 1973; Heath, 1983; Street, 1984). Print, from the very beginning of history, has had multiple purposes: accounting, record keeping, surveying property, and so on. Different societies have developed numerous uses for print and, by extension, have defined literacy according to their societal needs. Different usage patterns have also emerged among social groups associated with occupation, class distinction, ethnicity, or gender. Furthermore, differences in definition and cultural practice have been found at many levels: the broader social context, the community and family context, the school and classroom context (Moll & Díaz, 1985), the context of interaction (Erickson & Shultz, 1981), and the context of the transaction with the text (Rosenblatt, 1978). These varied cultural practices involving print have been called literacy events. Thus, to understand literacy events in the lives of a particular people, how they define literacy, and the purpose for which they use print, one must identify its context.

Teaching and learning literacy is no less a social phenomenon. The standards and behaviors associated with learning how to encode and decode print are communicated intergenerationally and negotiated in social interactions among adults, among adults and children, and among children in their homes, school, church, and other community institutions. In any of these settings, the social event called teaching/learning has been defined as an interactional accomplishment (McDermott & Roth, 1979). It is dynamic in nature and provides the child with the potential and opportunity to evolve from a learner of that culture, which is transmitted intergenerationally, into an individual who participates in generating culture in concerted activity with others (Moll & Díaz, 1985). New ways of defining and studying literacy go beyond the definition of literacy as a universally defined set of skills constant across time and place (Ferdman, 1990:186) and are increasingly challenging the content of the curriculum and the organization of classroom learning environments. Educators are confronted with the difficult task of deciding what a reading and writing curriculum should be and how to organize the learning in classrooms where the student population, and the context of literacy, are multicultural.

This chapter will develop a framework for organizing literacy in the classroom by examining relationships among culture, identity, and learning. Specifically, the chapter will deal with significant issues of multiculturalism, discontinuity, and miscommunication in cross-cultural interaction, culture in the classroom, and cultural repertoire.

MULTICULTURALISM: A MATTER OF DEFINITION?

For the most part, students participating in bilingual/multicultural classrooms share common histories and lived experiences that differ from those embodied in the school curriculum and those that often constitute the experience of school staff.

Neither the education of culturally and linguistically diverse populations, also referred to in the text as ethnolinguistic populations, nor the use of more than one language as a medium of instruction is a new topic in the history of education in this country.[1] We are experiencing a renewed interest in the issues of multiculturalism, literacy, and bilingualism.

Many educators, unfortunately, still think of culture in ways that render the concepts almost useless in bilingual/multicultural settings. In many well-intentioned programs attempting to incorporate the cultures of their multicultural populations, the following misconceptions about culture and cultural groups continue to emerge as organizers of curricula:

- Cultures are viewed as static rather than dynamic. (For example, the Mexican culture can be incorporated into the curriculum and school setting through the use of folk art [*piñatas, sarapes*, etc.], symbols [Aztec calendar], music [*jarabe tapatío* and other dances, etc.], and other similar expressions.)
- Homogeneity characterizes descriptions of culture. (For example, all Spanish-speaking groups are the same; all Chileans are the same.) *No, different groups, linked them by language*
- Some cultures are held up as models to which other groups ought to aspire. (For example, we need to enrich the cultural experience of Puerto Rican students in the Bronx by exposing them to Lincoln Center and the Metropolitan Museum.)

These assumptions, based on popular misconceptions and even scholarly presentations, perpetuate stereotypes and constrain our thinking about what culture looks like in the classroom. Let's take a closer look at these assumptions.

Ways of Viewing Culture

Viewing culture as a set of finite characteristics and behaviors of a people can lead to the inclusion of supplemental readers in social studies or reading programs and to activities involving foods, costumes, holiday celebrations, and displays of artifacts (Matute-Bianchi, 1980). While these token steps are in the direction of inclusion, this view of culture itself thwarts the effort. Culture is not solely the physical characteristics of a group of people, the artifacts (dress, food, music, etc.), and the behaviors associated with the group (the language they speak or the religious practices they engage in). We can describe the uniqueness of a particular cultural group by attending to some of these aspects, but we also need to attend to the relationships of specific cultural characteristics to each other and to the whole, and the conditions under which these relationships hold. For example, to draw on the image of the brown-eyed, straight-haired, dark-skinned "*cholo*" with baggy pants who likes to go cruising in a low-rider Chevrolet and eat *tacos* at the *taquería* (a fast food stand or place) does not begin to describe the range of Chicano adolescent experiences. Nor does it begin to describe under what conditions some, or all, of the elements may come together. It does not even give basic information about regional, gender, or class issues involved. This view of culture does not permit us to see its dynamic nature nor the role of individuals in the maintenance and change of cultural ways.

We rely on Goodenough's (1971) definition of culture as "the standards for ways of thinking, feeling, acting, and judging which are learned from and shared by a group of people." We recognize that people not only share patterns *of* behavior but they also share patterns *for* behavior (Erickson, 1987). The shared patterns help those who are members of the group, and those who are not, to understand how people act in consistent and recurrent ways. Understanding patterns helps the person from the cultural group, and the outsider, to determine what must be anticipated in a given situation with a given set of people in order to be judged as competent (Hymes, 1972b). The patterns of behavior are, in turn, standards for evaluation; the appropriateness or inappropriateness of an individual's behavior is judged according to the group's standards.

Acknowledging broad social patterns is important, but we believe it is vital to recognize that human beings are adaptive, creative, and dynamic. They constantly challenge the standards governing group behavior, placing their stamp on what occurs. When individuals or groups of people are confronted with the new or unknown, the cultural knowledge they have acquired through lived experiences and histories helps them to think about the new situation and frame new creations or solutions. Cultures are dynamic and undergo constant change. Variations and change occur in the relationships between individuals and groups over extended periods of time and when different groups come in contact with each other. It is important to understand both patterns and variations as a way of speaking about the dynamics of a group and the cultural context for literacy within it. Individuals need to be seen as cultural beings as well as individuals in the process of becoming; people must not be typecast, but discovered.

Whose Culture?

One of the major difficulties people have had with the reduction of culture to an established body of Western civilization ideas and works is that this simplification often negates the richness of the non-Western cultural traditions of the nation. Both Hirsch in *Cultural Literacy* (1987) and Bloom in *The Closing of the American Mind* (1987) propose that the essence of Western civilization can be captured in a dictionary-like presentation of facts, concepts, and "basic" terms, which is to say that culture is static and homogeneous in the United States. And this presentation of culture is what all members of this society would aspire to, in order to be judged literate.

One of the responses to Hirsch and Bloom that, at first glance, deals with the narrowness of their definition is Simonson and Walker's (1988) anthology of multicultural literacy. The anthology includes literature that is representative of non-Western cultural groups that are integral to the identity of this nation. It includes works by James Baldwin, Eduardo Galeano, Paula Gunn Allen, and Carlos Fuentes. At the end of the anthology, the editors include a preliminary list of places, terms, phrases, and concepts that are commonly excluded from U.S. educational textbooks, but that are part of the everyday life of the people of this nation, such as advertising, co-parenting, cool (personality attribute), nuclear waste, and Rosa Parks. Although Simonson and Walker deal with the pitfalls of reducing culture to a description of facts and a definition of terms, they don't depart significantly from the presentation of a few authors and terms themselves.

Even when multicultural literacy is attempted, as in the Simonson and Walker case or that of the Los Angeles Unified School District, where supplemental readers include literature from the Latino and Cambodian folktale traditions and others, literary treatment is incomplete. Only some aspects of culture are presented, usually the standard and upper-class versions, whereas others are ignored.

The threat of incompleteness is ever present. In your attempt to organize a literacy curriculum, and in our attempt to present to you a biliteracy approach in this book, we both confront this threat. To achieve the goal of authenticity, change and continuous reassessment become part of the process. We must always be vigilant against some basic misconceptions, however; the content of much of the multicultural education curriculum has as its reference the standard cultures of groups and is limited to what can be found in print and artifacts. In other words, the curriculum fails to present the importance of variations within and among groups.

One of the ways variation is excluded from school curricula is through simplification and generalization in the presentation of cultural groups. Latino populations, for example, are often presented as a homogeneous group. This lack of understanding of the complex characteristics of Spanish-speaking groups reflects the views of the larger society. A rendition of the musical *West Side Story* at Stanford University in the early 1980s, in which the Puerto Rican gang members' dance resembled a combination of the Mexican *bamba* and *tapatío*, is an example of how such misconceptions are publicly displayed. (See Guilliamin, 1972, cited in Ferdman, 1990, for a discussion of how majorities view minorities and vice versa.)

Latino[2] is an umbrella term for the populations of twenty-one different Spanish-speaking countries. The term also includes the Mexican and Spanish populations that reside in the U.S. Southwest, which was Mexican territory prior to 1848, and the indigenous non-Spanish-speaking populations in the Latin American countries. The differences among these groups can be compared to differences between an English-speaking Australian and an Englishman, both of whom speak English but are from distinct groups.

There are differences among Latinos not only because they come from different countries, histories, and national cultures, but because of their historical relationships to the United States as distinct national groups. In a comparative study of Mexican Americans and recent immigrants from war-torn countries such as El Salvador, Guatemala, and Nicaragua, Suárez-Orozco (1987) finds that the groups' perceptions of, and behaviors toward, schooling differ significantly. Mexican Americans, who had "experienced a long history of depreciation" (p. 161) in the United States, were more likely to see themselves as occupying the lowest-paying and most undesirable labor sector, as generations before them had. Recent immigrants from the other countries, however, seemed to believe in the possibilities of a better job and more desirable position in life in the United States than they had had at home. This different starting point of Latinos, Suárez-Orozco argues, makes a difference in their attitudes and behaviors toward school, teachers, and peers.

On a national level, the largest Latino groups are Mexicans or Mexican Americans, Puerto Ricans, and Cubans. The Dominican group is growing rapidly.

The largest concentration of *mexicanos* is in the Southwest, whereas Puerto Ricans are most numerous on the East Coast, as are Dominicans. The Cuban population is largely concentrated in Florida. Each group has a history, a political perspective, a literary tradition, and language and cultural features that are unique. Although many Latinos draw from these rich traditions to negotiate meaning, create identity, and achieve status, they also draw from their daily experiences in the *barrios* (communities), the *ranchos* (farm/rural communities), the suburbs, or wherever they have settled in the United States.

Similarly, excluding indigenous languages, the language used by the various groups is different, although mutually intelligible. An aspect of literacy programs in Spanish/English bilingual programs must be to encourage respect for linguistic diversity while promoting unity. Children must come to understand that language is arbitrary and that there is absolutely nothing wrong when Pepe writes *chiringa* (kite), whereas Sara writes *huila* and Carlos writes *papalote* for the word *kite*. All are not only legitimate ways of expressing the same concept, but manifestations of the richness of the cultural traditions from which they come.

Another way multicultural curricula exclude variation is by presenting unidimensional segments of a culture as models for the group as a whole. Usually, the models are representative of the social classes in power or what is perceived as high culture. For example, the curriculum of Puerto Rican history that presents the works of writers such as Virgilio Dávila, Evaristo Ribera Chevremont, René Marqués, Luis Lloréns Torres, and Ramón Méndez Quiñones or of historians like Salvador Brau and Ricardo Alegría would be a significant improvement over the total exclusion or the negative views of Puerto Ricans presented in many texts. But this presentation would be equally incomplete if it did not include the work of women, such as Lola Rodríguez de Tió and Julia de Burgos; of freedom fighters, such as Clemente Soto Vélez and Juan Antonio Corretjer; of Puerto Ricans in the United States, such as Nicholasa Mohr, Tato Laviera, Pedro Pietri, Martín Espada, and Sandra Esteves; and, most important, the experiences and untold histories of Puerto Ricans in the United States and on the island. Distortions of Puerto Rican culture abound because the multiple perspectives and complexity of the group's historical and social conditions are ignored.

In addition, Latinos perceive differences within groups that have ramifications in schooling and classrooms. Aside from the traditional ways in which status is achieved, that is, by having money, obtaining a college education, or being a white-collar worker or professional, there are other ways Latinos perceive status differences. When we were growing up, going to a Catholic girls' high school offered prestige to the working-class female living in the *barrio* for two reasons. Attending high school was already going beyond the level of education obtained by most of the community members; attending a private school required a family and personal sacrifice that warranted admiration. Although by U.S. norms this did not actually represent a change in social status, for the community members, achieving status was as much the experience of surpassing community norms as going from one rung of the social ladder to another. Who you are in relation to the *barrio* in this country, or who you were in your country of origin, is also important in relation to achieved status. For example, being a fourth- or fifth-generation Chicano living in the same *barrio* gives an individual a certain degree of pride and respect, and thus status. Being a leader in Chile against Pinochet in the 1970s also raised the status of some individuals who were political refugees in San José, California. Stratification based on social class, gender, family or personal histories, educational attainment, and the like have much to do with the attitude, competence, and behavior a student brings into the classroom.

The unsophisticated presentation of Latino groups and the preference for high culture convey implicit and explicit messages to children about themselves and their relationship to others. Theories about what children do with these messages, and how these messages are integrated in the *why* and *how* of children's success or failure in school, are the topics of the next section.

CULTURE AND SCHOOLING

We believe that promoting cultural diversity is an important school goal and classroom policy. Urban centers and, consequently, student populations in schools in the United States are becoming increasingly diversified both linguistically and culturally as the U.S. economy continues to develop into a more global economy. A case could be made for promoting multicultural curricula solely on this basis, but the critical issue goes beyond the goal of appreciation for other peoples and their cultures. U.S. schools have failed dismally in schooling children from linguistic, cultural, and social backgrounds other than those traditionally implicit in American classrooms. Answers to the whys and hows are not easy to come by. The complexity of sociopolitical and economic situations makes a simplistic response even more disheartening. In this book, we do not propose to address the various theories on culture and learning and their relationship to success and failure; instead, we will focus on those theories that are most relevant to presenting a guide to an integrated biliteracy program.

Cultural Identity and Schooling

One of the theories focuses on the variations among ethnolinguistic groups in school performance and on addressing the *why* question. Central to this theory is the belief that the community's approach to validating its own culture and the learning of a new one is important in explaining how children engage in school tasks and the outcomes of such engagements.

Ogbu (1974; 1987a; 1987b) proposes that students' internalization of social and economic structural inequities in the broader society and of the collective identities of their community group is important in their approach to schooling. Ogbu (1987a) distinguishes between groups that have historically entered the United States more or less voluntarily and those that have entered through force or involuntarily. By taking into account the historical conditions under which groups came together, he constructs a collective cultural framework that helps explain both intergroup relationships and community/school relationships. Ogbu (1987a) identifies what he calls castelike minorities[3] (African Americans, Mexican Americans, Puerto Ricans) and immigrant minorities (Costa Ricans, Hondurans, Punjabis) and proposes that

> among castelike minorities both the identity system and the cultural frame of reference are in opposition to those of the dominant group. Castelike minorities, furthermore, tend to equate school culture with dominant-group culture, so that the cultural frame of the school is also in opposition to that of the minorities. [They] view schooling as a one-way acculturation or assimilation process. . . . There is, therefore, the possibility of conscious and/or unconscious opposition and an "affective dissonance" toward learning in school or "acting White." The dilemma for an individual black student or other castelike minority student is that he or she has to choose between academic success or "success in the White way" and being a member of his or her group. (p. 274)

The immigrant does not necessarily employ the same cultural framework. (See the work of Gibson, 1983, 1987a, 1987b, with the Punjabi; Ogbu, 1974, with the African American, Mexican American, Chinese, and Japanese; Ogbu, 1987a, 1987b, and Matute-Bianchi, 1980, with the Mexican American and Japanese; and Suárez Orozco, 1987, with Central Americans and Chicanos.) Immigrants tend to separate "those aspects of the school culture which facilitate academic success and learn to conform to them in ways considered essential for school success within general white American culture" (Ogbu, 1987a, p. 274). By making such distinctions, many immigrants are able to maintain their language and culture while they acquire those skills necessary for educational success and economic survival. They learn about and integrate behaviors and perspectives appropriate for the school environment. The adaptation permits them to switch between home and school culture without the inner conflict of violating either one and without a crisis of identity. Immigrants, as opposed to the castelike minority, do not tend to act from an oppositional cultural frame of reference.

The explanation is a powerful one at the macro level because it exposes the sociostructural patterns that infiltrate everyday classroom life. It helps explain why some groups "experience persistent disproportionate school failure" (Ogbu & Matute-Bianchi, 1986, p. 73). However, the framework fails to present a dynamic view of culture and class and tends to perpetuate the view of individual members of a group as "cultural dopes" (Garfinkel, 1967). It does not explain why some members of a castelike group are able to maintain their language and culture while succeeding in school, nor why some immigrants choose resistance and oppositional behavior. It also renders insignificant the social realities in which individuals and groups opt for adaptive behavior, such as many second- and third-generation Puerto Ricans born in the United States no longer being able to speak Spanish fluently.

Culture in the Classroom

The second major explanation of the differential performance of ethnolinguistic groups in schools focuses on the interactional participation of teachers and students, schools, and communities in educational success or failure. It proposes that schools play a role in perpetuating or changing what occurs in a classroom made up of children from backgrounds that differ from the implicit American classroom culture. How teachers organize learning environments in the classroom can either provide access to, or create barriers to, children's learning. The connection between instruction and culture is critical to this view. The cultural categories used to organize instruction, and the symbolic and political significance of these categories within broader social relationships, become the filters through which a student reads the intent and meaning of social interaction within a lesson.

Numerous studies that have examined home and school culture have helped us to understand how culture and learning are dynamically interconnected (Philips, 1972; Mohatt & Erickson, 1981; McDermott & Gospodinoff, 1981). Philips (1972, 1982) found that the poor school performance of Warm Spring Indian children could be specifically linked to classroom contexts, or "participant structures," that demanded individualized performance, emphasized peer competition, and required that the teacher maintain control of performance styles and publicly display the incompetence of students by making corrections. The Indian children were more likely to show competence, on the other hand, in classroom contexts that were similar in organization to local Indian patterns of communication. In the community, the group rather than the individual was emphasized, cooperation rather than competition was valued, and demonstrating skill and ability through physical activity or display of material evidence rather than the verbal articulation of competence was expected. Similarly, when the Indian children were involved in group projects in school, they learned more and performed academic tasks more successfully than when engaged in academic tasks organized around the one-to-one teacher-controlled interactions characteristic of most classrooms.

Delgado-Gaitán (1987, 1994) proposes a similar relationship between home and school cultural discontinuity and academic performance. She identified patterns of learning environments found in Mexican American homes that differed from those found in schools. At home, the Mexican American children in this study were engaged in tasks that were collectively organized. The authority figure was not cueing and directing the task verbally, or identifying next steps: Adults assigned tasks and children asked questions for clarification. Children negotiated compensation with the adult and participation with other siblings. The adults exercised their authority by clearly establishing that the children show obedience and respect by complying with requests. The members of these households had a seemingly unspoken rule that a child could elicit help from other children and that, if the task called for collectivity, other siblings were expected to help. Furthermore, tasks were organized in ways that tapped into the reservoir of the children's multiple talents and resources (collective competition, resourcefulness, imagination, observation, decision making, and Spanish language proficiency). Delgado-Gaitán compared this to the learning environment of school-organized tasks, such as worksheets that focus on the cognitive competency of memorization, and concluded that the children who participated as competent members of their cultural group were likely to find engagement in the school-organized learning environments somewhat difficult. She concluded, as did Philips (1972), that the discontinuities between home and school can result in miscommunication between teachers and children, and that children may fail in school because the social conditions required for participation are not those they have become accustomed to in their communities.

Rodríguez (in progress) documents literacy events of working-class, Dominican preschoolers in an urban setting, including the ways in which literacy was part of their daily lives. For example, their dealings with public agencies such as the school, the church, the court, and the welfare system all created literacy events. In addition, she describes how the three families studied used music and dance, highly valued cultural forms in the community, in literacy situations. Rather than the middle-class bedtime stories, singing and praying were the bedtime routines. She suggests that songs and singing "play an important role in the development of vocabulary and the development of a schema of story" (p. 250). Print on TV is also a vehicle for literacy, and she uses TV to explore the children's hypothesizing about the meaning of print. It is clear from the children's responses that they were learning to interpret the print that appeared on the screen and that their interpretation was contextualized by family discussions associated with such print. Rodríguez documents how the exploration of print can be as enjoyable as any other type of play and compares this type of play with play as a literacy event in school. She concluded that "for these Dominican children, literacy appeared to be mediated by significant others who knew more about print, by the different media present at home and in society, such as television and music, and by daily activities such as play" (p. 251). She suggests that schools can use these as starting points for literacy assessment of young children and in the development of literacy programs.

Such studies of cross-context comparisons demonstrate that different communities organize learning in a variety of ways. They also organize literacy differently. For example, Heath (1983) found that literacy events in two communities were organized very differently and that both types of literacy events differed from school-related literacy.

> Roadville and Trackton residents have a variety of literate traditions, and in each community these are interwoven in different ways with oral uses of language, ways of negotiating meaning, deciding on action, and achieving status . . . in Roadville, the absoluteness of ways of talking about what is written fits church ways of talking about what is written. Behind the written word is an authority, and the text is a message which can be taken apart only insofar as its analysis does not extend too far beyond the text and commonly agreed upon experiences. New syntheses and multiple interpretations create alternatives which challenge fixed roles, rules, and "rightness." In Trackton, the written word is for negotiation and manipulation— both serious and playful. Changing and changeable, words are the tools performers use to create images of themselves and the world they see. For Roadville, the written word limits alternatives of expression; in Trackton, it opens alternatives. Neither community's ways with the written word prepare it for the school's ways. (pp. 234–235)

Not only were literacy events organized differently, but ways of communicating, as in the Warm Spring Indian case, were different. For example, the language use characteristics of the classroom differed from the language use in Trackton homes in three major ways: (1) children from Trackton had not had practice in responding to utterances that were interrogative in form but directive in pragmatic function (e.g., "Why don't you use the one on the back shelf?" vs. "Use the one on the back shelf"), (2) they did not have much familiarity with known information questions, and (3) they had little experience with questions that asked for information from books.

This view of the relationship between culture and learning is also powerful in another way. It focuses on how failure occurs in a situated way, in the context of the classroom. From a practical standpoint, as teachers, this is exactly where we want to focus our attention. As Ogbu and Matute-Bianchi (1986) point out, however, focusing on cultural and linguistic differences does not help us to explain why some groups "do quite well in school in spite of cultural and language barriers" (p. 74).

Erickson (1987) proposes that elements of both theoretical explanations can be integrated. Although students' refusal to learn and participate in school in ways that are expected of them has roots in broader sociohistorical and economic conditions and intergroup relationships, the school practices that perpetuate the perceived or real "domination and alienation . . . [do] not simply happen by anonymous workings of social structural forces. People do it. It is the result of choice (not necessarily deliberate) to cooperate with the reigning ideological definitions of what minority students are, what curriculum is, what good teaching is" (pp. 352–353).

Our decision to focus on literacy from a cultural standpoint and to conceptualize what happens in the classroom as a social interaction between teachers and students and among students is deliberate. We feel that the task of teaching literacy in bilingual/multicultural settings goes beyond the teaching of skills in decoding and encoding in two languages. The role of educational programs in helping students develop pride in who they are as well as improving their academic skills is critical to developing alternative social relations between groups and a better world for all. We agree with the conclusion of Erickson (1987) and other scholars (Ferdman, 1990; Cazden, 1988; Moll & Díaz, 1987; Vogt, Jordan, & Tharp, 1987) that "culturally responsive pedagogy is one kind of special effort by the school that can reduce miscommunication by teachers and students, foster trust, and prevent the genesis of conflict that moves rapidly beyond intercultural misunderstanding to better struggles of negative identity exchange between some students and their teachers" (p. 355).

Using Community Resources
to Transform Classroom Culture

Heath (1983), based on her understanding of the differences between communities and schools, worked with social studies teachers in Roadville and Trackton to develop lessons with questions that were more congruent with the students' ways of speaking and understanding. The teachers asked children for personal experiences and analogic responses (e.g., "What's happening there?" "Tell me what you did when you were there and who was with you." "What's this building like?") that were more like the questions parents asked at home. Thus, the community became a resource for transforming the classroom experience for the children. The students were also taught the language of school, thus enabling them to perform academic tasks that required them to name objects, provide descriptions out of context, and perform other such activities.

Au and Jordan (1981) also reported on a reading program based on the premise that, when organizational structures found in the Hawaiian culture are brought into the classroom, these can make negotiating the meaning of print more accessible to Hawaiian children. The Kamehameha Reading Program, while using a commercial English language basal reader, organized lessons similar to *talkstory* and *storytelling*, linguistic events of importance in the Hawaiian culture. The features were the following:

1. The teacher (an adult) was an established socially relevant figure whose status was earned both by demonstrating warmth for the children and by maintaining control, and whose approval the children valued highly.
2. The interactions of the children and the teacher were characterized by mutual participation, in which both narration and interpretation were jointly constructed and where co-narration of the story occurred as a speech event.
3. The lessons combined both school and informal learning as features, whereby the students' cultural knowledge was incorporated and whereby the interaction revolved around the successful completion of the task rather than on rule statement.

These lessons were organized to emphasize story comprehension, and the reading scores of the Hawaiian children, as measured by standardized tests, improved dramatically. This case demonstrates that children who come from cultural backgrounds other than those implicit in American classrooms, even when they speak English, may benefit from the organization of learning environments along lines that are more culturally relevant to them. Mohatt and Erickson (1981) propose that culturally relevant instruction has

> meaning even when the referential language of the children is English . . . [The] invisible cultural rules survive and remain quite strong long after the children lose their referential language, although this in no way implies that referential language is unimportant for culture. Systematic cultural differences appear in classroom interaction even when everyone speaks English. (p. 109)

Children who come from homes in which the use of print and the language patterns differ from those of the school are faced with the task of mastering the rules governing the literacy events as organized in the classroom. Students whose language as well as language use differs from that of the school are faced with a larger task: the need to master a new code altogether. Not only do these children differ with regard to the type of experiences they may have had with print, and how they make meaning and talk about print, but they also face the added complexity of differences in language and culture. Silva (1983) refers to the associated issues of access to school literacy that these linguistic differences present.

> Because reading is a language-related process, the meaning of a text has to be accessible for a reader to interact with it. A reader needs to read in a familiar language to interact successfully with an author's message. Unless a child reads in a

language that he or she understands, the language-related strategies necessary to obtain meaning cannot be utilized. (p. 198)

Moll, Díaz, Estrada, and Lopes (1992) studied Spanish-dominant bilingual students participating concurrently in reading lessons in separate Spanish and English language classrooms. They found that the English reading instruction did not take into account the total language abilities of the students. Based on the assessment of English language proficiency, students were placed in low reading groups even when they came from top reading groups in the Spanish language classroom. They found that a similar discrepancy in instruction occurred in other areas and concluded that the students were not using higher-order skills, nor being challenged instructionally. Their findings about reading are a microcosm of the learning environments established in English-only classrooms.

A second study, by Moll and Díaz (1985), focused on the relationship between social interaction and individual cognitive development. Reading instruction in English was made accessible to students by tapping into developing and maturing behaviors beyond the children's level of independent problem solving and by making the lesson linguistically comprehensible. This accessibility helped students perform at the most advanced level possible and gave them the time to practice and to appropriate for themselves strategies for learning that eventually helped them direct their own behaviors. Thus, shifts in control of the task were organized.

Initially the responsibility for decoding the text was that of the instructors; the students were to listen. The emphasis was on comprehension, skills that the students had already developed in Spanish. The lessons were reorganized to address two of the students' needs: the development of oral language skills in English and the development of decoding, encoding, and negotiating meaning around print in the second language. The students were able to draw on their native language to demonstrate their understanding of the story. This is how Moll and Díaz (1985) explain their intervention:

It is best to teach children in the language they know the best.

In our bilingual situation, the students have at least *two entry levels* for reading: one in English, plagued by difficulties in verbal expressions, vocabulary, and so on, and a more advanced level as manifested in their Spanish reading lessons. For reading instruction to be proximal in *English* it has to be aimed at those levels manifested in *Spanish*. That is, English reading must be taught in the context of what the children can do in Spanish. What the children are doing in Spanish reading creates the *proximal* conditions for learning in English. As our data suggest, failure to relate Spanish reading to how reading is taught in English leads to lessons aimed at reading levels *beneath* the student's performance capabilities, levels that do not facilitate development. (pp. 137–138, italics in original)

Reading is a language

Although there are important differences in these studies as to language use, there are some commonalities that we would like to stress. All the studies examine literacy and the learning of literacy within a cultural context. The studies describe discontinuities of language use (within and across codes) and how learning environments are organized in the home, the community, and the school. In the Au and

Jordan (1981) and Heath (1983) studies, the rules for language use and the meaning associated with the different uses of language were significant. In the Moll et al. (1992) study, the language code itself was a source of discontinuity. All the school interventions described in these studies start from the premise that more effective communication and learning would occur if the resources of the community were incorporated in instruction. Because there is variation even among broadly defined cultural groups, the single-group studies provide insufficient information for organizing classroom instruction in multicultural classrooms (Nieto, 1992). Nonetheless, classroom interaction ought to be organized for sense making and understanding, as is evident in the previous studies. The organization of reading for comprehension (Moll et al., 1992; Au & Jordan, 1981) provides a flexibility that introduces community learning patterns and helps engage the student in encoding and decoding more successfully.

CULTURAL REPERTOIRE
OR CULTURE AND POWER

Promoting cultural diversity rather than ignoring it, in our opinion, is an important classroom policy. On an individual level, the goal is to develop an extensive *cultural repertoire*. An individual who acquires understanding and develops competency in different linguistic and cultural systems is said to have an extensive cultural repertoire (Guthrie & Hall, 1981). In this chapter, we have argued that in the development of literacy programs in bilingual/multicultural settings it is important to:

- validate the child's experience,
- acknowledge linguistic and cultural differences, and
- integrate the community as a resource in development.

In addition, we believe it is vital that students critically learn the language and culture of the dominant group so that they can participate in the affirmation and redefinition of self, the community, and the broader society (Nieto, 1992; Menchu, 1985). Thus, developing a cultural repertoire among students in bilingual/multicultural classrooms is, by definition, one of the goals of such a classroom.

We advocate a curriculum of cultural diversity that is transformative and futuristic in nature. Thus, developing a cultural repertoire through literacy refers to understanding the rules governing different contexts (such as those that govern participation at a salsa dance, a concert at Carnegie Hall, or communication through cyberspace) and understanding the different cultures (Salvadoran, Guatemalan, Dominican, Chinese, and others) embedded in the printed matter related to them and their evolving images (Rosaldo, 1989). In addition to knowing the rules, developing a cultural repertoire in a bilingual situation refers to enabling each individual to participate in cultural practices of more than one group, in more than one language, while maintaining, negotiating, and creating his or her identity at multiple levels. Although broader social constraints still impinge on the daily life of individuals, the possibilities of affirming, integrating, taking oppositional stands (Freire, 1970; Giroux, 1983; McLaren, 1989), and creating still exist. One of the major tasks in developing a literacy program is to enable individuals to assess their world critically and entertain the possibility of a different future.

We encourage you, in your role as a teacher in a specific community and with a specific set of students, to choose in favor of breaking with stigmatized views of children from backgrounds other than those embedded in the school culture and to be a learner and observer of the cultures and cultural ways that students bring into your classroom. We acknowledge that knowing about the culture will, in itself, be insufficient for you and your students; to be effective students of a culture, you must live the culture and study *in* it rather than *about* it (Bredo, Henry, & McDermott, 1990). We encourage you to attempt living genuine relationships with your students, and throughout the book we will suggest different ways of bringing cultural forms into your classroom to promote an environment of authenticity, creativity, and cultural diversity.

SUMMARY

The literature reviewed suggests the importance of the role of culture in learning. An assumption permeating the reviewed literature, and this book, is that school failure is *not* rooted in the language and cultural background of the children; the sources of failure can be found in both school organization and in more general societal processes. The reviewed literature assumes that children bring a richness of linguistic and cultural backgrounds into the classroom, thus making the search for their strengths a classroom imperative. In the programs described in the reviewed literature, culturally responsive alternative learning environments for developing literacy focused on comprehension skills and making meaning of the printed text and its context. These programs also assumed different relationships between teachers and students, students and students, and classroom and community, suggesting that schools underutilize the resources of their communities and students. Furthermore, we suggest that a different relationship should be fostered between published material and the children's experiences. Most important, we suggest that promoting cultural diversity can be a principle upon which to build more effective literacy programs.

ACTIVITIES

This chapter has focused on cultural issues. There are many ways of discovering culture in your surroundings. You can speak to people or observe them. Both are legitimate ways of finding out about what they do and how they think about what they do. Doing oral histories, observing the unfamiliar, or rendering the familiar as strange by making explicit those rules taken for granted are important ways of understanding culture. There are advantages to each of these ways. The following activities can help you reflect on various aspects of culture. Doing all the activities will give you a perspective different from doing only one of them. If you do all three, before going on to the next activity, reflect on what you have already learned. You may find you have new eyes or that your own interpretations get in the way of seeing something new. It is preferable that you write about what you have learned; later, you can go back to see what shape your own learning has taken.

Journal Writing

1. Keep a log of what you notice as you move through the day. Do this for a week. What senses did you use when you noticed things around you? What patterns do you find? How much is routine? Can you find anything that you do because that is how you were taught in your family?

2. Watch a regular news program and keep a log of cross-cultural or culturally/ethnically marked news items for a week. Make sure you write down details of pictorial images and words spoken. From this log, do an analysis of the public images of cultural diversity provided through the news. A variation would be to focus on sit-coms, sports, prime-time commercials, or music programs.

3. Write about how you felt as you undertook the second field-based activity at the end of the chapter. Be as honest as possible about what was triggering your feelings. Distinguish between your emotional state and reactions at the time of the interview and what was communicated by the interviewee or the individual observed. If you were to take your emotional state out of the observation or interview description, would your analysis differ? How judgmental were you?

Discussion Activities

1. In a small group, discuss what your thoughts about culture are and how they are similar or different from the definitions provided in the chapter. Was there any idea in the chapter that was new to you or that captured your attention?

2. Discuss in a small group or in pairs one area of knowledge you have that the curriculum in school never reflected, such as knowledge about cars, about cutting meat and meat parts, about sewing, about living on an island, or about fishing. What is the most unusual knowledge area in the class? Brainstorm about a literacy activity that you would develop using that knowledge.

Field-Based Activities

1. Observe parents and children at a park. How does the parent communicate to the child? What does the parent say and how does the child respond? What gestures (nonverbal, such as eye contact, smiles, etc.) are exchanged? What is their tone of voice? What kind and degree of physical contact occurs? (Are there kisses or hugs? Does the child run and play and frequently get close to the adult for a touch on the head? How often does this happen? How far does the child venture?) What function does silence serve? What can you speculate about the adult/child relationship from the observation of these interactions?

2. Interview parents from a cultural background different from your own. Ask them to describe how the family celebrates the children's birthdays, the naming and christening of

an infant, or some other family event. Let them talk about the celebration and, based on what they say, probe in areas you don't understand. When you think you know what they mean, ask them to confirm your understanding. For example, if they tell you they invited family members and some neighbors, you may want to ask how the guests were invited. In one type of family, telling the mother—if the mother is the conduit for family communication—may be the equivalent of sending out written invitations in another type of family. Think of the event in three segments: preparation, actual event, and afterward. Compare your findings with others who interviewed parents from the same cultural group.

3. Interview a classmate to find out what cultural experiences he or she may have had. Some of the questions you might ask are: What is his ethnic background? Where was she born? Where has he lived? What places has she visited for extended periods of time? What experience does he have with people from a different ethnic group? Reflect on the interview: Would you have guessed what you learned by looking at your classmate? How much of what this classmate said was surprising to you? Why? How does this change the way you think and feel about your classmate?

NOTES

1. In 1953, the United Nations Educational Scientific and Cultural Organization (UNESCO) recognized the need for native language instruction (vernacular education) in many parts of the world (Engle, 1975). Mackey and Orstein (1977) provide a capsulated picture of the linguistic diversity found in the world when they point to the 5,000 languages spoken in approximately 250 sovereign nation-states.

    In the United States, public bilingual/bicultural education began during the 1840s. A backlash because of the large number of non-English-speaking populations entering the United States in the late nineteenth and early twentieth centuries resulted in restrictive laws prohibiting instruction in other than English. A renewed interest in such education developed in the 1960s with the civil rights movement, which resulted in new efforts to protect minority rights. Title VII of the Elementary and Secondary Education Act, or Bilingual Education Act, of 1968 provided federal aid for transitional bilingual-bicultural instruction. In 1974, the Supreme Court of the United States in *Lau v. Nichols* ruled that public schools must provide special programs for students who speak little or no English. There have been several reauthorizations of and amendments to the Bilingual Education Act through 1994.

2. We prefer the term *Latino* to *Hispanic* in referring to all Spanish-speaking groups. The latter is not a well-received term by some groups because it is a political term associated with government functions and did not originate with the people themselves. Also, it excludes the legacy of the indigenous population. See Bean and Tienda (1987), *The Hispanic Population of the United States*, for a discussion of the historical development of the term *Hispanic*. The term and degree of acceptance are subject to regional and ethnic variation. Some people prefer other umbrella terms such as *La Raza*. Latinos are rapidly becoming the largest non-white group in the United States. There are over seventy languages, including Chinese, Vietnamese, Greek, Polish, Spanish, Russian, and Native American, used in federally and state-funded bilingual/bicultural programs in the United States. Approximately 60 percent (the number is estimated to be as high as 8,034,000) school-age children who speak a language other than English are from households in which Spanish is spoken. Although the context, broadly speaking, is the bilingual/multicultural classroom, the examples are primarily drawn from the experiences of children in Spanish/English programs.

3. Ogbu (I987a, b), Ogbu and Matute-Bianchi (1986), and Suárez-Orozco (1987) identify castelike minorities as groups originally incorporated into a society against their will who have been exploited and depreciated systematically over generations through slavery or colonization (e.g., Mexicans, Puerto Ricans). Immigrants (Costa Ricans, Colombians, Dominicans, Venezuelans, Punjabis, etc.), on the other hand, chose to leave their original environment, presumably intending to enter a more self-advantageous social realm.

CHAPTER 2
The Child Learner

Chapter Overview

Language Development in Bilingual Home Environments

Developmental Trends in Children's Learning

Language Acquisition Process

Observing Children

INTRODUCTION

As all good teachers (or prospective teachers) know, quality teaching requires that you know your students. You should know your students as persons and know about their general developmental, social, and cultural ways. When you meet a new group of students, you usually have expectations about their abilities and interests. In addition, their age level and cultural group help shape the character and direction of your instruction. Understanding children's cognitive development within cultural contexts, with particular emphasis on understanding first and second language development, is the foundation for helping Spanish-speaking children learn to read and write. The complexities of a child's language background may be obscured by erroneous assumptions of homogeneity among Spanish speakers, as we proposed in Chapter 1. To say that a child is a Spanish speaker or is bilingual is not enough to describe and identify the cultural and linguistic background that the child brings to the task of literacy. It is very important that each child be observed for specific strengths. The teacher must discover the child's cognitive, linguistic, and cultural strengths.

The topics explored in this chapter include the development of language in bilingual home environments, theories of cognitive development, the characteristics of language development during early childhood, and ways of observing and providing for children's unique differences.

LANGUAGE DEVELOPMENT IN BILINGUAL HOME ENVIRONMENTS

From birth, children are immersed in a sea of language through which they interact with people and things. Adults use language to communicate with infants and young children for various purposes: to make contact, give comfort, and direct behavior. These are authentic events in the life of the child. In home/community life individuals learn the language of their group, using it with ease, efficiency, and authenticity. And that language (*home discourse*), acquired readily and naturally, is the basis for all social activities, for enlarging any field of learning, and for acquiring and preserving useful knowledge.

In the Spanish-speaking communities of the United States, the language used by parents and caregivers of infants and young children may be Spanish, English, or both, to varying degrees. However, even when the home language is predominantly Spanish, the child is still exposed to English through radio, television, and community life (e.g., visiting the doctor, shopping, riding the bus). Some Spanish-speaking children come from homes where efforts have been made to separate languages, but the majority come from homes where children are daily exposed to bilingual linguistic environments with no conscious effort made to separate languages. The separation of languages in these homes occurs spontaneously when family members use one language with the child more frequently than the other. Parents and grandparents, for example, may use Spanish more often, but the child may be frequently spoken to in both languages by extended-family members and older siblings. When children live in Spanish-speaking *barrios*, communication in their community life may occur almost exclusively in Spanish. When children live in integrated neighborhoods, they will be constantly exposed to English. Children in either of these environments advance through the same language-learning tasks as children who learn one language (García, 1983a). Exposure to two language systems does not seem to alter the process of linguistic development (Hakuta, 1986). In other words, the children from these Spanish-speaking homes go through the same experimentation, construction, invention, and testing as do all children when acquiring language. In fact the use of both codes (Spanish and English) becomes one language system for the young child.

A number of studies of children who learn a second language during early childhood years document the ease with which many children learn more than one linguistic communicative form in many societies (Carrow, 1971, 1972; Padilla & Liebman, 1975; Bergman, 1976; Lindholm & Padilla, 1978). Most of these studies found little deleterious effect or confusion caused by bilingual language development. Children use the appropriate form (rule or structure) for both languages even in mixed utterances.

Huerta-Macías (Huerta, 1977; Huerta-Macías, 1983) conducted a longitudinal study of a bilingual (Spanish-English) child beginning when the child was two years old. She reports a comparable pattern of continuous development in both Spanish and English, although identifiable stages appeared in which one language forged ahead of the other. Christopher, the little boy studied by Huerta-Macías (1983), simultaneously acquired two languages in a context in which the one language-one person principle (one parent speaks Spanish to the child and the other speaks English) was not in effect; both languages were often used indiscriminately by the adults around him.

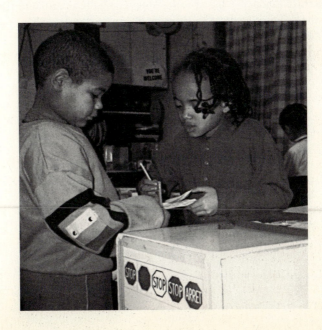

The Huerta-Macías study focuses on the effect of a mixed language environment upon the sociolinguistic and linguistic patterns emerging in the child's speech. The child differentiated sociolinguistically between the two codes. He separated them and developed a model of when to use each of his languages. The two languages interacted linguistically in his speech, but he adhered to the grammar of both Spanish and English, particularly in his mixed language utterances. In general, the child's linguistic environment was reflected in his speech and influenced his language development. He also displayed an awareness of the social context of language.

Sociolinguistic Awareness

Children develop a sense of sociolinguistic awareness; that is, they begin to separate their languages and differentiate the use of Spanish and English according to the speaker addressed. This generally occurs by the age of three, when children begin to separate their codes along the lines of the one language-one person principle. Children begin to use Spanish with perceived Spanish speakers and English with perceived English speakers. This awareness develops in homes where separation of language by speakers is not commonplace, where the mixing of languages is not discouraged, or where children are not told that they should use a certain language with certain speakers. The reasons children most often switch to a given language are the following:

1. The child uses the language most frequently used by the adult in interactions between them. For example, a child might speak Spanish to an aunt who consistently addresses and responds to the child in Spanish.
2. The child associates the use of a language with a particular person because this person is perceived to be more fluent in that language (Genishi, 1976; Fantini, 1974).

Linguistic-Code Awareness

Early in their language development children also develop an awareness of the use of two distinct language codes. They begin to explore "different ways" of saying things. Huerta-Macías (1983) describes Christopher's awareness of his use of two languages at $3\frac{1}{2}$ years old:

PARENT: *Quiero que usted me hable en español.* [I want you to speak to me in Spanish.]

CHILD: OK. *Casa, juguete, troca, carro.* [OK. House, toy, truck, car.]

PARENT: *Pero platíqueme en español.* [But speak to me in Spanish.]

CHILD: I am! *Troca!* [Truck!] You see?!

At a later time, while looking at colors in a book, he asks:

CHILD: How do you call brown *en español* [in Spanish]? (p. 23; our translation)

By $4\frac{1}{2}$ years old, Christopher was showing awareness of the differences in language codes in his own speech production. There was also some evidence that the differences were not always clear. At times, he was not sure whether to classify a speech act as Spanish or English and sometimes he refused to talk about differences between the language codes (Huerta-Macías, 1983):

ADULT: Look! Your grandpa bought tangerines.

CHILD: (about thirty seconds later) They're *naranjas* [oranges], but in Spanish we call them tangerines.

ADULT: And what do you call peaches?

CHILD: *Duraznos* [peaches].

ADULT: In English or in Spanish?

CHILD: I don't know.

ADULT: In English?

CHILD: I don't know.

ADULT: In Spanish?

CHILD: I don't know. (p. 23; our translation)

Studies of other children have found similar patterns of awareness by children speaking two languages and asking for translations (Fantini, 1974; Swain & Wesche, 1975).

Linguistic Contact

The mixed language utterances or "code-switching" of young children follow the grammatical applications of each of the languages (see Chapter 3 for a discussion of code-switching in the classroom). Children also seem to code-switch for reasons other than the absence of a given code (word) in a given language. For example, Christopher at $3\frac{1}{2}$ years old says *semillas* and then later within the same dialogue uses "seeds," while flipping through a story book on Sylvester and Tweety (Huerta-Macías, 1983):

. . . to eat it, that's why . . . then got some pie put *semillas* [seeds] and grandma put it on. Grandma says, "it ready," . . . Then Sylvester . . . throw a big *clavado* [dive], then step on truck and fall down, *y luego, y luego* [and then, and then] got *escalera* [steps] off and he hit him *así* [like this], and then *pa*! Got pie with *pescado* [fish] and seeds and then eat it, . . . (p. 25; our translation)

The mixing, however, is rule bound. Padilla and Liebman (1975), who studied the Spanish-English acquisition of two 3-year-old children, conclude that

the appropriate use of both languages even in mixed utterances was evident; that is, correct word order was preserved. For example, there were no occurrences of "raining *está*" or "a *es* baby" but there was evidence for such utterances as "*está* raining" and "*es* a baby." There was also absence of the redundance of words in the mixed utterances as well as the absence of unnecessary words which might tend to confuse meaning. That is, "*dámelo* that" or "*es un* a baby pony" did not appear, whereas "*dáme* that" and "*es un* baby pony" did occur. (pp. 406–407)

Garcia (1983a) summarizes the unique conditions under which Spanish-speaking children develop language in the following way:

1. Children are able to comprehend and/or produce some aspects of each language beyond the ability to discriminate that either one language or another is being spoken. [Linguistic character] . . .
2. Children are exposed "naturally" to the two systems of languages as they are used in the form of social interaction during early childhood. [Social character] . . .
3. The simultaneous character of development must be apparent in both languages. [Psychological/developmental character]. (pp. 13–14)

DEVELOPMENTAL TRENDS IN CHILDREN'S LEARNING

Learning is a dynamic process that is both social and mental. The learner acquires new knowledge and ideas and sees connections between ideas by actively forging mental representations, finding relationships, interpreting, retelling, and making meaning. Bruner (1994) defines learning as "a view that takes as its central premise that 'world making' is the principal function of mind . . ." (p. 28). In this constructivist perspective, children are the active transformers of their experiences with the world, picking and choosing what they need to recreate or to make their own world in their head. They use representational systems (e.g., symbols, language) to interpret and reinterpret their experiences. Bruner and other cognitive psychologists are concerned primarily with the mental construction of meaning or the building of knowledge structures. Anthropologists and sociolinguists view constructivism as social construction and negotiation of meaning among individuals within a specific cultural context. Some researchers suggest that children's learning occurs on a sociocultural plane and is internalized to the intrapsychological or internal cognitive plane. Hiebert (1991) explains that the ". . . labels that scholars use for this 'new' perspective, that is, constructivism, vary as a function of their disciplines. However, the diversity of labels should not obscure the similarity in the underlying views of literacy and learning held by these scholars" (p. 1). In these underlying views, children are active participants in creating their knowledge and in forging the representational systems they use to convey that knowledge.

Children's representational system (the symbols they relate to concrete concepts and experiences) is culture/community based. Language processes and their products (spoken word, scribbling, writing, stories) reflect children's underlying cognitive abilities and their social and emotional growth. Children's acquisition of language processes during early childhood years is a component of their developing representational system. Further, because language and thought are interacting systems, such representations function as a catalyst for intellectual growth.

thinking

Piaget's Theory of Cognitive Development

Piaget (1959) originated a theory of cognitive development. He theorized that intelligence develops as children adapt psychologically to their environment and reconcile discrepancies between current forms of understanding and new physical experiences that contradict those forms of understanding. According to Piaget, psychological adaptation has two components:

1. *Assimilation*—new information is transformed and incorporated into already existing structures.
2. *Accommodation*—already existing structures are modified to adjust to new information.

Initially, for example, a child may call all foods *papa* [potato]. Beans, rice, potatoes, and even meats are assimilated into the child's already existing structure or concept of *papa*. Later, as children begin to draw distinctions among different kinds of foods, they call foods by the names acceptable to their social-cultural group. Accommodation occurs as they expand their intellectual categories or cognitive structures to include different labels for different classes of foods.

Piaget referred to the cognitive or mental structure as a *scheme*. An individual uses *schemata* to adapt to and organize the environment intellectually. The information, conveyed verbally, visually, or in written form, does not in and of itself provide meaning. Meaning is construed by the observer based on previous background *knowledge structures*. These previously acquired knowledge structures, which we carry with us and have acquired through our own experiences, are called schemata. Schemata are created through interaction with the environment as an individual actively seeks to organize experiences and information according to internally construed common characteristics.

Schemata, then, are truly the building blocks of cognition. They are fundamental elements upon which information processing depends. They are like scripts waiting for a particular cast of characters to read them. They are personal theories about the universe that individuals carry around in their heads. Hence, the process of understanding new phenomena is the process of finding a configuration of schemata that offers an adequate account. For example, upon seeing a chicken for the first time, a young child may call it a bird because the chicken and the bird have some features in common: they both have wings, feathers, and appear to fly. But schemata are continually being changed and refined as the child assimilates and accommodates new experiences. When a stimulus or experience cannot be assimilated into an already existing scheme, the child accommodates by either modifying an already existing scheme or creating a new one. In the previous example, the child would ultimately develop a new scheme for chicken that encompasses both chicken and birds. Through active interaction with the environment, then, the child creates knowledge.

Table 2.1 provides examples of the various stages of development as conceptualized by Piaget. The importance of these stages for developing a literacy pro-

TABLE 2.1. PIAGETIAN STAGES OF COGNITIVE DEVELOPMENT

Stage	Characteristics	Example
Sensorimotor (birth to 2 years old)	Organizes sensations, controls muscular activity; learns about objects and forms ideas about world through physical manipulation	A toddler, in order to think about throwing a toy, must actually do it
Preoperational (2–7 years old)	Develops symbolic representation; manipulates symbols; engages in symbolic thought; ability to think without solely relying on trial and error	A child can examine measuring cups and imagine how they would relate to each other if stacked. The child can think before acting rather than having to think about the relationship while stacking
Concrete operational (7–11 years old)	Begins to understand construction of logical operations and their application to solution of concrete problems	A child can decenter perceptions from a single aspect of a problem and attend to several aspects and relationships between them (e.g., concepts such as conservation and reversibility)
Formal operational (11 years old and beyond)	Develops abstract thinking skills	A child can evaluate, hypothesize, and analyze

gram is the recognition that the child's ability to integrate symbolic referents (objects or experiences) to decipher and interpret the written word is also developmental. For example, children about six years old, at the preoperational stage, tend to fix their attention on a single aspect of a relationship. If two rows of the same number of coins are lined up one-to-one, equally spaced, and children of this age are asked if the number of coins in the two rows is the same, they are likely to judge the two to be equal. When the appearance of one of the rows is changed, by either spreading the coins out or bunching them up, the child is more likely to judge them as being unequal. A major criticism of Piaget's theory has been that young children are generally more skillful than he concluded. For example, Piaget believed that preoperational thought is highly egocentric, particularly in its earlier stages. When Piaget explained a very simple experiment to a preoperational child, warning the child in advance that he would have to explain the same experiment to someone else, the child simply repeated what he remembered of the directions without taking the listener's needs into account. However, more recent research does not support this conclusion (Donaldson, 1978). Donaldson describes how very young children have been found to show empathy for their peers, and some three-year-olds have been shown to adopt the special speech register called baby talk when speaking to infants.

In addition, Piaget did not believe that language is necessary for the development of intelligence. He did acknowledge that language provides a useful medium for symbolic functions. Representational skills, one of which is language, enable a child to think more quickly and efficiently. Yet according to Piaget, language and thought are separate, and it is not until the period of formal operations that language plays a direct role in the acquisition of knowledge.

Vygotsky's Language/Thought Relationship

Today, many researchers who believe that there is a closer relationship between language and thought than acknowledged by Piaget often refer to the work of the Russian linguist Lev Vygotsky for a theoretical rationale on the language/thought relationship. Vygotsky saw an interactive relationship among language, thought, and social conditions. Although language and thought are distinct and develop independently, it is not until the two systems fuse with the development of inner speech that logical reasoning develops. Young children use language not only to communicate, but also to plan and guide their behavior in a self-regulatory manner within the context of their society. The interpretative rules of language use are acquired through social interaction at a very early age.

Vygotsky's approach focuses more on social and cultural contexts and the use of language to solve problems. He described the function of language in a child's early years (Vygotsky, 1978):

> The specifically human capacity for language enables children to provide for auxiliary tools in the solution of difficult tasks, to overcome impulsive action, to plan a solution to a problem prior to its execution, and to master their own behavior. Signs and words serve children, first and foremost, as a means of social contact with other people. The cognitive and communicative functions of language then become the basis of a new and superior form of activity in children. (pp. 28–29)

So for Vygotsky, unlike Piaget, language initially serves a social function, and the cognitive and communicative functions evolve from this first general use.

Children's approaches to problem solving are socially mediated through formal and informal interactions with members of the culture group within what Vygotsky described as the "zone of proximal development." He defined it (Vygotsky, 1978) as "the distance between the actual developmental level as determined by independent problem solving and the level of potential development as determined through problem solving under guidance or in collaboration with more capable peers" (p. 86).

Gradually children become more independent in their ability to solve problems, although their style of cognitive functioning continues to be influenced by the cultural group. Children who develop language and problem-solving skills within bilingual contexts learn sociolinguistic, cultural, and cognitive systems that are likely to be different from those encountered in classrooms. Moll and Díaz (1985) have used the concept of the zone of proximal development to study second language learning in classrooms. They found that the native language could be used to bridge the gap between the level of cognitive functioning of the Spanish-dominant children and their linguistic performance in English. In other words, if the lesson were conducted totally in English, the children would understand more about the stories they read than what they could demonstrate. When they were given the opportunity to respond in their native language, the level of comprehension that they demonstrated was considerably higher. Thus, children were able to go beyond what they could do independently in English.

Successful achievement of each developmental task along the way to full maturity results in the child's ability to advance to higher, more demanding levels; failure leads to difficulty with later related tasks. Several influences from elements within the developing child and from sources outside may contribute positively or negatively to the child's growth. Like all children, the Spanish-speaking child follows an orderly progression of growth according to his or her own inner timetable of maturation. They reach the significant milestones of sitting, standing, walking, talking, and adapting on the basis of their innate capacity to do so and the cultural expectations placed on them. This progression may be altered slightly by specific environmental conditions that may enhance or delay development.

LANGUAGE ACQUISITION PROCESS

Language acquisition is one of the most important developmental tasks. All human cultures use language (at least in its spoken form) as a highly organized and systematic way of symbolically representing experience. The processes and skills required for mastering a language are basic and universal, unrelated to the specific language (English, Spanish, Italian, etc.) in which they are exercised. Because language helps children make sense of and master their world, it is intimately and interactively related to cognition. Language is a product of culture and an instrument of thought. Undoubtedly, language enhances and refines intellectual development and is necessary for higher abstract reasoning. In the first section of this chapter we introduced some characteristics of language development in bilingual home environments, and in the last section, we reviewed Piaget's and Vygotsky's theories. Now let us take a closer look at the process of language development from infancy through the primary grades.

Infancy

An infant's prespeech vocalizations exert a powerful influence on their caregivers. Crying, for instance, will bring an adult to the infant. The adult will check to see if the child is ill, needs feeding, needs a change of diapers, or needs comforting. When the child's needs are met, the infant stops crying and the adult is reassured of the baby's well-being. Prespeech appears to have three stages. The *crying* stage begins with the birth cry. About the end of the first month, the infant enters the *cooing* stage, using the organs of articulation (i.e., mouth, lips, tongue) to produce more varied vocalizations than the cry. The vocalizations sound like cooing because they are produced at the back of the mouth with the lips in a rounded position. *Babbling* begins about the middle of the first year. It sounds more like conventional speech than do earlier vocalizations because it consists of consonant-vowel combinations (e.g., ta ta ta, da da da, ga ga ga). The distinctive pitch contour of a baby's native language shows up very early during the babbling stage. Weir (1966) has reported that five- to eight-month-old babies of Chinese-speaking and American English-speaking parents had different intonation patterns in their babbling. The infants, even at this early age, could already be identified by their distinctive pitch patterns.

From birth, infants engage in the reciprocal play of communication. They employ systematic ways of expressing various intentions: they gesture, point, and use supports to pull objects nearer. What is more, their "conversations" with adults are even characterized by turn-taking features of the cultural group to which they belong. Thus, the communicative function of language is present in a baby's earliest vocalizations. Language develops in the service of fulfilling varied needs: predicting the environment, interacting with others, and reaching goals with someone's help.

As language develops the young child acquires labels for a rapidly growing store of facts and concepts about the world. At about a year old, the child begins to use one-word utterances, called *holophrases*, to represent an entire thought. Holophrases are an accompaniment to action; the child uses them to demand, declare, question, or describe a relationship. The initial use of language supports and is closely linked to action. Holophrases are entirely context-bound. Thus, if a child said *leche* [milk] without any specific clues from the environment, it would be impossible to know if the child meant "I see my bottle of milk" or "Give me some milk" or something else entirely.

Frequent *overextension* of a word to inappropriate categories is another characteristic of the very young child's speech. We are amused when a child calls any liquid *agua* [water]. This occurs because children begin to use words before they have acquired an adult sense of their full meaning. For the young child, the meaning of each word is comprised of a bundle of features. Children gradually add more features of a word's meaning to their understanding of the word until their combination of features for the word approximates that of an adult. Words acquired first are the most general. Initially, toddlers may label all hairy, four-legged creatures *gato* [cat]. Later, as they add more specific features to their concept of *gato*, they will discriminate among *gatos*, *perros*, *conejos* [cats, dogs, rabbits], and the like. Some researchers believe that perceptual features such as shape, size, or movement account for much of a child's early overextension.

Toddlerhood to Preschool

During this preschool period a child's linguistic development will increase dramatically as an incredible quantity of linguistic behavior is exhibited. Children will generate many words and combinations within a short period of time. By school age, they will not only learn what to say, but what not to say as they learn the social functions of their languages.

Telegraphic Speech. Usually between eighteen months and two years of age, a child begins to combine words into two-word utterances. This is a major achievement because it marks the beginning of the use of language to express relations and intentions. Between two and three years of age, children speak in sentences that consist mainly of nouns and verbs (*pájaro canta* [bird, sing; bird sings]), with some adjectives and adverbs. Prepositions, conjunctions, articles, and auxiliary verbs are usually absent. Speech at this stage is called *telegraphic* because it has the characteristic abbreviated form of the telegram.

Rule-governed and Systematic Development. Children process the speech that surrounds them and induce from this a latent language structure of their own. They explore the structures of their language-making constructions and the applications of these structures. For example, three- to four-year-old Spanish-speaking children say *yo lo poní*, instead of *yo lo puse* [I put it]. It is unlikely that the child has actually heard and imitated this form, and most Spanish-speaking children around this developmental stage make the same kind of error. The child has probably unconsciously overgeneralized by applying the past tense construction of regular verbs to irregular verbs. After all, if you get *comí* [ate] from *comer* [to eat] and *corrí* [ran] from *correr* [to run], why shouldn't the past tense of *poner* [to put] be *poní*? The errors in young children's speech are not random; they are consistent with the grammar children generate at a particular stage of language development.

Reading and Print Awareness. Just as children develop language through their earliest efforts to understand and control their world, so do they learn to organize and make sense of print in literate societies and cultures where print bombards the senses. As children encounter print in stores and supermarkets, along streets and highways, and on TV, they learn to read by themselves. Children learn to give meaning to authentic print and pictures in context. Young children will often point to print and ask, "What does that say?" They are aware that print communicates. They begin to perceive written text as "talking sheets," as Morrison (1987) so vividly puts it. Reading begins at this point of awareness.

Anderson and Teale (1982) describe how María, a three-year-old Spanish-speaking child, initiates her own attempts at prereading when she consults a TV guide in search of a program listing. The mother is watching *telenovelas* [soap operas] and María spends ten minutes going through the TV guide. Anderson and Teale (1982) describe the print event this way:

MARÍA: *Voy a ver otra cosa* [I'm going to watch something else]. (Goes to the TV and gets the TV guide. She returns to the sofa and begins to leaf through the TV guide)

MARÍA: *Mamá, ¿Qué día es hoy* [What day is today]?

MOTHER: *Viernes* [Friday].

MARÍA: (Turns five more pages and focuses on one page) *Voy a ver Popeye* [I'll watch Popeye] (pointing to a spot on the guide), *y voy a ver Bugs Bunny* [and I'll watch Bugs Bunny] (pointing to another part of the page).

MARÍA: *No, voy a ver La Mujer Maravilla a las 3:00* [No, I'm going to watch Wonder Woman at 3:00]. (Pointing to the 6:00 listing, she walks up to the TV, pretends to change the channel, places the guide on the TV, and returns to the sofa and pretends to watch her program) (p. 293; our translation)

María's parents had not taught or talked to her about the use of the TV guide, but they had used the guide to consult program listings and had occasionally used the guide to look at the pictures with María. María's awareness of the use of the guide was obtained through her observations of the use of print, in this case the TV guide, in her environment.

Through such active experiences with print, children develop principles about reading and written language. They begin to feel that the transaction with the text has a meaningful personal purpose. A person becomes a reader by virtue of a relationship with a text that is within the person's cultural experience.

Development of Writing. Developmentally, writing and reading share common origins, but writing, rather than reading, develops earlier (Chomsky, 1971; Durkin, 1966; Emig, 1982; Graves, 1978). Writing activity can begin as early as eighteen months, with the toddlers handling writing instruments and scribbling. The scribbling may then continue for several years. Preschoolers engage in several kinds of scribbling. Children vary in how long they employ a particular variety of scribbling (Heald-Taylor, 1984). A description of types of scribbling is outlined in Table 2.2.

Although the child's early writing may seem to bear little relationship to conventional writing, close inspection reveals a number of characteristics that indicate growth toward meaningful print. For example, rather than being randomly drawn, the scribbles may display such important features of print as linearity (horizontal and vertical movement), horizontal arrangement on the page, and similarity in segmentation. Figure 2.1 illustrates a child's linear arrangement of writing (scribbles) for a shopping list. When children start experimenting with the combination of lines to form letters, their writing will show less scribble and more of what Clay (1975) labels *mock writing*—letterlike forms together with conventional letters. Children begin to recognize that the forms of the writing system are arbitrary (letters do not directly relate to the form of the objects), and that they are ordered in a linear fashion.

The way in which children use space when they write provides still another index of their growth toward conventional print. Children begin by writing words as continuous strings of letters with no spaces. Later, they come to understand that words are discrete entities; children begin to use dots or some other kind of mark to separate the words. Figure 2.2 shows a kindergartner's use of slanted lines to separate words in his writing.

TABLE 2.2. TYPES OF SCRIBBLING

Precommunicative	The scribbles convey no message but have qualities of writing such as correct directionality.
Sense of story	The child is able to reread scribbles after an interval of time, matching a retelling of the story to a particular segment of scribbles.
Sentence and word matching	The child matches a line of scribble to a complete thought or puts spaces between scribbles to match each scribble to a word.
Mock writing	The child combines letters with scribbles.
Scribble integration and segmentation	The child integrates awareness of syllables, letter/sound relationships, words, syntax, and punctuation with scribbling.

Figure 2.1. *Lista de compras de María* [María's shopping list]

As with spoken language, the mastery of writing requires an understanding of the purpose and nature of symbolic representation. Initially, children use writing to symbolize known objects rather than to represent speech. At this point, they interpret letters as direct representations of objects (Dyson, 1981). They are probably more interested in creating a message than in communicating it. This process—rather than product-orientation—is also evident in their play with tempera, sand, clay, and other media. Sometime between three and five years of age, when they become aware of the existence of print as a representation of language, preschoolers start to accompany their drawings with a special scribble they call "writing." Some children read only a general message from their print and do not understand that each symbol or symbol cluster represents a specific word; others read a spe-

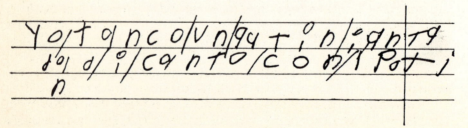

Figure 2.2. Using Slanted Lines to Separate Words

cific message from their writing and are able to match their written symbols to words. Children will attempt to represent nouns before verbs in their writing (Ferreiro & Teberosky, 1982; Tolchinsky Landsmann & Levin, 1987). Children construct hypotheses about the conditions that a piece of writing ought to have in order to be "readable." For example, Spanish-speaking children choose three as the ideal number of letters needed to make print readable (Ferreiro, 1990). If there are only two letters, children are doubtful that those symbols can represent a word, and most will say one letter cannot represent a word. Children also hypothesize about the organization of the letters in a string in order to make a word, that is, the combinations between vowels and consonants.

Spanish-speaking children look for correspondences between graphic and linguistic units based on a *syllabic hypothesis*. That is, children may write as many letters as syllables, but the letters are chosen randomly. For example, *zapato* [shoe], which has three syllables, requires three letters. Others use particular letters, often the initial letters of familial proper names. Thus, the *P* of Pedro could be used to encode the *pa* in *pato* [duck] or the *piz* in *lápiz* [pencil] (Ferreiro & Teberosky, 1982; Tolchinsky Landsmann, & Levin, 1987). According to Ferreiro (1990), it is also relatively common to find vowels used to stand for syllables. These syllabic written productions make use of the regularity of Spanish vowel sounds (i.e., five letters for the five vowel phonemes). Ferreiro (1990) further explains the constructive processes children must explore:

> From the cognitive point of view, the syllabic hypothesis represents the first attempt to deal with a very important and general problem—the relationship between the whole (a written string) and the constituent parts (the letters themselves) . . . As satisfactory as it could be from the point of view of the child, the syllabic hypothesis will be repeatedly invalidated externally by environmental print and by adult productions. Without abandoning this hypothesis, children begin to try out a new hypothesis, the syllabic-alphabet, where some of the letters may still stand for syllables while others stand for smaller sound units (phonemes). This is a typical unstable solution that calls for a new constructive process. (p. 22)

As they develop, have more experiences, and have some cognitive conflicts over inconsistencies and contradictions in the concepts they hold about writing and reading, they grasp the *alphabetic principle*—that is, that letters represent vowel and consonant phonemes. English-speaking children explore the syllabic hypothesis less. They frequently use their knowledge of letter names (*r* for *are*, and *u* for *you*) and use more consonants in their pre-alphabetic writing than do Spanish-speaking children. All children report that formal rather than everyday language is expected to characterize print (Edelsky, 1986; Teberosky, 1990). What is clear is that in acquiring writing, children are not "breaking a code" but rather building a complex system for representation (Bisset, 1980; Chomsky, 1971; Ferreiro, 1986). This means that children have to define the system's units, the syntactic rules of its composites, its semantics, and the pragmatic conditions for its utilization internally.

The oral and written aspects of language develop in a parallel rather than strictly serial fashion. Moreover, they influence one another, each feeding into and enriching the other. The content of children's writing often evolves from the talk that pre-

(handwritten in left margin: language plays important role. +)

TABLE 2.3. LANGUAGE DEVELOPMENT PROCESSES

Processes	Examples
1. Crying, cooing, and babbling	Consonant-vowel combinations, turn-taking
2. One-word stage and overextension	*Mío* [mine], *dáme* [give me]; *agua* [water] or *leche* [milk] for all liquids
3. Telegraphic speech	*Dáme papa* [literal translation: give me potato; meaning: give me food], *voy bye-bye* [I'm going bye-bye], *carro azul* [blue car], *es mío* [it's mine]
4. Rule-governed, systematic development	*Yo lo poní,* for *yo lo puse* [I put it]; *andé/fui a tienda* [I went to store]
5. Sociolinguistic awareness	Speaking Spanish to perceived Spanish speakers (e.g., *abuelitos* [grandparents]) and English to perceived English speakers
6. Linguistic-Code awareness	Asking to say something in Spanish or English: *¿Cómo se dice mesa en inglés* [How do you say table in English]?
7. Scribbling and drawing	Directional scribbling; drawings with scribbling; writing letters; pretending to write
8. Reading, print awareness	Pretends to read; calls out street/environmental signs (e.g., "stop," "K-mart," "Coca-Cola")
9. Syllabic writing	Writing at least as many letters as there are syllables (e.g., *p o ta* for *pelota* [ball])
10. *Alphabetic* writing and invented spelling	*Staban* for *estaban* [were]; *felis* for *feliz* [happy]; *aser* for *hacer* [to make; to do]

cedes the writing. Also, reading and writing are related; experience in one enhances growth in the other. Writing is the enabling process for literacy (encoding). If children learn to write, they will learn to read; but it is through extensive reading that their writing will develop sophistication.

Spelling. Just as with spoken language, development in written language is rule-governed and systematic. This is particularly obvious in the development of children's ability to spell. Children *invent spelling* in much the same way that they invent words in oral language development. They are sensitive to rules but then overextend them. They understand the relationship between speech and print and that letters represent speech sounds, but they think writing consists of recording these speech sounds as precisely as possible in the order in which they are heard. For example, *kasa* for *casa* [house] or *aser* for *hacer* [to make; to do]. Of course, written symbols do not correspond precisely to the sounds of spoken words; there are rules that govern spelling, and many exceptions.

Until children become more familiar with print, they will use invented spellings in their writing. As exposure to print continues, invented spellings gradually yield to standard forms.

By the time children enter school, they speak their home discourse almost as well as the adults in their immediate environment (Shanahan et al., 1995). They have mastered a good deal of Spanish grammar (and maybe some English grammar); are quite adept at the social conventions of communication in their speech community, such as taking turns, code-switching, and knowing when to respond and when not to; and may be scribbling and using some invented spelling. They have developed *metalinguistic* terms (words, letters, writing) to request assistance and discuss their own and others' language use. These are remarkable achievements, considering the complexity of language and the short time span (five to six years) in which all of this is accomplished.

Table 2.3 summarizes and gives examples of these language development processes. However, these processes are not necessarily consecutive or sequential stages in development; much simultaneous and overlapping development occurs. For example, a child can be working on sociolinguistic awareness, scribbling, and print awareness processes at the same time.

As both a cultural product and an instrument of thought, language, once acquired, shapes the successive mental structures and behaviors that constitute the growth of intellectual development.

OBSERVING CHILDREN

In taking a child-centered view you must allow the children to provide you with the information on their linguistic, cultural, and cognitive development that will dictate the design of your literacy program. How can you begin to know the unique strengths and needs of your students? First, observe them, then couple the observations with what you already know and understand. Observation of the children's development can help you find answers to the instructional questions you face: how to get Alicia interested in reading; why Manuel is so bored; which children will work best together; which language to select for what activities. Good observation helps teachers to get to know their children and to meet their needs.

Through knowing the kinds of things children are doing with language, how they relate to print, and what cultural referents they bring to literacy interactions, more meaningful opportunities can be provided to stretch language use to more advanced levels. Chapter 7 will discuss various ways to assess language development, but here we want to suggest the need for classroom observation. You can learn much more about children by permitting them to be your linguistic informants and carefully observing them than by formal assessment. Listen to children having a casual conversation; create small-group interactions around a theme and observe the level of interest and use of language by different children; watch children's interaction with print; listen to children's conversations on the playground; conduct one-to-one conferences with children about reading or writing; listen to children talk about their home and community; and ask children to evaluate their literacy development. Make anecdotal records of your observations, noting the children's interest in selecting language tasks, problems the children perceive, strategies they use to circumvent or solve problems, and the construction processes they use. Information gathered about children in this way can aid you in knowing what kinds of language and thinking skills children are using and in what contexts these are exhibited.

The first weeks of a new school year provide a valuable opportunity to meet and get to know the children in your class, and although you will revise and update your knowledge throughout the coming months, this initial impression is essential for planning the specific experiences needed to assist each child's development toward full literacy. Think about a favorite teacher who made you feel special, who really listened and somehow reached out to you alone. Not surprisingly, students at all educational levels note a special, personal (teacher-related) quality in describing meaningful learning experiences.

SUMMARY

Although there are many unanswered questions, Piaget's theory (universal developmental stages) and Vygotsky's theory (mediation between the child's independent knowledge base and the adult's culturally influenced knowledge structure) have important implications for assisting children to develop literacy. From Piaget's research we have learned that young children construct their understanding in the context of their own activity. They progress from concrete thinking to the more abstract, from the figurative to the operative aspects of cognition. That is, young children experience the here-and-now time frame. They therefore learn more easily when they can manipulate objects rather than use abstract symbols that stand for the object.

Because of the interactive relation between language and cognition, it is important that the child's home language be preserved and strengthened in order to support the continuity of cognitive development. It is also important to preserve cognitive continuity. This means that the concepts and ideas as well as the language are familiar. The context of literacy tasks must be meaningful and express the values of the child's own culture.

The language development processes discussed in this chapter help us to understand that (1) children's language is concrete and context bound; (2) children apply problem-solving tools to language by searching for patterns, meaning, and rules; and (3) children begin to develop sociolinguistic and code awareness as they develop language.

ACTIVITIES

Journal Writing

1. Reflect on what "world-making" or "re-creating experiences in your head" means to you.
2. If you are doing a case study (see field-based activity 4), reflect on your expectations, concerns, or questions you might have about doing a case study.

Discussion Activities

1. In small-group discussion, brainstorm ideas and recollections about how you learned to read and write. Did you first learn to read and write in Spanish or English? Compare your ideas with the theoretical perspectives discussed in this chapter.
2. Discuss examples of how parents and more capable language/literacy users create a "zone of proximal development" for children and less capable language users. In your own ex-

perience, are there areas of learning in which you would benefit from working with more knowledgeable persons? List three such areas and discuss one with the group members. Do you have any areas in common with another member?

Field-Based Activities

1. Conduct a cooking activity with a young child or a small group of young children. Making soup or some other dish that requires a number of ingredients and a certain amount of cooking gives you the opportunity to observe the children's stages of language and cognitive development. Discuss, observe, and note the children's responses to questions such as: What is soup made from? What are the names, colors, textures, and smells of the different ingredients? What do we need to do first, next, last? What do we need to do to the ingredients before we put them in the pot? How does it smell while it is cooking? What is happening when it is cooking? How does it taste? What do the ingredients look like after cooking? Write up your notes and assess the children's levels of cognitive and language development.

2. Tape-record three children from three different grade (age) levels telling a story based on the same wordless picture book. (One example is *Anno's Flea Market*, by Mitsumasa Anno.) Transcribe your tape. Compare the three different stories for complexity of grammar and meaning, fluency, inclusion of detail, and explicitness.

3. Collect samples of young children's scribbles or writings (ask them to tell you a story or read to you what they wrote) that illustrate their early attempts at using writing as a communication tool.

4. Begin a case study of one child's language development. Identify a child that you may observe. Decide how long you will conduct your case study. (Observing the child a couple of times a week for two or three months should result in some rich data to study.) Observe and record detailed notes (without interpretation) on language usage and context. At the end of your observation, analyze your notes and describe the language and thinking abilities of your case study.

CHAPTER 3
Biliteracy

Chapter Overview

Characteristics of Language

Native Language Instruction

Classrooms as Contexts for Biliteracy

INTRODUCTION

In Chapter 1, we looked at the sociocultural context of literacy and its ramifications for developing a literacy program in a bilingual/multicultural context with the explicit goals of promoting cultural diversity and developing the linguistic and cultural repertoire of the students. Chapter 2 centered on the learner-child, specifically focusing on issues of language and cognitive development and their relationship to the sociocultural context in which they occur. We discussed why, within bilingual contexts, children use both codes (English and Spanish) as one language system. In this chapter we will discuss the goals of the integrated curriculum by focusing on language and language teaching.

Developing a bilingual context for learning is complex. The hidden messages about language stemming from program structure and goals, the tensions regarding code-switching and language separation, the similarities and differences of the English and Spanish language systems, and the practices that result from historical traditions of Spanish reading approaches are some of the issues that converge in the bilingual classroom. We believe that the contexts of the classroom and the school influence how children approach and learn how to use language. Examining these issues will guide you in the development of an integrated biliteracy approach.

CHARACTERISTICS OF LANGUAGE

Based on what we have presented in previous chapters on the acquisition of language in the context of home and community environments, we can say the following about language.

Language is a medium of communication. Language enables us to communicate with ourselves, one another, and our environment. Language use is always functional, purposeful, and context bound. Part of understanding language as communication is also understanding the cultural referents or context of the language users. For example, the word *estrenar* has a unique cultural referent for Spanish speakers—an equivalent word does not exist in English, but its meaning is to handsel, to use or to do something for the first time. For communication to take place, language users, speaker and listener or reader and writer, must understand each other's referents, values, ways of thinking, and potential points of difference.

Language has many functions. Language is used for many purposes: to advise (meddle), influence (bias), entertain (divert), intimidate (browbeat), confuse (baffle), regulate (govern), and so forth.

Halliday (1973) showed that language develops as a problem-solving response to the child's evolving needs and developmental tasks. Children learn the language of their group or community as a by-product of striving for these other goals. As children acquire new concepts, develop cognitively, and manipulate their experiential knowledge, language becomes the means by which they reflect on their learning. Language, in all its functions, helps children refine thought, extend imagination, and cultivate relationships. Thus, language develops as a mediator to social functions in the child's life. If children do not experience a need to communicate in a particular way, then the corresponding linguistic structure will not develop (Bruner, 1975a, 1975b; Hamers & Blanc, 1982; Karmiloff-Smith, 1979; Purcell-Gates, 1995). The child's *home discourse* develops in response to the social and problem-solving tasks posed in the home environment.

The function of literacy develops similarly: it will "not take root in individuals unless it serves some already existing function for them" (Downing, 1987: 30). Thus, literacy will not grow in individuals unless they experience literate activities that increase their competency with existing functions.

Language is an organized system of symbols. In oral language, the symbols (speech) are auditory; in written language, the symbols (print) are visual. The symbols of a language are intended to represent and convey experience, but the symbols in and of themselves are not necessarily embedded in what they represent. In alphabetic languages, the system of symbols is said to be arbitrary. Neither the letters nor the sounds of the word *gato* [cat], for example, bear any relationship to the furry, four-legged animal. However, in non-alphabetic languages, like Chinese, which is based on characters, the symbols more closely illustrate the referent they represent. All languages are bound by rules that govern the way meaningful units are put together to form the language. Although the rules vary from language to language, their presence is a universal characteristic of language. These rules determine how the major systems of a language—its sound system (phonology), its grammatical system (syntax), and its meaning system (semantics)—work. Although the rules governing the Spanish and English language systems cannot be adequately presented here, some essential differences are discussed in the following section.

The Spanish and English Language Systems

Language systems are symbolic representations of spoken language. Spanish and English are alphabetic systems. The alphabetic system attempts to create correspondences between units of writing and units of speech. In spite of its varying complexity in the different languages, the basic *alphabetic principle* that letters represent the smallest units of sounds, called phonemes, is the same across all alphabetic systems. For Spanish and English, the representation of sound by the alphabet is only approximate. Spanish has more graphemes (letters) representing a single phoneme (sound) than English, but neither has a one-to-one correspondence. Thus, neither is phonetic in the sense that one can sound out a word reliably solely by knowing the rules of correspondence. Both languages have *phonological* (sound), *syntactic* (grammatical), and *semantic* (meaning) systems.

Phonological System. The phoneme is the smallest unit of sound in a language.[1] For example, the number of phonemes in Spanish depends on whether the Spanish is that of the U.S. Southwest, Latin America, or Spain; there are between 22 and 24 phonemes. The majority of phonemes are consonants; in Spanish there are five vocalic phonemes (/a/, /e/, /i/, /o/, and /u/). There are many more phonemes in English than in Spanish. The relationship between sound symbols and written symbols is called phoneme/grapheme (sound/symbol) correspondence. Phonemes are abstractions rather than natural physical segments of speech (Liberman et al., 1967).

Therefore, it is difficult for a teacher to teach a sound accurately, especially consonants in isolation. It is very difficult for children learning to read to isolate, discover, and associate the isolated abstract phoneme with a specific grapheme.

There are phonological variations among Spanish-speaking groups. For example, among some Puerto Rican students one is likely to find that the *r* at the end of a word is pronounced as /l/, for example, *amol* for *amor* [love] and *comel* for *comer* [to eat].

Syntax. Syntax refers to the rules that govern how words are combined to form meaningful phrases and sentences. The largest construction is the sentence. In both Spanish and English, how words are ordered is very significant. They both rely heavily on word order to convey meaning. Because word order is so critical, rearranging words usually affects meaning or may destroy it altogether. This is illustrated in these sentences:

- *¡Qué dolores de piernas!* [What leg pain!]
- *¡Qué piernas de Dolores!* [What legs Dolores has!]

The fact that words are sequenced in certain ways places constraints on the kinds of words that may be used at given points in a sentence. These constraints allow for syntactic cues. Both Spanish and English have *content words* (nouns, verbs, adjectives, adverbs), *function words* (prepositions, conjunctions, relative pronouns, adjectives, auxiliary and linking verbs, and articles), and *affixes* (meaningful word elements that are attached to nouns and verbs and indicate person, number, and tense). Word order is relatively predictable, but a few variations on the syntactic level have been found among Caribbean Spanish speakers. Valadez (1981) documents the following example from Puerto Rican Spanish:

Puerto Rican Spanish   (1) *¿Adónde tú vas?* [Where are you going?]
World Standard Spanish   (2) *¿Adónde vas?*
                                              (3) *¿Tú adónde vas?*
                                              (4) *¿Adónde vas tú?* (p. 169; our translation)

Syntactic knowledge is acquired naturally as part of the language development process (see Chapter 2). Most children, and many adults, will use the standard syntactic forms of their native language without being aware of or able to state the rules of syntax formally.

Semantics. Semantics deals with both word meaning and the attitudes that people have toward particular words and expressions. It includes both the denotation and connotation of words. People are sensitive to *pragmatic cues*, that is, the genre and social context of words. The same word may have a variety of meaning associations to different children based on each child's background knowledge. For example, *lift* means *elevator* to the British, whereas it means *a ride* or *picking up something* to Americans; *chavo* means *penny* to Puerto Rican children and *boy* to Mexican children; likewise, *guagua* means *baby* in Uruguay and *bus* in Puerto Rico and the

Canary Islands. Differences on the semantic level are abundant with lexical items. Differences in semantics go beyond differences in the terms used and include the cultural knowledge associated with the term.

The term *parts of speech* refers to the function of words according to their position in a sentence. This means that when the form of a content word changes according to its function in a sentence, it signals a change in meaning as well: for example, *lustre* [lustre, clear, gloss, noble] is the noun form, *lustroso* [noble, glossy] is the adjective form, and *lustrar* [to expiate, to purify, to make brilliant] is the transitive verb form. Thus, a word's form is a clue to its function in the sentence. The context of the sentence also denotes which form of the word is most appropriate.

Semantics includes not only vocabulary, but also how words are used and understood at various stages of cognitive development and in different contexts. Chomsky (1969), for example, shows that younger children have greater difficulty with the concept *promise* than do older children. It is the knowledge gained through prior experience that provides that child with the referents for words encountered in a variety of reading contexts.

NATIVE LANGUAGE INSTRUCTION

There is considerable evidence (Chu, 1981; Mace-Matluck, 1982; Hakuta, 1986; Ramirez, 1992) that quality literacy instruction in the native language facilitates overall academic achievement and the development of English-literacy skills. Given that literacy is a process of constructing meaning from text, it makes sense that readers will manipulate the context and cueing systems (the graphophonic, syntactic, semantic, and pragmatic cues) of a language they speak fluently better than those of a language they do not know well (Goodman, Goodman, & Flores, 1979).

A successful bilingual/multicultural education context minimally meets the following three characteristics described by Krashen and Biber (1988):

1. High quality subject matter teaching in the first language, without translation.
2. Development of first language literacy.
3. Comprehensible input in English. (p. 25)

Even in bilingual classrooms that share these minimal characteristics, however, children's development of literacy, in Spanish and in English, is mediated by variables of institutional and sociocultural context (Hornberger, 1992). The teaching of literacy in the classroom is laden with the intentional application of an ensemble of pedagogical and political practices emerging from decisions about the type of bilingual program model[2] to be implemented, instruction, assessment, and related daily classroom interaction. A hidden curriculum is established that may augment, enhance, complement, and, in instances, contradict the messages expressed in the Spanish literacy texts and methodology used.

A number of studies (Garcia, 1983b; Milk, 1980 & 1993; Cazden, 1988; Hornberger, 1992) have examined different situations and the cultural dynamics of teaching and learning in bilingual contexts. In bilingual classrooms, the contexts are created by 1) the goals of the bilingual program, 2) the teacher's attitude toward native language instruction, English, and code switching, and 3) the continuing influence of traditional Spanish reading approaches.

Literacy Goals of Bilingual Programs

The design of bilingual/multicultural programs will differ according to local and state social-political and literacy goals (Arias & Casanova, 1993). Programs organized to protect the educational rights of language minority children may vary in purpose, from developing the native language to making a quick transition to the second language. In a seminal article, Kjolseth (1973) presents a continuum of program models that are based at one extreme on assimilationist structures and social goals and, at the other, on pluralistic ones. Social-political goals influence the objectives of the literacy program.

The pluralistic model, because of equal language time and treatment, "encourages students to become active in a variety of settings, use a number of linguistic varieties, and become experienced in switching between them [languages]" (Kjolseth, 1973:11). This model promotes linguistic and cultural diversity. In programs with such a purpose, students who are not proficient in English are provided learning experiences in their native language while they learn the second language. These programs also provide opportunities for English-speaking counterparts to learn a second language. Organized to develop full literacy in both languages, they are known as two-way or dual language models.

In each of these models the messages students receive are different. In the pluralistic model, each language and its speakers are valued. In contrast, the assimilationist model

> emphasizes the superiority or inferiority of different varieties of language and culture and encourages restricting use to correct forms of school-approved varieties in all domains of usage. . . . Preexistent stereotypes . . . held by youth and adults in both groups are unaltered or reinforced; . . . the bilingual program [is viewed] as bringing cultural enrichment and a literate standard language to the "culturally deprived" and illiterate. (Kjolseth, 1973:15)

At this point, most bilingual/bicultural education programs describe themselves as maintenance or developmental, enrichment or dual language, or transitional bilingual education (TBE) programs, with many variations. The goal of maintenance and enrichment bilingual programs is full literacy in both languages for both ethnolinguistic and mainstream children. They vary in how the second language is introduced, simultaneously or successive. In transitional bilingual education programs, non-English-proficient students are taught for several years using the native language until the student is fluent in the second language. The eventual goal of transitional bilingual education programs is exclusive instruction in the second language. Teachers must be aware of the hidden messages that they and the program structure convey to students about the identity and relative statuses of the languages (Escamilla, 1994), literacy, and the language users.

Code-Switching and Language Separation in the Classroom

The ability to *code switch* (alternate between two language systems in an utterance or conversation) develops very early and naturally when young children are learning language in a bilingual environment. Bilingual children acquire code-switching rules based on norms operating within their speech community. Code-switching may occur at the word, phrase, clause, or sentence level and is governed by functional and grammatical principles (Valdés-Fallis, 1976b; Faltis, 1989). The switches can serve various situational or stylistic functions (e.g., to resolve ambiguities, for clarification, or as a mode shift—narration to commentary—topic shift, or attention device). The function of code-switching for the bilingual is similar psycholinguistically to stylistic switches among monolinguals (Grosjean, 1982). Code-switching behavior can vary widely because of such factors as language proficiency, context, and the formality of the situation.

A fourth-grade girl's explanation of how she saw the need for the use of English vocabulary and Spanish pronunciation of English words demonstrates some of the functional and grammatical principles involved:

> . . . *cuando vamos a acampar en las montañas, lo llamamos* "camp," *y no le llamamos bolsas para dormir, pero le decimos* "eslipin bags"—*para* "sleeping bags." *Entonces yo le digo a Esther* [her friend], "*Cuando vamos a* camp *tienes que llevar tu* eslipin bag, O.K." . . . [When we are camping in the mountains, we call this "camp" and we don't translate it as sleeping bags, but we say "eslipin bags." Then I tell Esther, "When we go to *camp*, you must bring a *eslipin bag*, O.K."].

In this example, the context in which the vocabulary was learned, that is, the cultural concepts guiding her thinking about the conditions under which one sleeps outdoors, was a factor influencing the choice of the word *camp* and the language used. The choice of language would have been different had *hamaca* [hammock], rather than sleeping bag, been the alternative rest place or had the organization of sleeping out in the mountains or wilderness been different. Furthermore, the speaker adhered to the phonological rules governing the use of *s* in a beginning position in Spanish [in *eslipin*], the language governing the speech act.[3]

Although most bilinguals are likely to participate in code-switching behavior, its use and the attitudes toward its use may vary. Peñalosa (1981) states:

> Hispanics have somewhat mixed feelings about language mixture. They are aware that many purists frown on it and that Anglos use a derogatory terminology to re- fer to this mixed speech, such as "Tex-Mex," or "Spanglish." But the rise of eth- nic power movements such as the Chicano movement has done much to rehabili- tate the image of mixed speech, *caló*,[4] and the nonstandard varieties which have become for some the mark of ethnic pride. Apparently, however, the Chicano com- munity attitudes toward nonstandard varieties of Spanish are more positive than at- titudes toward Chicano English. (pp. 157–158)

The divergence in views about code-switching has been particularly sharp among scholars of bilingualism with respect to its use in instructional settings. Most bilingual educators consider code-switching an inappropriate vehicle for school in- struction (see Anderson & Boyer, 1970; Saville & Troike, 1971; Legaretta, 1979; Wong Fillmore & Valadez, 1985) and strongly argue in favor of the separation of languages. Yet language alternation options have not been adequately researched (Zentella, 1984; Jacobson, 1990). There are instructional situations where code- switching is appropriate. Valdés-Fallis (1976a), for example, provides a description of how code-switching is used effectively in poetry; Olmedo-Williams (1983) de- scribes the positive role code-switching can play in peer teaching situations; and Jacobson (1982, 1990), Milk (1981), and Faltis (1989) document a planned class- room code-switching approach called the New Concurrent Approach, which was developed from the perspective of local community use and proved to be as effec- tive as, and in some subjects more effective than, the language separation approach. Although many educators separate languages, they accept the code-switching behavior of students because, as Zentella's research demonstrates, the students' re- sponses reveal an understanding, sensitivity, and creativity that reflect the sociolin- guistic rules learned in their speech community (1984). Zentella also points out that by banning code-switching from classrooms, "we do not know what we are ban- ning along with it" (p. 130). In addition, Zentella (1984) and others make a strong argument for tolerance of code-switching behavior in the classroom because of the connection made between code-switching and identity. Elías-Olivarez (1983) makes the following point:

> The alternation of Spanish and English in bilingual discourse has been regarded by many, especially educators, as a disintegration of Chicano and Puerto Rican Spanish

language and culture. However, most bilinguals view this mode of communication as a feature that is characteristic of their identity. (p. viii)

The issue of identity and learning is important in developing literacy. Ferdman (1990) states:

> Teachers can discover ways of encouraging students to explore the implication of their ethnicities and to engage in self-definition. Explicitly and positively linking classroom activities to the students' cultural identity can also be a way of motivating students. . . . (p. 201)

Teachers' attitudes toward and tolerance for code-switching as well as the language practices of the classroom are likely to influence the degree to which classroom code-switching behavior occurs.

Edelsky (1986), in studying writing samples of bilingual children, found that there is a difference between the use of code-switching in oral and written channels. She discovered that bilingual children did not use code-switching with high frequency in their writing. About this finding, she makes the following speculation:

> The rarity of written code-switching can be attributed to children's sociolinguistic sensibilities—perhaps they saw the written channel as more formal, certainly as constraining the use of some typical oral resources. The same dimension—formality—may have been operating to make code switching even less frequent in English than Spanish texts. (p. 98)

In other words, literacy environments create a context that discourages code-switching behavior. Another element that may be related to the use of code-switching in writing is that although texts for adults use code-switching, particularly in the genre of poetry, such texts are nonexistent for children. The lack of such models may also cue students as to the "inappropriateness" of code-switching in writing.

There is an increasing tendency to separate languages as a strategy for the conservation and protection of Spanish, for ensuring equity in language use, and for providing richer linguistic environments in both languages. However, there are viable instructional situations in which switching codes is a legitimate activity reflecting the student's speech community. The alternation of codes for instructional purposes should be explored and must be planned and grounded in community use.

Traditional Reading Methods in Spanish

Whereas Bellenger (1979) studied the reading methods used to teach Spanish reading in Spain and Latin America, Thonis (1976), Peña & Verner (1981), Flores (1981), and Freeman (1988) studied Spanish reading methods used in the United States. Different reading approaches reflect different traditions or assumptions about the reading process. The following is a summary of the different methods they describe that are used to teach reading in Spanish.

El método alfabético o de deletreo (alphabet or spelling method) is one of the oldest methods. It was introduced in Latin American countries by the religious orders involved in the Spanish christianization of the conquered peoples. It begins with the teaching of letter names, starting with vowels and followed by consonants. The letters are then put together to make syllables and words. For example:

ma—eme (m) a (a)—ma
no—ene (n) o (o)—no
mano—eme (m) a (a) ene (n) o (o)—mano [hand]

El método onomatopéyico (onomatopeic method) develops a system of sound associations for graphemes and phonemes based on natural or environmental sounds. The Mayan culture used this method in developing its printed language. For example, the sound /i/ may be associated with the shrill sound made by a monkey or a mouse, the /a/ sound may be associated with the laughter of people or a scared cry, the /r/ sound may be associated with the car motor sound, and the /m/ with the sound made by cows. Stories are created as contexts for introducing and reinforcing the sound. For example, to introduce the /i/, the story *La ratita inteligente* [The Intelligent Mouse] is told. One of the passages goes like this (Torres Quintero, 1973): "*¿Cómo piensan Uds. que lloraría la ratita? ¿Lloraría diciendo iiiiiiiiii?* [How do you think the mouse cries? Does it cry saying iiiiii?]" (p. 79; our translation)

To reinforce the /i/ the teacher has the children first identify words they know in which they can identify the /i/ sound and, only then, introduces the written symbol. The last thing they learn is how to write it. The focus is on making as many associations as possible for the child in order to facilitate the remembering of the decoding skills.

El método fónico o fonético (phonics method) teaches the system of phonemes (sound symbols). The child is first taught each sound in isolation and then taught to combine sounds. The vowels and vowel combinations are taught before the consonants are introduced. The sounds are combined to make syllables, words, phrases, sentences, and paragraphs.

El método silábico (syllabic method) goes beyond isolated sounds and uses the syllable as the basic unit for introducing the process of decoding. The Egyptians developed hieroglyphics based on the syllabic system. The vowels are taught first, but they are immediately paired with consonants to make syllables and words. As in the *método fónico,* after learning the vowels, the child is introduced to the consonants. For example, the chlid learns /p/ in syllables such as *pa, pe, pi, po, pu,* then combines syllables, such as *papá, pipa, Pepe,* and proceeds to make sentences, such as *"Pepe es mi papá"* [Pepe is my father].

El método de palabras (whole word method), also known as *palabras generadoras* [generative words]) first presents a complete sentence. Thus, it is a deductive method, unlike those previously presented. It aims at analyzing and synthesizing. The sentence is broken into words, syllables, and finally, individual sounds. Then the child is asked to form new words and new sentences using the letters and syllables. The entire sequence of steps is generally presented as shown in Figure 3.1. This method was so widely adopted in Latin American countries that the humorist Quino pokes fun at it in the cartoon in Figure 3.2 (p. 52).

El método global o ideovisual (global method) uses words and phrases to teach reading and writing without analyzing their component parts. However, most teach-

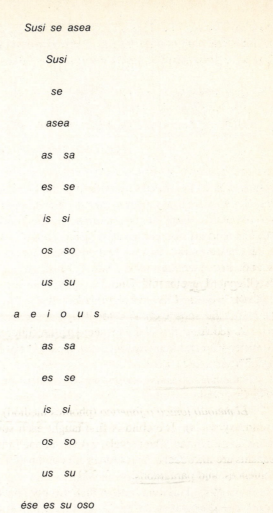

Figure 3.1. *Método de palabras* [Whole word method]; our translation

ers begin by teaching the five vowel sounds as part of a reading readiness program. The development of sensorimotor experiences, concepts, and affective development is also part of a readiness program. When children have mastered the readiness program, they begin reading with whole words or phrases. This method includes elements of the language experience approach as well as sight reading work. The teacher involves a small group of children in an experiential activity in which the children draw pictures based on topics the teacher suggests. The children dictate ideas that the teacher writes on sentence strips and then copy the phrase or sentence onto their pictures. They practice reading their phrases and sentences until decoding is mastered. In subsequent lessons, words are lifted from the children's sentences and are learned as sight words.

El método ecléctico [eclectic method] includes elements from various methods. The child might work on activities or exercises that develop skills in visual discrimination, motor coordination, auditory discrimination, attention, memory, and oral

Figure 3.2. *Mafalda* by Quino

language. Then the child is introduced to the sounds, names, and visual forms of letters. Children are also taught to take dictation, copy, create new words, visualize letters and words, write letters, and associate the oral to the written form. This is perhaps the most utilized approach of Spanish basal reading series in bilingual programs in the United States. This method does not have an explicit guiding philosophy.

El método integral is the whole language approach, which is more of a philosophy than a method. The emphasis is on meaning derived from interacting with language presented in a natural context. It goes from the whole to the parts, with the individual parts such as letters or syllables analyzed in context and the encoding and decoding processes presented in an integrated way. The focus is on authenticity—on children creating their own texts and engaging in the purposeful reading of other texts.

El método de temas generadores, also called the syncretic reading method (Ada, 1987:18), brings together a variety of the methods already mentioned: *método integral, método de palabras,* and *método silábico.* Used with adults and out-of-school youth in Latin American communities and in high school and adult literacy programs in the United States, it is based on Freire's (1970) theory of *critical literacy.* The formal and informal systems of literacy instruction rest on the assumption that the development of literate competence within specific cultures plays an important role in people's daily lives and in their struggle for liberation. As in the *método integral,* the emphasis is on meaning. A generative word is selected because of the importance it has as a theme in the lives of the learners, such as *favela* [slum] in the Brazilian context. The dialogue between educators and learners about both the concrete context of the slum and its theoretical context, in which they explore the reasons for slum reality, is used for instructional purposes. Through the dialogue, the educator introduces the process of decodification. Educators and learners explore the relationship of the whole to its parts, the semantic relationship between the word and its meaning, the image of the word, and the syllables into which it can be separated. The presentation of syllables, however, is analytical. Through a problem-solving mode, the educator asks such questions as: What are the similarities and differences between the parts? What can we call each part? The last stage is a creative one. The aim is to have the learners discover the syllabic composition of words in their own language and to have them put the syllables together in a variety of new, meaningful combinations.

Through critical literacy, students and teachers have the opportunity and the means to do more than learn language; they learn to think and act as critically conscious beings. Students are more likely to develop intellectually and linguistically when they analyze their own experiences and create their own ways to describe and better understand these experiences, as also proposed by *el método integral*. Teachers allow access to this constructive process through interactive literacy and critical dialogue. Freire defines critical dialogue as "an encounter among men [and women] who name the world; it must not be a situation where some men [or women] name on behalf of others" (Freire, 1970:77). Through dialogue, learners and teachers with different experiences and knowledge critically reflect on beliefs and information; in such dialogue, both have the opportunity to build knowledge. The most important thing is to focus on the meaning that learners construct. By engaging in critical dialogue about *generative themes,* learners connect concrete knowledge from their lives to more abstract themes (Freire, 1970; Freire & Macedo, 1987). For example, a teacher conducting a brainstorming session with a group of second graders as part of a prewriting exercise used some of these principles. The children had selected *ayudar* [to help] from a list of words suggested by the teacher to generate a semantic map as shown in Figure 3.3. (Semantic maps are explained in Chapter 6.)

The teacher was sensitive to the needs of the child who suggested "*recogiendo cartón,*" "*en el yonque,*" "*cuando necesitamos dinero.*" (See Figure 3.3 for translation.) She encouraged the child to explore the value and benefits of his contribution to his family. The child wrote a story and drew an illustration about a trip to the junkyard with his father to collect recyclable cardboard. During the week that followed, the child made several entries in his writing journal about the role he played in helping his father collect various recyclable materials.

By focusing on a generative theme the teacher assisted this child in exploring and critically building his own ideas and views about his role in his family. Through dialogue the student connected concrete knowledge from his reality to literacy. This teacher and student made the literacy task genuine. The child came to understand an element of the world that was relevant to him (Pérez, 1994a).

The reading methods described represent both an evolution of tradition and a tension of opposites. For example, in the *método fónico,* the introduction of syllables follows the tradition set up in the *método silábico.* Although they are both inductive methods, they differ with respect to starting points. The deductive approaches, such as the *método integral* and *global,* do not start with the isolation of

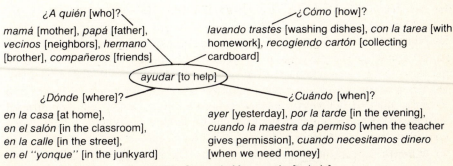

¿A quién [who]?
mamá [mother], *papá* [father], *vecinos* [neighbors], *hermano* [brother], *compañeros* [friends]

¿Cómo [how]?
lavando trastes [washing dishes], *con la tarea* [with homework], *recogiendo cartón* [collecting cardboard]

ayudar [to help]

¿Dónde [where]?
en la casa [at home], *en el salón* [in the classroom], *en la calle* [in the street], *en el "yonque"* [in the junkyard]

¿Cuándo [when]?
ayer [yesterday], *por la tarde* [in the evening], *cuando la maestra da permiso* [when the teacher gives permission], *cuando necesitamos dinero* [when we need money]

Figure 3.3. Semantic Map *ayudar* [to help]

language structures, but present whole words or the context from which the word derives meaning. The *método ecléctico* randomly uses elements of the other approaches, whereas the *método de palabras generadoras* is systematic. In bilingual classrooms, Spanish reading texts reflect the use of a variety of methods, but the *método silábico* still prevails (Freemen, 1988).

The teaching of writing in most Spanish-speaking countries also is based on some strong traditions. In the primary grades the focus of instruction is *handwriting;* children are expected to practice their handwriting by copying exercises composed of words and sentences. Some countries, like Mexico, use a "script" or cursive system to teach handwriting, whereas others use a manuscript system. The teaching of *orthography* (the rules for punctuation, spelling, etc.) is the focus of writing lessons in intermediate elementary grades. Through a series of exercises and dictation children are expected to copy and memorize the rules of orthography. Rockwell (1982) in an analysis of Spanish writing instruction describes the most common practice as:

> se asigna la 'copia' de una lección del libro de texto, para que 'practiquen la escritura' (el docente califica letra, ortografía, formato) . . . En cualquier tarea de 'escribir', se da una referencia constante, por parte del docente, a los aspectos formales del ejercicio: la letra, la posición de las palabras, los renglones, etc. [(the student's) assignment is to copy a lesson from the textbook, for writing practice (the teacher evaluates letters, orthography, and format) . . . In any writing assignment, there is constant reference, by the teacher, to the formal aspects of the exercise: the letters, word position, lines, etc.] (p. 305; our translation)

Rockwell also describes many other occasions in which she observed children writing in schools, but not as part of the learning activities. She describes how children were often involved in writing notes to each other, writing on the blackboard, copying poems and prose for reciting, and the like. In recent years, the research conducted by Ferreiro (1982, 1989), Teberosky (1982, 1990), and others on emergent writing and the influence of group work on writing development has begun to challenge and influence traditional approaches. More developmental and integrated reading/writing approaches are beginning to be discussed in professional literature and to appear in school texts.

CLASSROOMS AS CONTEXTS FOR BILITERACY

By biliteracy we mean the acquisition and learning of the decoding and encoding of and around print using two linguistic and cultural systems in order to convey messages in a variety of contexts. We agree with Hornberger (1990:213) that "any and all instances in which communication occurs in two (or more) languages in or around writing" is biliteracy. Literacy events are rule-governed, and their different situations of occurrence determine the rules for talking—interpreting and interacting—about a piece of writing. The use of two languages and culture systems is integral to these literacy events.

Anderson, Teale, and Estrada (1980) define a literacy event as "an action sequence, involving one or more persons, in which the production and/or comprehension of print plays a role" (p. 59). They categorize literacy events into two types: reading and writing events.

In a reading event, an individual either comprehends or attempts to comprehend a message that is encoded graphically. Anderson and Teale (1982) describe how María, a three-year-old Spanish-speaking child and her mother interact around print. As the mother dresses María's younger brother in a T-shirt that has print, the following conversation takes place:

MOTHER: María, *¿qué dice ahí?* [What does it say there?] (pointing to the print on
　　　　　the infant's T-shirt)

MARÍA: Mmm . . .

MOTHER: *¿Te acuerdas?* [Do you remember?]

MARÍA: No.

MOTHER: María, *¿qué dice ahí?* [What does it say there?]

MARÍA: Mmm . . .

MOTHER: *Dice: "Yo soy . . ."* [It says, "I am . . ."]

MARÍA: *Tú dímelo.* [You tell me.]

MOTHER: *Yo soy, ¡Fa . . !* [I am, Fa!] (pointing to the last word)

MARÍA: "*¡Fabulosa!*" [Fabulous!]

MOTHER: *¿Eso es!" . . . pregúntale a mi papá.*" [That's right! ". . . ask my dad."]
　　　　　(p. 286; our translation)

The second type of literacy event involves writing. Here an individual attempts to produce graphic signs. Heath (1982) suggests that literacy events have social interactional rules that regulate the type and amount of talk about what is written and define ways in which oral language reinforces, extends, or sets aside the written material.

What differentiates classroom literacy events from daily uses of literacy is that whereas the latter may indeed influence the development of particular language practices, the former are especially designed for teaching and learning language. That is, they are intentionally didactic and deliberately structured to emphasize this didactic function. Teachers lead children to particular kinds and levels of reading practice, discursively structuring what will "count" as a legitimate classroom reading (Baker & Freebody, 1988). Even when teachers organize language learning in ways that resemble more authentic literacy encounters in a broader societal sense, how they structure the event serves to open or constrain students' access to texts. Through this the students learn what "counts" as writing and reading, what "counts" as response and interpretation, and what "counts" as a legitimate function and use of literacy.

Literacy events in classrooms are *situated* in a social context guided by culturally bound ways of thinking. Bloome (1985) observed that

when students are asked to read a story, they must do so in socially appropriate ways: silently or orally, individually, competitively, or cooperatively with other students, in a round-robin manner, etc. Students who read orally without error or who appropriately answer teacher questions may gain social status within the classroom. Students who read with error, give inappropriate answers, or who sit quietly, may be viewed as outcasts or nonparticipants. (p. 135)

Not only do children have to know the rules of behavior for various literacy events, they must know how to talk about them in appropriate ways. Cook-Gumperz (1986), in her notion of "situated meaning," recognized the relationship among knowing the rules, being able to talk around print material, and being judged competent:

> After the achievement of literacy, the child's communicative ability is judged not only by criteria of effectiveness—do the requisite actions get performed?—but by whether the communication meets adult criteria of contextually relevant and appropriate speech. (p. 110)

In classroom discourse, certain characteristics of literacy are linked to social environments, that is, the particular roles that students and teachers play. These roles are, in part, determined by the specific function of the language and the sociolinguistic rules in operation, both of which are usually set by the teacher. Ramírez (1985) describes the language use in classrooms as "a highly constrained form of communication" (p. 155). For example, many teachers rely on an initiation-response-evaluation interaction structure as a pattern for conducting lessons. Teachers initiate questions (to which they have preconceived right answers), students respond, and the responses are evaluated by the teacher (Mehan, 1979; Cazden, 1988). This classroom discourse (initiation-response-evaluation interaction) limits the amount and use of language and literacy. It also reinforces the roles played by the teacher, as knower and imparter of knowledge, and by the student as the recipient of such knowledge. The teacher initiates and evaluates, and the student not only receives the "right" answer, but must remember this for the purpose of evaluation.

Teachers' and students' social roles in the context of the classroom and the power associated with those roles, in turn, shape language use. Role relations in literacy are so powerful, in fact, that rightness in literacy relates to the power involved in different social interactional roles. When students' social roles are expanded their literacy use changes accordingly (Delpit, 1986; Milk, 1980). To promote literacy, teachers need to expand, not limit, students' roles. Literacy instruction in the classroom should reflect the communicative functions of language and create the kinds of social contexts and conditions in which literacy can and will flourish.

Interaction with Text as Context

Erickson and Shultz (1981) propose that people in interaction become environments for each other. When readers are interacting with print, Rosenblatt (1978) proposes, the interaction is between the reader, the author, and the text. Social environments, including those presented in the text, enter into the sense making of what is read. In a study of an alternative high school, Torres-Guzmán (1989) found that the positioning of students as experts vis-à-vis the text influenced how they, as readers, negotiated the meaning of the text. Linguistic, situational, and social-cultural contexts contribute to the literacy event.

Linguistic context refers to the way something is written (or said); how it relates to what was previously written (or said) by the writer (or speaker); and how it relates to what will follow later in the text (or dialogue). The reader uses three cue systems to analyze the linguistic context of any text: the graphophonic cue system, the syntactic cue system, and the semantic cue system. Through graphophonic cues the reader relates the language's written forms (letters) to its oral forms (sounds); syntactic cues help the reader to interpret the arrangement (word, sentence order) of the written parts of the text; and semantic cues give meaning to particular words within the text. All three cue systems function in the cultural situation in which the reading and writing are taking place.

Situational context refers to the physical form and environment in which the written language is encountered. Non-English-speaking people around the world can read the English symbols *Coca-Cola* on a bottle because of the symbols' situational context. The language user will form hypotheses about a text based on an association with the situation in which the print is usually encountered, for example, a newspaper, recipe, grocery list, bumper sticker, street sign, school book, or novel. When the language learner knows that a text is a letter rather than a newspaper article, that knowledge accompanies the text as context.

Pratt (1977) proposes that knowing that a text is "literature" is a context for interpreting the text. He argues that genre in literature is signaled through book cover, advertising, publishing house, and so on. Similarly, types of reading and writing in the classroom are signaled by context features. For example, when encountering a new storybook young Spanish-speaking children who have experienced traditional children's stories in Spanish will try to begin the story with "*había una vez*" [once upon a time].

Harste, Woodward, and Burke (1984) and Edelsky (1986) showed that children use situational context in their writing. The children used different forms when they wrote stories, letters, songs, and lessons. Even the materials affected the decisions the children made—crayons were more often used for drawing, and pencils were used for writing. Journals, lined or unlined paper, and crayons or pencils elicited different responses and variations in the genre of writing.

Social-cultural context refers to the background knowledge the language user brings to the text and to the purpose of interacting with text. It refers to what is known or implicitly understood about a topic, background information or experience with the referents for particular words, and the importance or relevance of the topic. Abstract terms such as *respeto* [respect] or *ser educado* [to be educated] have a different social-cultural context from the same words in English.[5] On a concrete level, Spanish-speaking children from different cultural groups will describe the common primary-grade classroom experience of growing bean sprouts from different perspectives. Contained in the terms (*frijól, habichuela, ejote*) that they use to talk about the bean will be the context of each child's experience about the cultivation, selection, and preparation of beans. Figure 3.4 illustrates a Puerto Rican child's writing from her social-cultural perspective about this experience.

Linguistic, situational, and social-cultural contexts also vary from print environment to print environment, from classroom to classroom, from community to community (Pérez, 1994b). Included in these contexts are community beliefs, motivations, language functions, perceptions of literacy, and expectations for children's

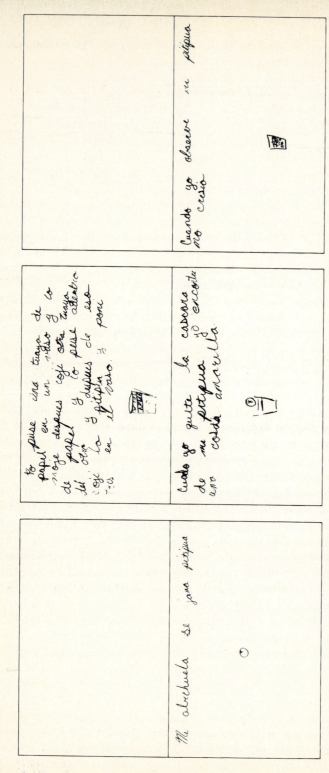

Figure 3.4. *Mi habichuela* [My bean]

[My bean's name is green bean. I put a paper towel in a glass and I wet it afterwards. I took another paper towel and put it inside the other and after that I took the green bean and I put three in the glass. When I took off the outer layer of my green bean I found a little yellow thing. When I observed my green bean, it did not grow.]

success with literacy. In studying the writing of bilingual first, second, and third graders, Edelsky (1986) found that

> . . . it is not merely in each of these overlapping contexts that children generated hypotheses about the various subsystems of written language, but through them. Some constellations of contexts encouraged hypotheses with certain systems of written language while discouraging attention to others. . . . But it is only through contexts that growth in writing occurred. (p. 158)

SUMMARY

In this chapter we have presented information that will assist you in developing a context for biliteracy. Knowledge of the language systems to be learned is one of the three foundational bases (the child and the culture being the other two) for making instructional decisions. Additionally, the goals set forth by the particular bilingual/bicultural program model at your school, the language policies about code-switching and language separation, and the methodology that you adopt and that is presented in the texts used for teaching literacy influence the diversity of literacy instruction.

Reading and writing, like oral language, are social activities, always occurring in some context, for someone or to someone, even if that someone is yourself and the reason is personal and private. In this chapter we have seen that context is central to the acquisition of meaning in the literacy process. In a piece of text, the words that readers know and the experiences related to those words combine to form a context. This context permits them to make inferences about unknown words.

The importance of context regarding interaction, print environment, classroom organization, and community is slowly beginning to influence the designs of school literacy programs in bilingual education. However, Spanish literacy, for the most part, has followed the models of basal readers in English using decontextualized print and language activities. Teachers are very important in setting up learning environments for children that not only focus on comprehension of materials, but that go beyond the text, beyond the relationship between the reality and fantasy they read, and beyond the children's aspirations. Children are helped to use what they capture, what they fantasize about, and what they hope for to create a vision of a better future.

ACTIVITIES

Journal Writing

1. For a week, keep a journal of questions you would like to ask your family if you were to write a story about them. Also, write about incidents or situations you remember as important. At the end of the week, write a fictional story based on your family's history or on that which you remember.

2. Keep a log of your language activities for at least one day. Include only those that involve interactions with others. Note whether you were reading, writing, or using oral language, as well as the following factors about each communication:
   (a) place (home, school, work)
   (b) nature of communication (classroom discussion, the giving of directions, requests)
   (c) party or parties involved (friend, parent, grocery clerk, teacher)

   Once you have a daily log, write a short response to the statement: "Reading, writing, and oral language occur independently of (or are dependent on) the contexts in which they occur." Cite specific examples from your log to support your response.

Discussion Activities

1. In a small group, discuss what you remember of the method by which you learned to read. What were the difficulties? What were memorable moments in that process? Who was your support?

2. Discuss your own writing. Do you like it? Not? Do you remember how you were taught to compose? Talk about your development and how you feel now about it.

Field-Based Activities

1. Work with a group of three or four children. Ask the children to interview a community member—their mother, aunt, cousin, a neighbor, the mother of another member of the class, or an adult friend or acquaintance. They are to ask questions about what the person reads and writes, when, and so forth. Help the children come up with their own questions. In doing so, encourage the children to ask questions in different ways and have them role play, ask each other questions, formulate possible answers, and use a variety of vocabulary. As the culminating activity, ask them to make a presentation about their experience as "researchers."

2. Choose a story that has a great deal of action and emotional words such as fear, annoyance, surprise, amusement, impatience, and happiness. Work with about eight students, divided into two groups. Tell the students that one group will read and the other will act out the story. Tell the students who are acting out the story that they must let the others know what is going on without saying a word. Discuss with the students the context clues they used to portray or guess emotions.

3. Observe two classrooms, preferably one a primary grade and one an intermediate grade, and note the types of literacy events you are able to observe. Who is involved? What materials are they using? Is what you observe an activity organized for literacy or is it an activity in which literacy is used to accomplish another academic or social goal?

NOTES

1. When phonemes appear in text, the symbol for a phoneme appears between slanted bars: //.

2. For a discussion on types of bilingual programs (concurrent translation, alternate approaches, immersion, or active language [L1] and second language [L2] approaches) and issues related to literacy instruction in L1 and L2, see Hakuta (1986), Krashen (1985b), Milk (1993), and Lindholm (1992).

3. For further study of code-switching among bilinguals in the United States, see Gumperz and Hernández-Chávez (1975); Genishi (1976); Valdés-Fallis (1976a, 1976b, 1978); Pfaff (1979); Poplack (1979); Elías-Olivares (1983); Pedraza (n.d.); and Alvarez (1988).

4. *Caló* is one of the variations in language use that mixes or alternates codes, known as jargon developed by youth gangs, whether delinquent or nondelinquent, that is most notably used among males and by Chicano groups such as *pachucos, cholos, tirilones*, etc. (see Peñalosa, 1981).

5. For a discussion of *respeto*, see Carrasco (1984). He defines *respeto* as an implicit notion in all interactions. In the classrooms he studied, *respeto* was "often demonstrated by [the students' and teacher's] choice of a second person singular form of address, i.e., "*tú* and *usted*" and by "how [they] fit into the social order of the society around you, i.e., community, etc." (p. 12). It goes beyond being polite and deferential—beyond the connotation of respect in English. It implies taking special care about how you speak and treat the other person as a human being. It also means to maintain dignity and honor in the treatment of others, whether you agree or disagree with them in the positions or roles they assume. *Ser educado*, which is literally translated as "to be educated," means to be well-behaved and well-mannered.

PART II
El salón y la práctica

CHAPTER 4

Early Years of Reading and Writing

Chapter Overview

The Instructional Environment and Authentic Literacy Events
Creating Meaningful Enabling Environments
Integrating Language Instruction

INTRODUCTION

Goodman (1986) proposes that language development is really the same in and out of school; whatever makes language easy to learn outside of school will also make it easy to learn in school. And what makes it hard to learn is the same, in school or out. Therefore, it is important to know what discourse, print, and literacy environments the child has been exposed to in the home and community. There are unique language functions, literacy events, and classroom discourses that relate to the school's character as a community of learners and to the school's focus on specific areas of knowledge. Facilitating the transition from home discourse to school discourse will make language and literacy learning more natural and easier to learn.

Kindergartners, first graders, and second graders are in the process of moving from preoperational to concrete operational stages of cognitive development (Piaget, 1957) and are beginning to acquire the ability to solve problems by constructing theories, testing, and generalizing from concrete experience. They require an environment and a literacy program that allow for physical activity and learning by doing, talking, reading, and writing. They need quiet periods to relax after periods of mental concentration or physically strenuous activity. Adults are still the primary source of direction, comfort, and reinforcement; but youngsters are beginning to make more lasting friendships with their peers. As they enter school, children associate schooling with learning to read and write and thus are predisposed and motivated to become readers and writers. The literacy skills that children develop during the primary grades will be the foundation for future learning.

This chapter suggests ways that primary-grade teachers (kindergarten, first, and second grade) can create environments for the development of biliteracy. Specifically, the chapter will deal with seizing moments of authenticity to promote literacy and designing meaningful learning experiences. Furthermore, it deals with integrating language skills and language systems.

THE INSTRUCTIONAL ENVIRONMENT
AND AUTHENTIC LITERACY EVENTS

The instructional environment (the routines, the organization of lessons, the types of learning activities selected) will tell children about the purpose and expectations of learning and literacy. A carefully constructed instructional environment creates opportunities for reading and writing. Authentic moments occur in classrooms when the acts of reading and writing are meaningful and purposeful to the children. The stories children bring to school about their experiences of the previous evening are authentic. Children are in the process of defining themselves and reinventing their world.[1] When they communicate about the previous evening with the teacher, an important adult in their lives, they are attempting to engage the teacher in genuine communication from their standpoint. Unfortunately, teachers are taught to direct children away from the self, the stories of the previous evening, to the other, the task of the day and the functioning of the class. Thus, frequently, neither the child's nor the teacher's goals are effectively accomplished. Kindergartners, first graders, and second graders are very much centered on the self and the here and now, but they also live in a world of fantasy and enjoy role playing and pretending. By building the literacy program on what you know about the children's developmental characteristics and their individual stories, you will be guided toward authenticity.

Authenticity does not imply a classroom in which children decide by themselves what and when to read or write. As Vygotskian theory proposes, children need adult guidance in developing beyond their current capabilities. The teacher is the key to the children's development (Pérez, 1993). There are times when it is appropriate for children to choose what and when to read and write and in what language, but it is the teacher who creates the environmental context, provides opportunities for social mediation, and creates challenging encounters to guide the learning.

The integrated biliteracy approach is based on the assumption that children need to use their language (local and standard Spanish and English) and literacy skills to communicate with varied audiences for varied purposes. The focus of the learning emphasizes function and content, not language forms. Children will need to integrate reading and writing with most learning activities. Learning is organized through the use of oral and written language while working on projects (constructing projects, dramatic presentations, storytelling, etc.). And teachers are encouraged to seize teachable moments as they arise and in setting up classroom routines. Teachers will also need to base what is taught on the context of a particular activity and organize lessons around thematic units. In other words, the oral and written language learning/teaching in and through the use of Spanish and English in these classrooms will not consist of oral or written language drills.

Seizing Teachable Moments and Setting Up Classroom Routines

Teachers must recognize those moments when children have real purposes for learning a skill, reading a passage, or writing a note. It is through the optimum use of these authentic purposes that the most learning occurs. Questions students ask are often the best cues to their interests and can lead to a project for study by the individual student, a group of students, or the whole class.

Response to Teachable Moments.   Teachers must be able to respond to developing classroom situations. They should be able to take advantage of unexpected opportunities, *teachable moments*, to teach something that is both educationally significant and needed. Teachable moments happen often in any classroom; they arise in the context of activities. Teachers who find opportunities to pick up on and extend children's curiosity and/or immediate instructional need have learned to recognize and fully utilize teachable moments.

As students show interest in print, they may ask how a word is written, why print appears differently in different books, or why a question mark is upside down. The teacher must seize the moment and respond with the appropriate instruction so as to guide children in solving the intellectual problems posed by their questions. The teacher can help a child to discover relationships between letter and sound patterns and to search, generalize, or hypothesize about usage and spelling rules. Developing generalizations in the context of reading and writing language will strengthen the children's use of the graphophonic (sound and letter pattern) cue system.

Some teachable moments are pursued immediately; some may require that the teacher jot down a note for further study and development. Recurring interests and questions may suggest a future unit of study. The teachable moment is a spontaneous insight into students' learning and growth. The students' quest for immediate knowledge provides opportunities for authenticity.

Using Routines as Literacy Lessons. Everyday classroom routines can be organized for language and literacy use. Teachers can establish daily routines not only in ways that encourage children to interact with and experience print, but also in ways that allow them to assume the role of the leader. For example, in a bilingual kindergarten (which one of us observed for a period of time) the taking of attendance, the calendar activity, the daily weather report, and the assignment of routine classroom tasks were organized so that the leader of the day (based on alphabetical order of the children's last names) was responsible for selecting and assigning students to participate. Although at first the noise level was very high and the length of time that the leader took to make the decisions seemed excessive, eventually the power of this classroom routine in developing leadership skills became apparent. The outstanding characteristic of this kindergarten classroom was leadership development, and one of the things these children had to do to exercise leadership was to learn to identify the tasks associated with the activities they led. They had to learn how to read the charts and to delegate tasks to other members of the class—to understand, for example, that they couldn't simultaneously take attendance slips to the principal's office and continue to lead the class.

Children may already be familiar with several kinds of print when they enter the primary grades. In kindergarten and first grade, some children can identify their names in print. The classroom abounds with opportunities to facilitate the writing and reading of children's names. Parents can be asked to identify possessions with name tags. Cubbyholes and other storage areas can be labeled with names along with an additional identifying symbol, such as a picture of the child's favorite thing, favorite flower, or favorite animal. Names and charts can be used in assigning routines and tasks. For example, you can construct an attendance chart as shown in Classroom Activity 4. 1.

An attendance chart is but one way that children can gain familiarity with their names; they can also be encouraged to sign all of their work. Create another chart for the assignment of classroom housekeeping tasks, such as taking balls and jump ropes to the playground during recess, passing out papers and other materials, or checking out library books to be used in the classroom. Many opportunities for language use arise when students are responsible for maintaining and distributing supplies and materials. Children can use print and patterns of written language when sorting out games or putting away painting supplies. You can exploit everyday classroom routines to provide the children with authentic opportunities to interpret print. By being involved in the literacy events of the day-to-day functioning of the classroom, children will experience the need for and use of reading and writing.

CLASSROOM ACTIVITY 4.1   Attendance Activity

1. At the beginning of the year, write the children's first names on cards and explain to them that every morning they will assist in taking attendance. Each child's name is hung on a hook. At the bottom of the chart is an envelope labeled "*PRESENTE*." One of the children's routine tasks upon arrival is to locate their name tags on the chart and place them in the envelope. Perform the expected behavior for the children.

2. Every morning the children indicate their presence by selecting their name cards and putting them in the envelope. This simple routine can teach the children to read their names and others' names as well. In addition, it helps the teacher learn which children remember—read—names easily, which have more difficulty, and which remember few names.

3. Later on, when the children gather around for sharing time or the opening exercise, the leader or another child can read aloud the name tags of those children who are absent. These will be the ones left hanging on the chart.

Other suggestions for kindergarten, first grade, and second grade children include the following:

- Have a child or a team of children, on a rotating basis, record events on a class calendar (the weather, holidays, birthdays, community or school events, or other accomplishments).
- Have children assist in making daily/weekly schedules, charts, and bulletin boards.
- Announce activities using written signs, for example, Math Time or Clean Up Time.
- Use notes to communicate with children, to praise them, to provide them with information, and to make suggestions.
- Create a simple form for children to report minor infractions, such as when a child wants to report to the teacher that another child has borrowed a paper/pencil/book without the owner's permission or when a child wants to report that during group work another child disrupted with continuous talking. At the end of the day the teacher can deal with all of the infraction reports.
- Create a communication center to encourage children to communicate with you, parents, and other students in writing. Provide an assortment of small notepaper, pencils, rubber stamps, pens, and other materials.

- Use written language to tell children what things mean and how they are used, and encourage them to anticipate and construct the meaning of written language using contextual cues.
- Use written communications between school and home, and make children aware of the messages they contain. Emphasize the children's importance as message carriers.

Routines also provide the teacher with an opportunity to observe the children's approaches to reading and writing carefully and get a better idea of their understanding of print and emergent literacy. The ways you can use these observations for assessment are discussed in Chapter 7.

CREATING MEANINGFUL ENABLING ENVIRONMENTS

Beyond routines and spontaneous teachable moments, teachers can design lessons that are authentic or attempt to reinvent authenticity. The following are some ways in which teachers can attempt to do so.

Lessons Generated by Grade Curriculum

The grade curriculum (reading and content textbooks) can be an important guide for the teacher and is probably the starting point for most teachers. The grade curriculum generally establishes the expectations for learning for the grade/age level set forth by various policy bodies (school board, state education agency, or textbook publisher) based on what experts (usually teachers and teacher-educators) think those expectations ought to be. Many school districts and schools have their own adaptation of the grade curriculum. You will want to be familiar with the expectations for the grade, but keep in mind that if you decide (or you have to comply with school policies) to use the grade curriculum (1) the material does not have to be covered starting from page one forward, (2) your students may not be interested in much of the material, (3) the suggested way of teaching may not be appropriate, purposeful, or meaningful for the children in your classroom, and (4) children vary greatly in interest and performance. Thus, the graded text may be used as a source of information, ideas, and suggestions. The best use of the grade curriculum is as a reference tool.

Lessons Generated by Eliciting Students' Interest

Students' interests are the best place to begin curriculum planning for your classroom. When children are exposed to activities and texts of high appeal, they will stretch to understand and make meaning, and they will enjoy learning. Once a positive association between learning and an area of interest has been made, the teacher can attempt to help children generalize these positive feelings to other types of content. The consideration and monitoring of interests can initiate a process in which children read/write more frequently and as a result become better readers/writers.

Children's interests can be elicited in several ways: (1) observation, (2) interest inventories, (3) student interviews, and (4) parent interviews. Parents of young children can provide valuable information on students' interests. Often they can provide data that are not or cannot be offered by the child. Listen carefully when children tell you about the television programs they have watched, the movies they have seen, the sports events they have attended, and the music they listen to most frequently. It will be necessary to elicit interest information throughout the year because children's interests change constantly as they grow and as their knowledge about a specific topic develops.

When observing for the purpose of assessing interests, here are some things you might look for:

1. What are some recurring themes from the "previous evening" stories?
2. What types of books does the child choose?
3. What are the child's emotive expressions when being read to?
4. Is the child willing to discuss materials that have been read?
5. What topics does the child prefer to write about?
6. How does the child use fantasy?
7. What does the child choose when alternative activities are available?

As children's interests are determined, you can plan lessons/activities and select materials to display in the learning environment.

Setting Up the Lesson

By using the children's interests, you can design a process that attends to the elements of instruction, which will in turn assist the children in discovering and practicing literacy concepts and strategies. There are many ways of setting up a learning activity that gives the students options for interacting with texts in various ways and for various purposes. In this chapter we will explore our Integrated Biliteracy Lesson.

The Integrated Biliteracy Lesson[2]
  I. Creating Context

Begin with an activity that is conceptually and experientially based. An essential aspect of the activity is that it include the concept or skill you want to teach. For example, a bilingual kindergarten teacher placed a white sheet of paper beside the faces of several children in the class, asking the questions, "Is s/he the same color as the paper?" "What color is the paper?" This teacher wanted to address the issues of ethnicity, culture, and color of skin, important topics to the Spanish-speaking children in the class. She started with a simple question about color that she wanted the students to think and talk about. The design of the activity can be simple—a discussion guided by the teacher, such as the one above—or complex and self-directed, depending on the topic and the time available.

II. Expanding Knowledge
   A. Observe during the creating-context phase in order to identify the issues
      emerging around the concept and to facilitate the discussion that follows.
      Ask questions about the topic and the thinking process. As students discuss
      their decision-making processes, you follow up with statements that echo
      their findings and bridge their way of speaking. One of the functions of the
      knowledge-building phase is to validate the knowledge of the learners. For
      example, the kindergartners knew how to identify the color white. The stu-
      dents working in groups explored, discovered, and created knowledge. They
      determined that the color white is not the same when said in reference to a
      person.[3] The aim is to start with a certain level of affirmation and success,
      but this is not the totality of the lesson.
   B. A second function of the knowledge-building phase is to bridge the knowl-
      edge produced by the students' common experience. It is important that you
      permit the students to speak in their own words about the knowledge they
      produced as a group. You should continue to use their words while you guide
      them into other ways of saying the same thing that they would find in texts
      or other materials, so that not only are you building vocabulary, but you are
      also creating a repertoire. You can ask questions that connect the students'
      focus with other aspects of their experience that they do not know how to
      discuss or do not know whether it would be appropriate to discuss. These
      may be topics that you, as the teacher, could bring up later for them to con-
      sider.[4] As the teacher working with ethnicity, culture, and color of skin es-
      tablished through a discussion of color, no one is actually as white as pa-
      per. This permitted the children to unlock other aspects of ethnicity. They
      were able to focus on various aspects of culture and discuss their feelings
      about being Latino and being different. The discussion of ethnicity in this
      kindergarten class was part of a larger discussion on culture. You can do
      other things at this stage—write key words on the board, draw a semantic
      map, or compose in a group. These activities give a teacher the opportunity
      to engage the learner in new ways of thinking while incorporating the knowl-
      edge generated by the learner. Remember, new information can be intro-
      duced in several ways: through direct dialogue, demonstration, or experien-
      tial instruction.
III. Action—Practice
   A. At this point you can design guided practice with chunks of new informa-
      tion or the new skill that has been acquired. Guided practice gives students
      a chance to use what was learned under the supervision of the teacher. For
      example, in the lesson dealing with ethnicity, culture, color of skin, and be-
      ing different, after reading a section of *Gente* [People] by P. Spier (1987),
      the children made drawings of their families. The teacher here acts as a re-
      source person, facilitating the children's performance, but with the aim of
      allowing students the time to think about and work on problems indepen-
      dently. Positive feedback and cues from the teacher and other students en-
      courage students to tackle the work of learning.

B. Independent group or individual practices use the chunks of new information as a base. Whether it be recoloring a picture of children playing together
or using clay to mold shapes of houses of different cultures, there are many
interesting independent activities that can be provided.

IV. Reintegration through Application
This can be an activity similar to the first or one in which you alter some aspects of the activity so that you can summarize and apply what has been learned
or generate higher-level questions about the topic. The bilingual kindergartners
were introduced to the term *rainbow* as it is used to refer to various groups of
people coming together. Students might also act out a story that is related to
the topic or theme; they could retell stories into a tape recorder so as to include
their own experiences; or they might work at a "Publishing Center" and make
a booklet of their original stories. Giving students an opportunity to use what
they are learning in the context of "authentic" reading and writing relates learning to the students' lives and motivates subsequent learning.

Organization of Lessons in Thematic Units

Developing units based on themes that include students' interests can help the teacher
organize various authentic and integrated literacy events; the teacher will have a
sense of direction and the students will feel a greater sense of ownership of what is
going on. The flexibility of larger organizational units provides the possibility of
developing a robust and rich context for integrating learning, exploring sustained
learning, and giving a common purpose to a variety of activities. The use of themes
also allows for purposeful collaborative learning and accommodates individual differences without singling out individual students. Thematic units can offer many alternatives for organizing time, materials, and resources. It can be a major class project that engages the whole group for a specific amount of time, or it may be an
individual project developed around a student's or a small group of students' interests. Thematic units can involve (1) the whole class, (2) a small group of students,
or (3) individual students. The unit of study can last a short time or take a whole
semester. It can culminate in a closure activity (a presentation, production, demon-
stration) that would give the children a sense of accomplishment and success.

First, select a theme that suits your students' ages and interests, such as the
history of our neighborhood, my place in the food chain, how to organize a flea
market, or where music comes from. The theme may derive and integrate concepts
from literature, science, social studies, and math (see Chapter 6). A theme supports
planned integration and becomes the focal point for inquiry, the use of language,
reading and writing, and cognitive development. It involves students in planning
and gives them the choice of authentic activities relevant to their interests and needs.
The sophistication of the thematic unit increases and types of activities broaden as
students' interests grow. Classroom Activity 4.2 gives an example of how a thematic unit can be developed.

Once the class has selected a theme, schedule time and provide resources for
its cross-curriculum activities. Allow the theme to become the focus of story time,

---

CLASSROOM ACTIVITY 4.2   School as a Work Place—A Thematic Unit

1. Students examine the purpose, role, and function of the school as a work place. Either the whole class or small groups brainstorm lists of persons, jobs, and functions related to the school. Prompt and encourage the students as needed.

2. Assist the students in categorizing their lists.

3. Discuss and plan how the class can be organized to study the theme. One good idea might be to conduct interviews. Children working in teams of two or three can interview school staff (the principal, secretaries, cafeteria workers, bus drivers, janitors, teachers, students, parents) to find out what they do, how they like what they do, what the favorite part of their role or function is, and how they contribute to the total school community. The children may record the interview using a tape recorder, a camera, or video equipment. If an aide or parent volunteer is not available to assist with the group work and interviews, the school staff can be asked to come to the classroom at appointed times for in-class interviews (not presentations).

4. Encourage students to make their own decisions. It is important that the children decide what questions they want to ask, what they want to know, who is going to ask the question, and the like—through the thematic unit the children are developing a whole array of skills in an integrated way. The students are making decisions (whom to interview and what to ask), speaking (asking questions and reporting to the class), listening, and writing or making notations.

5. The children follow up the interviews with reports—written, dictated, and/or illustrated.

6. In the second phase of the unit, the children can develop a school within the classroom. They can create/write skits and role play a variety of different situations.

---

a writing assignment, a science experiment, or a math activity. You may also wish to set up learning centers where individuals, partners, or teams can engage in theme-related studies. The key is to help the children create knowledge through their participation in diverse literacy activities.

INTEGRATING LANGUAGE INSTRUCTION

Integration of Speaking, Listening, Reading, and Writing

One of the objectives of your design and selection of activities should be the integration of language skills. When one is listening, opportunities for writing evolve (e.g., writing a note to remember something). When one is reading, opportunities for speaking arise (e.g., wanting to share what was just read). Integrating the four language skills is natural. Literacy instruction needs to build on the natural integrated language experiences children bring to school.

Oral and Written. The child's previous experience, oral language, and knowledge are the main contributors to acquiring meaning from written text (Durkin, 1989) and are the foundations for learning to read and write. By the time children come to school they have a remarkable oral *communicative competence*, that is, they know how to predict and use language appropriate for the social context (Hymes, 1972b). The prediction strategies acquired by young children while interacting with oral language and their environment provide a natural precursor to making predictions about written language. Experience with oral language continued through the primary grades provides a natural complement and transition to reading for meaning. However, it is important that oral language development (speaking and listening) not be isolated from children's experiences and from experience with print. Edelsky (1978) voiced concern about the practice of teaching oral language separately:

> These programs often define oral language development simply as substitution of standard for non-standard forms or as exercises in building vocabulary or in learning set phrases. Worse yet, such programs frequently become "operationalized" as a set of discrete sequenced objectives . . . This discrete, part-task learning/teaching approach to oral language effectively denies the essence of both the nature of oral language and the process of language acquisition, of which, presumably, "development" is a part. (p. 291)

Oral language development in the classroom can be supported by activities structured so that the interaction between teacher and students takes the form of *instructional conversations* (Tharp and Gallimore, 1988). In instructional conversations, teacher and students can learn from each other in a shared, open-ended discussion on a topic of mutual interest: "The teachers' interactions with students provide different forms of modeling and feedback, expand utterances, and provide purposeful questioning to guide and support students' learning" (McCollum, 1991:113). The following are some of the ways in which you can accomplish the integration of oral and written language while engaging children in instructional conversations in the classroom.

Reading to Students. Because the experience of being read to has great potential for developing both print awareness and an understanding of metalinguistic terms (words and letters), it should be a regular component of the strategy for integrating oral and written language. A strategy readily available to any teacher, reading aloud is not just a special treat used to give students a break or the last resort of a tired teacher to calm noisy students. The daily reading aloud of quality literature that is appropriate to the age and interest of students is an excellent technique for showing students how to read and engaging them in instructional conversations. For example, reading a poetry book like *Listen to the Desert: Oye al Desierto* (Mora, 1994) can demonstrate to children the importance of rhythm and phrasing in reading. An open-ended discussion of the book will provide opportunities for children to use oral language. Reading aloud to students helps develop their imagination, interests, and prediction strategies. It can encourage them to select books by the same author or on the same topic for silent reading. For older students, teachers can choose humorous or scary sections of a particular book to whet appetites. Listening to the oral presentation of a book will encourage students to check out the book.

Reading stories aloud provides an ideal medium for children to practice prediction strategies that will assist them in making meaning. When reading a story the

teacher can stop at a strategic point and ask students to tell or write about their predictions concerning the story's conclusion. For example, after reading the first part of *El gentil dragón rojo* [The Gentle Red Dragon] (Velthuys, 1982) you might stop after reading the following passage: *"El culpable fue conducido a la ciudad. Durante el recorrido, la gente insultaba al dragón y aplaudía a los bomberos que lo habían capturado."* [The guilty (dragon) was taken to the city. On their way there, people insulted the dragon and applauded the firemen who had captured him.] (p. 12) Ask the children to predict what will happen to the gentle dragon and how the story will end.

In order to take full advantage of reading aloud as a teaching strategy, the teacher can guide students to question and recognize what they are hearing and learning. As you read aloud to a class, the students can be learning:

1. what fluent reading sounds like—the cadence of Spanish/English sentences, the varied intonation appropriate for questions or a sense of excitement, and the way words are pronounced;
2. that reading can be an enjoyable experience. Laughing or emoting together about the character's escapades makes for cohesive group dynamics;
3. how to make meaning, predict, interpret, infer (empathy with characters, moods, etc.), generalize, and evaluate;
4. how to think critically about the writer's perceptions, familiarity with the setting, and issues presented;
5. aspects of writing style, for example, the interesting ways in which the author uses language, figurative language, and imagery;
6. characteristics of different forms of writing (genre): prose fiction (plot development, characterization, setting, mood, theme, and dialogue), poetry, drama, and expository writing; and

7. what book language and grammar sound like, how sentences are structured, and sentence variety.

The teacher and students can plan follow-up oral or written activities, such as designing a mural, creating a diorama, writing and illustrating alternate endings, or writing a script and dramatizing the group's favorite section of the text. Every literature selection—short story, novel, poem, article, or essay—can connect with other activities/concepts/themes to be developed across the curriculum. However, it is not always necessary to have extensive follow-up activities. Occasionally, your students can simply be allowed to feel the sheer enjoyment of hearing a good piece of literature. (See Chapter 8 for examples of children's literature you might use for this purpose.)

Dictated Material. The children's individual and group-dictated stories written on experience charts can also comprise a useful strategy for integrating oral and written language. It can help to bridge their oral experiences to reading and writing. Moreover, dictated material and self-composed material have two important qualities: they are highly motivating, because they are so personal and immediate, and they illustrate the connective link between the spoken and written aspects of language.

The teacher can record the students' dictation or ask them to talk into a tape recorder. When the teacher is recording the stories, saying each word aloud while writing it down can be helpful to the student. When reading it back in a natural-sounding voice, pointing to each word as it is pronounced is also recommended. To assist children in developing knowledge of clauses and phrases the teacher in rereading the story can place a hand under each phrase as it is read. Students can be encouraged to locate specific words and word patterns, and to reread the story in unison, pairs, or individually. Because the stories have rich associations for their authors, many of the words will be meaningful and interesting to the children who dictated them. Usually, it is the meaning-bearing or content words, that is, nouns, adjectives, and action verbs, that children remember first. But as children recombine these words to encode new sentences, function words—conjunctions and articles—become necessary, and these too become part of the child's growing reading vocabulary.

Reading and Writing. It has only been in the last decade that widespread attention has been given to the connection between reading and writing. Previously, "making meaning" was considered a writer's responsibility. The need for successful readers to assume the same posture came to be appreciated much later. Even when reading and writing were thought to be significantly different, and thus were contrasted rather than linked, they often received similar treatment in the classroom (Duin, 1987; Durkin, 1989). For example, students commonly read and wrote to satisfy a single, external demand, that is, complete an assignment. As a consequence, neither the reader nor the writer had a real purpose except to comply with the assignment. Nor was there any genuine audience except for the teacher.

Reading and writing can begin from the very first day of the school year. Even first-time kindergartners will have some awareness of print, and some will be reading and writing, to varying degrees.[5] Beginning readers and writers will use their developing skills more when they are provided with a safe and nurturing environment that encourages them to take risks. In such environments, children are encouraged to read, and their reading miscues (attempts/errors in decoding) are celebrated if they contribute to making sense and show developing strategies. Children are encouraged to write as best they can, inventing spelling if necessary, but using the words they need when they need them. No one is perfect, and sense making rather than error-free performance is the main point of reading and writing. If reading and writing are made a part of normal, day-to-day classroom business, children are likely to make rapid progress in literacy.

Writing and Sharing. When children write, they are also reading. Writing notes, preparing reports, drawing up lists, composing stories and poems, and writing letters are just a few of the many kinds of writing primary children can do. The process of (1) thinking about what they are going to write, (2) putting the words down on paper while deciding how to write and spell them, (3) reading what they have written, and (4) possibly revising and rereading gives the children the kind of meaningful repetition of written forms that is so important in learning to read. Children can be encouraged to write for themselves and for others, thus developing a sense of audience and perspective. It is not only the varied forms of writing that are important in order for children to grow as writers, but also the different audiences. Children can write notes, reports, letters, poems, and the like, but if the only real audience is the teacher and the only real purpose is to comply with an assignment, children will not be challenged to consider their reader. Opportunities must be created in which children spontaneously write with purpose for a real audience (see Edelsky, 1986). Even the teacher can become a real audience, as was the case for a second grader who wrote to a student teacher. Figure 4. 1 is an example of a child using the words, invented spellings, forms, and punctuation he needed in writing for a real purpose and audience.

Writing experiences can be integrated across the curriculum as children search for knowledge through their thematic units (discussed earlier in this chapter). They can keep journals, make signs, labels, and lists, and write letters to audiences other than the teacher (requesting field trips, thanking a class visitor, etc.). They can record and keep notes on their own physical growth and the growth and food intake of classroom pets. Imagine all the fine literacy opportunities provided by a trip to the grocery store or supermarket to buy ingredients for a cooking activity:

- observing street signs along the way;
- noting the store name;
- looking for specific ingredients;
- checking prices;
- identifying familiar products and brand names;
- checking off items on the shopping list; and
- watching as the prices are rung up on the cash register.

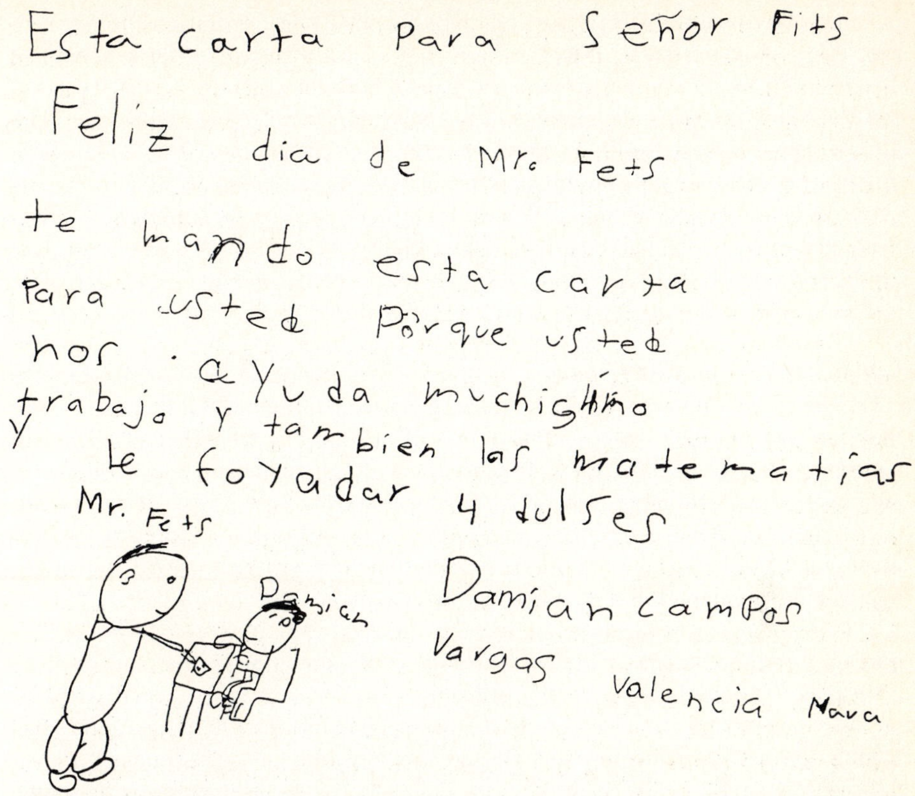

Esta carta para Señor Fits. Feliz día de Mr. Fets. Te mando esta carta para Ud. Porque Ud. nos ayuda muchísimo (con el) trabajo y tanbién (con) las matemáticas y le voy a dar 4 dulces. Damián Campos Vargas Valencia Nava

[This letter is for Mr. Fits. Mr. Fets' Happy day. I send this letter to you because you helped us a lot with our work and also with mathematics and I am going to give you 4 candies.]

Figure 4.1. Damian's Letter to Mr. Fitz

As children expand their writing repertoire, they learn to describe, to report, to raise questions and answer them, and to share real experiences. As their writing develops, their sense of audience increases. The need for writing to be meaningful and used for real purposes becomes more significant. Writing newsletters that will be circulated to other classrooms or sent home; writing plays and scripts that will be performed; and writing letters that will actually be mailed all provide a real need for audience awareness, revision, editing, and rewriting. (See the writing as a process approach in Chapter 5.) These types of activities provide for dramatic developments in the child's use of conventional segmentation (words/spaces), punctuation, and spelling.

Part of being able to write independently is gaining a mastery of the physical act of writing. The act of producing writing is laborious for young children and requires a great deal of physical coordination. The best way for children to learn handwriting is naturally and functionally. Scribbling around, signing their names to pictures, and labeling their possessions will eventually lead to increasing approximations of standard forms. Handwriting is not a skill that can be learned first and then used. Instruction in letter formation can be built into literacy events. Teachers can assist children in the development of handwriting by selecting a particular manuscript alphabet system—the system may have been selected for you by your school—but there are only slight variations among the different systems and no apparent effect on ease of learning. Whichever system you use, be sufficiently skilled to be able to write on chalkboard and paper easily and quickly. A manuscript chart can be prominently displayed in the room at the children's eye level, and each child can have a personal copy of the manuscript alphabet as well.

Self- and Class-Composed Books. Children's own individually or class written texts constitute a very important source of reading material. Once the children realize that they can write on their own, read what they write, and that what they produce will be enthusiastically received, they often become very excited about independent writing and tend to write more frequently. Composing class books represents truly authentic functional writing because the book is a record of the children's observations and/or findings incorporating daily events and real experiences with useful and interesting information in the children's own language.

Class books are collections of accounts dictated or written by individual children on a common theme. Children can write books imitating the patterns of some of their favorite predictable stories. In reading their own and their peers' writings, novice writers can learn to read from the perspective of the writer; they notice surprising spellings, become alert to style and structure, and know that books have authors because they've experienced authorship themselves. Beginning with simple topics each child contributes a page with a single sentence or phrase. Children can be encouraged to pattern their book after one they have read. Figure 4.2 demonstrates some sample pages from a class book composed by first graders. Each child dictated a sentence using the pattern from *El oso más elegante* [The Best Dressed Bear] (Blocksma, 1986) and illustrated it. The teacher bound the pages into a book and affixed a library-pocket to the back of the book. Children were encouraged to check the book out overnight to take home to read to their parents.

More ambitious group books can evolve naturally as children are involved in more sophisticated units of study.

The development of texts that will be read by others will promote the need to develop spelling skills. Spelling in the texts of beginning readers is generally so creative and unique that even the writers may not always be able to read what they've written. Children invent spelling[6] in much the same way that they invent words in oral language development. They are sensitive to rules but then overextend them. But soon they will develop consistencies so that both they and the teacher can read what they write.

When do you directly teach spelling? Not at the first sight of misspelling or even after continued misspelling. Observe what strategies the child is using; most invented spelling will be self-corrected as the child reads and becomes more aware of different ways of writing words. Children will use different strategies for different languages. In Spanish, for example, children will use more vowels than conso-

EL OSO
MÁS ELEGANTE

EL OSO MÁS
ELEGANTE
escrito por:
Glenn
Joel Edgar
Reynaldo
orlando
Erik c.
Arturo O.
María.G.

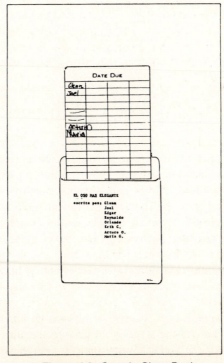

EL OSO MAS ELEGANTE
escrito por: Glenn
Joel
Edgar
Reynaldo
Orlando
Erik C.
Arturo O.
Maria G.

Figure 4.2. Sample Class Book

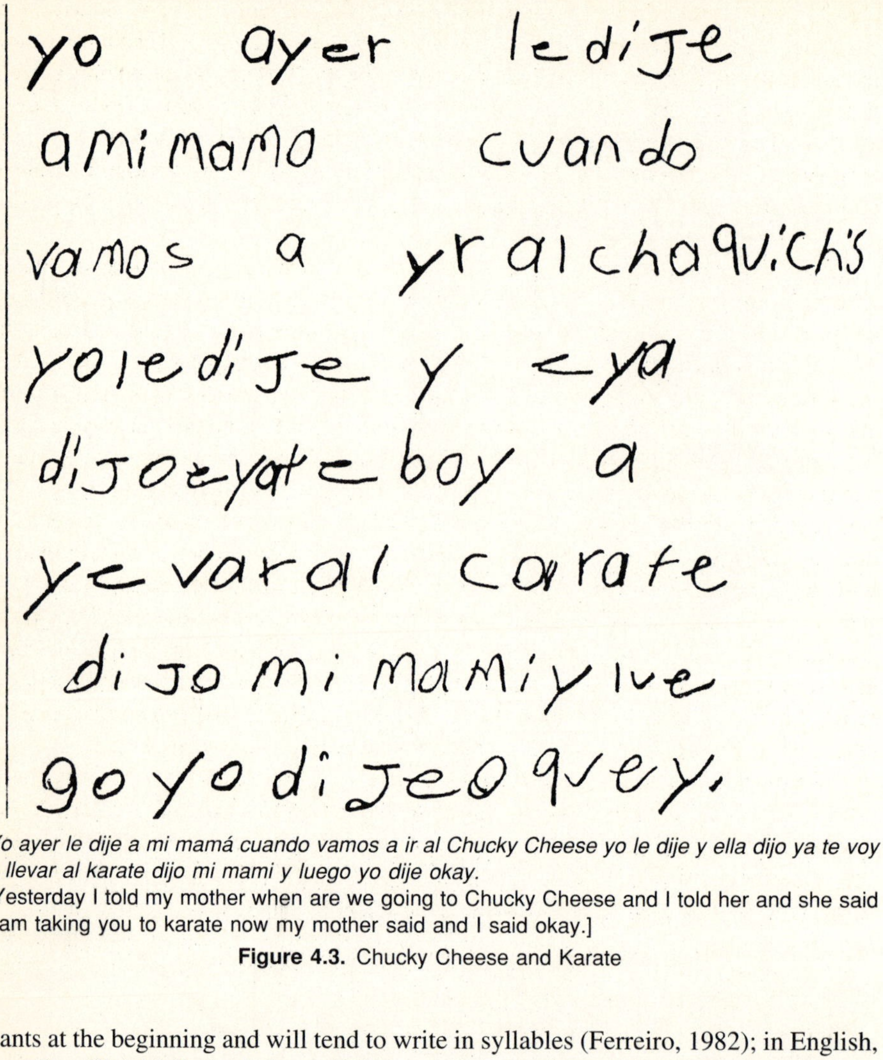

yo   ayer   le dije
a mi mamo   cuando
vamos   a   yr al chaquich's
yo le dije y c ya
dijo e yot e boy a
ye var al carate
di jo mi mamiy lue
go yo dije o qvey.

Yo ayer le dije a mi mamá cuando vamos a ir al Chucky Cheese yo le dije y ella dijo ya te voy
a llevar al karate dijo mi mami y luego yo dije okay.
[Yesterday I told my mother when are we going to Chucky Cheese and I told her and she said
I am taking you to karate now my mother said and I said okay.]

Figure 4.3. Chucky Cheese and Karate

nants at the beginning and will tend to write in syllables (Ferreiro, 1982); in English, vowels will initially be left out (Bissex, 1980). In either case, children will begin to use a combination of letter names and sounds to spell words. If they feel supported and encouraged, they will continue to invent spellings for the new words they need. As children read extensively from books and literature they become aware of more conventional spelling. Developing writers will realize that the spelling in the material they read is standardized. It is through extensive reading of standard written language that children will learn conventional spelling. Soon they will develop more consistency, and teachers and parents will be able to read the children's work.

Figure 4.3 is a sample of a second grader writing about his favorite topics, Chucky Cheese and karate, using a variety of invented spelling strategies. The child is applying his knowledge of Spanish orthography to spell the English /k/ in Chucky, karate, and okay.

In assisting children in their writing development teachers ought to look at the strategies[7] that the children are using for their invented spelling. Teachers can use metalinguistics (talk about the characteristics of words, letters, symbols) or metacognition (talk about the thinking process) strategies to help children become more aware of the graphophonic cues needed for conventional spelling. If a correct spelling is requested, the teacher can provide correct spellings for young children; for older children the teacher can suggest that the child use a dictionary.

Interactive Journals. Journals can be a powerful learning tool, starting in kindergarten. Writing in journals gives children the opportunity to use language authentically in a literacy context. Interactive journals provide a vehicle for children and teachers to communicate on a daily basis about student-selected topics. Some children illustrate their writing with quick line drawings. The guidelines that will facilitate journal writing are: (1) having a consistent time designated each day for journal writing, (2) making students feel they can use their own mechanics and invented spelling, and (3) having teachers authentically interact in writing with each child. The teacher and the class can decide beforehand who will be allowed to read the journal. In most cases the children understand that their teacher and their parents will read it. Some students will want to share their journals with other students.

Because the purpose of journals is written communication, teachers should not correct children's journal writing but should write comments on content and provide encouragement and reassurance. It is important that teachers respond regularly to what children write in their journals in order to reinforce interactive written communication. Figure 4.4 illustrates a teacher's response to a journal entry.

Some children begin to see the journal as a unique way of communicating with the teacher. For example, a second grade boy who quickly realized that the teacher would respond to whatever he wrote in this journal began asking the teacher questions. Later, to facilitate the teacher's quick response, he began to put in response boxes for her reply. One such entry went something like this:

Mi mamá me compró un camisa nueva. ¿Te gusta?
sí [ ] o no [ ]
[My mother bought me a new shirt. Do you like it? Yes or no.]

The teacher would check the appropriate box and make any other comment she thought appropriate.

According to Flores et al. (1985) journal writing gives children the opportunity to: *advantage*

1. learn that written language communicates;
2. experience making choices about topics and develop a sense of ownership of the written product;
3. develop their writing within meaningful context;
4. integrate language skills and experience its function and processes;
5. develop a personal interaction with the teacher through writing; and
6. use this safe environment to experiment with the second language.

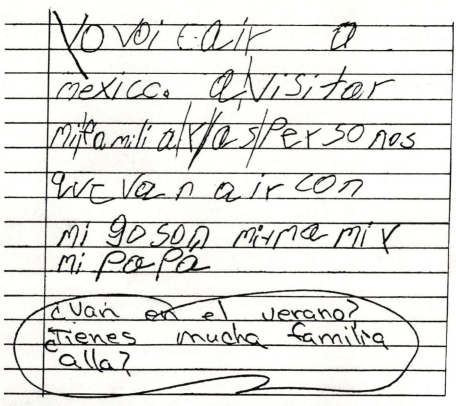

Student: *Yo voy a ir a México. A visitar mi familia y las personas que van a ir conmigo son mi mami y mi papá.* [I am going to Mexico. To visit my family and the people that are going with me are my mother and my father.]
Teacher: *¿Van en el verano? ¿Tienes mucha familia allá?*
[Are you going in the summer? Do you have a lot of relatives there?]

Figure 4.4. Teacher's Response to Journal Entry

Journals give teachers an opportunity to:

Advan to teacher

1. learn about each child's interests, ideas, and everyday concerns;
2. interact and communicate on an individual basis with each child;
3. model standard conventions of writing in the context of authentic communicative use;
4. assess the use of knowledge and skills that each child is developing; and
5. assess when the child is making a transition into the second language.

Integrating Different Types of Material and Technology

Literature and Trade Books. Through extensive interaction with a variety of literature and books, children can develop diversity in their purpose and use of language and literacy skills. Teachers can create the need for children to interact with a variety of published texts in Spanish and English, thus permitting children to observe the skilled and standard use of language. A place to start with kindergartners and first graders is with predictable books. Their familiar content and structure and the often repetitious, cyclical sequencing make them predictable. *El Oso Más Elegante* [The Best Dressed Bear] (Blocksma, 1986), *Los Seis Deseos de la Jirafa* [The Six Wishes of the Giraffe] (Ada, 1989), or *Los Tres Osos* [The Three Bears] (Claret, 1986) are examples of predictable books for beginning readers. It is easy for children to get a sense of where the book is going and to predict what is coming next. Predictable books provide children with rich contexts for vocabulary development and for the development and use of decoding skills with predictable print. Fortunately, young children seem to love rereading familiar predictable materials that give them productive, self-motivated practice. Classroom Activity 4.3 illustrates how a predictable book can be used to teach reading and writing.

By using literature, you can show students how to write more effective sentences and also longer forms such as paragraphs, fables, and short stories. Conventional spelling, punctuation, and grammatical structures can also be taught using literature as a tool to call children's attention to the mechanics of writing.

As children develop more independent reading skills, they will need a wider selection of literature. You will want to prepare by including a variety of different literature—different genres—with a wide range in reading difficulty. Select books designed to interest and motivate children to read. The books should have lovely, colorful illustrations, and the print should be large and readable. For example, *Hairs: Pelitos* (Cisneros, 1994), illustrated by Terry Ybáñez, and *Moon Rope: Un Lazo a la Luna*, written and illustrated by Lois Ehlert (1992), are beautifully yet very distinctively illustrated. Both will beckon children to pick up the book and explore the text and the illustrations repeatedly. The classroom literature collection can include traditional stories, modern stories, fantasy stories, folklore, poetry, plays, and other genres. Different types of literature can be used to demonstrate a variety of styles of writing and various literary forms. Chapter 8 of this book offers more suggestions on the use of literature in the literacy program. The following are some selected anthologies of folklore, poetry, and plays appropriate for primary students:

Folklore
Bravo-Villasante, C. 1981. *China, china, capuchina, en esta mano está la china.* Valladolid, Spain: Miñón.
Corona, P. 1978. *Pita, pita cedacero: Cuentos de nanas.* México: Novaro.
Mendoza, V. T. 1980. *Lírica infantil de México.* México: Fondo de Cultura Económica.

Poesia/Poetry
Acevedo, M. 1988. *Llamo a la luna sol y es de día.* México City: Editorial Trillas.
Freyre de Matos, I. 1979. *ABC de Puerto Rico.* Illus. A. Matorell. Sharon, CT: Troutman Press.
Vega, B. de la. (ed.). 1960. *Antología de la poesía infantil.* Buenos Aires: Editorial Kapelusz.

Teatro/Plays
Armijo, C. 1981. *Bam, bim, bom: Arriba el telón.* Valladolid, Spain: Miñón.
Leza, M. J. 1988. *La bruja cigüeña.* Madrid: Editorial Escuela Española, S. A.
Vázquez Vigo, C. 1984. *Jugar al teatro.* Valladolid, Spain: Miñón.

**CLASSROOM ACTIVITY 4.3   Integrated Reading/Writing
and Predictable Books**

1. In context with a unit on *osos* [bears] read the story *El Oso Más Elegante* [The Best Dressed Bear] (Blocksma, 1986). The children will soon begin to pick up on the predictable characteristics of the story. For example, the teacher reads, *"Si el más elegante quieres ser, calcetines nuevos te debes poner. Nuevos calcetines me voy a poner. Y el más elegante voy a ser."* [If you want to be the most elegant, you should wear new socks. New socks I will wear. And the most elegant I will be.] As the story continues, and during subsequent readings, the children will predict what comes next.

2. Discuss the style of writing, asking children to infer and relate the bear's experience to their own experience. Answer and discuss any observations, comments, or questions about graphophonic cues, orthography, or vocabulary. Reread the pattern, helping students to become aware of and familiar with its predictable characteristics, and discuss how the author uses these characteristics.

3. After the teacher reading, children may read and reread the story in pairs and small groups. The children can be instructed on how to ask each other prediction, inference, and application questions.

4. Begin the prewriting activity in small groups by encouraging the students to offer ways of adapting the pattern using their own experiences, words, and themes. Some suggestions from a first grade class were:
   "Si el más gordo quieres ser, frijoles debes comer. Frijoles guisados voy a comer. Y el más gordo voy a ser." [If you want to be the fattest, you should eat beans. Baked beans I will eat. And the fattest I will be.]
   "Si el más feo quieres ser, bigotes te debes poner. Bigotes grandes me voy a poner. Y el más feo voy a ser." [If you want to be the ugliest, you should wear mustaches. Big mustaches I will wear. And the ugliest I will be.]
   "Si el más listo quieres ser, ejercicios debes hacer. Muchos ejercicios voy a hacer. Y el más listo voy a ser." [If you want to be the most active/clever, you should exercise. Many exercises I will do. And the most active/clever I will be.]

5. Follow with the writing of a class book (in which each student writes a page for the book), a group book (each group member writes a page), or an individual book (each child writes several pages for his or her own book). The drafting of the book may be done at a center or over several days during the daily writing time.

6. The bound book(s) can be displayed alongside the original book for the children to read. A library-pocket can be affixed to the back of class or group books so that children can check out the book(s) to read with their parents.

A suggested list of children's literature appropriate for the primary grades can also be found in Chapter 8, as can a list of U.S. distributors of children's literature and trade books in Spanish. This is a starting point and by no means an all-inclusive list. Most of these materials can be found in public libraries.

Technology, Reading, and Writing. Technology such as Polaroid cameras, overhead projectors, filmstrips, video cameras and recorders, videocassettes, and computers can be used as an integral part of a literacy program. Pictures of the children's first day at school may later be used to assist them in writing and illustrating an account of their first day at school. Videos of field trips, examples of printed matter from the community, school events, or ordinary school surroundings can often be used to stimulate discussions for writing activities, for example, script writing. Teachers and students can use overhead projectors for story dictation and brainstorming. Filmstrips and videos can be used to provide students with the vicarious experience of a topic, assisting their comprehension when reading materials on the same topic and stimulating writing interest.

The visual media of television, film, and video can play a role in classroom reading instruction. First, such media can serve as a source of language models for children, and second, they can bring experiences and concepts to children that they might not encounter in their daily lives. The on-screen print of some children's programming and of commercials also serves as environmental print that children learn to interpret (Rodriguez, in progress). Spanish language television is now available in most areas of the United States, but its programming consists primarily of *telenovelas* [soap operas], variety shows, and local news. Some programming for children is beginning to appear, mostly modeled after English-speaking cartoons and game shows. And, of course, English language television is also viewed by most children whether they speak English or not. Television serves as a language model (both for Spanish and English).

Davies (1986), in a synthesis of British research on reading, concluded that television viewing does not directly compete with reading in real time but may actually serve to stimulate reading. As a source of many vicarious experiences for children, it can be used to stimulate reading and writing. For example, a committee of three or four children can recommend a program for the class to view—the "pick of the week"—from the current television guide (which you have brought to the classroom). The class "pick" can be discussed and the committee's recommendations evaluated after the programs are seen. This activity allows for the critical discussion of programs and acknowledges television as an integral part of children's lives.

The computer is another communication tool that, used along with reading, writing, speaking, and listening, expands children's communication range and effectiveness. The computer and its instructional programs, called courseware or software, can enable children to interact with and generate ideas, concepts, and literacy. Spanish language software and cooperative student learning techniques (discussed in Chapter 5) can assist in integrating the computer in the reading/writing process and in providing computer access to Spanish-speaking children (González-Edfelt, 1993; Pérez, 1987).

Word-processing packages, for example *Fred Writer* (available in Spanish and in the public domain), *Mi Primer Editor* [Primary Editor], *Milliken's Word Processor*, or *Bank Street Writer*, enable students to integrate reading and writing with the result that printed selections can be compiled into "published" class works for the other children to read.

The use of computer writing networks in classrooms and across campuses, cities, and even countries creates a whole new concept of "writing" (Peyton & Mackinson-Smyth, 1989; Sayers, 1989). Through a computer writing network called

De Orilla a Orilla [From Shore to Shore], children in bilingual classes have been communicating with each other throughout the United States, Mexico, and Puerto Rico. Communication is accomplished through writing messages on a word processor and transmitting via modem using the Computer Mail System-SchoolNet (CMS-SchoolNet). Using this technology, children begin to see writing as a natural and essential way of communicating in many varied situations. On the network they experience extended times during which their primary identity is established through writing or creating texts. Sayers (1989) reports that children find a written identity and create a written manner of expression in a lively, creative, and spontaneous context.

A number of reading/writing software packages are available in Spanish. The Spanish reading and language arts packages, like the English language software, range from drill and practice (fill in the blank/worksheet or one correct response software) to more interactive packages that encourage students' thinking, reading, and writing. When choosing software the teacher or school can decide on the criteria for selection that are appropriate for the biliteracy program. The primary criteria ought to be the availability of interactive reading-related activities that have the child both read and write (Anderson-Inman, 1987). A list of distributors of software in Spanish is included at the end of the chapter.

English software can also be used as children develop their English language skills. For example, software packages, such as *Story Tree* or *Explore-A-Story*, that incorporate word-processing technology and story creation allow children to complete program-generated stories or create their own stories and reports. These types of programs include the use of graphics and icons, which can act as contextual clues for children beginning to write in English.

Voy a Leer Escribiendo (VALE) [Writing to Read] is a computer-based instructional system designed to develop the writing and reading skills of kindergarten and first grade students. The program is designed to assist students in writing what they can say and reading what they can write (Torres-Guzmán, 1990). Building on the foundation of their natural language development, students work at a series of learning stations using the words they can say to write words they can read. In the first step, the system uses a "voice" to introduce students to each of the phonemic sounds that make up the Spanish language. The students then proceed to the *Cartilla* [The Work Journal], *Escribiendo a mano/a máquina* [Writing/Typing], and *Formar palabras* [Make Words] stations where they immediately use the phonemes they have learned to create words and stories. The *VALE* system also includes a *Biblioteca Auditiva* [Listening Library] with which students listen to Spanish literature stories on audio cassette while they follow the story's text in the corresponding book. Figure 4.5 illustrates a child's story written using the *VALE* system.

a series of skill there are to be developed.

Basal Reading. A basal reading program is a sequential reading approach usually K-8 based on the assumption that learning to read consists of mastering a hierarchy of skills. It is the kind of program that is used most frequently in teaching reading. Spanish basal reading programs are modeled after English reading programs and usually employ either a phonetic or syllabic approach to the teaching of reading. Basal readers consist of a series of graded reading textbooks, generally from the

each one builds upon next one.

Advancy very detail activity, supplementary reader.

Habia una ves KiKo y Roberto
y Carlos fuimos al boske i nosotro
encontamos un rio pescamos pezes
y preparamos fuego enpesamos
a comer. Idespues nos fuimos
a miami.

[Once upon a time Kiko and Roberto and Carlos went to the woods and we came upon a river. We caught fish and prepared a fire and began to eat. Afterwards we went to Miami.]

Figure 4.5. *VALE* Story

kindergarten readiness through the sixth grade level. The teacher's guide is a key to understanding the organization and underlying assumptions of the series. The guide generally describes in precise detail how and when to introduce new material, what skills to teach and how to teach them, and how to review and reinforce these skills. Supplementary materials frequently include workbooks, duplicating masters, charts, films, records, filmstrips, and tests. The newer basal series may also include selections from literature either as parts of readers or as accompanying literature books.

Because the content of the texts and the directions for the teacher are so clearly sequenced and programmed in a basal reading series, a beginning teacher may find this kind of program a useful resource. However, its use as an authentic tool for developing literacy is questionable, although not impossible.

One example of the successful adaptation of the use of basal materials is the Kamehameha Early Education Program (KEEP) described by Au and Jordan (1981). The KEEP program served native Hawaiian children who were having difficulty with reading. The teachers modified the use of the basal reading lessons by integrating the traditional Hawaiian talkstory (home/community discourse). The lessons were structured so that children began with reading from the basal, but the discussion that followed invited children to bring in or create their own meaning through the use of talkstory, a traditional form of didactic storytelling.

Teachers will need to look at ways of adapting and integrating basal texts to the experiences of their students if they decide to use them. A suggested organizational pattern for teachers who wish to begin integrating literature and other print experiences into their basal reading program might be to begin with the traditional three reading groups that meet with the teacher every day. As the children indicate a need for diversity of experience and the teacher feels comfortable enough to begin to experiment, the pattern might change to permit the children within the groups to read literature, work on independent reading, or group reading/writing projects in some of the time periods originally devoted to round-robin reading. The teacher might start, for example, by adding some core children's literature or other trade books to the basal readers. The children can select their favorite passage to read, or teacher and children can have book-sharing discussions during round-robin reading. Gradually, the teacher may find that the basal readers have become a subordinate feature of the literacy program as more and more literature experiences are provided that are tailored to the needs of individual children.

Oral Reading and Silent Reading. Some teachers and many parents still equate "teaching reading" with asking children to read aloud. The fact that oral reading is sometimes helpful when young children are just beginning to read must be put into perspective. Oral reading can be used to assist children in (1) understanding that what is said can be written or that text stands for spoken language, (2) comprehending the meaning of metalinguistic terms like *word* and *sentence,* and (3) identifying the clauses and phrases of the text upon which the development of fluency and comprehension are dependent (Goodman, 1986). Nonetheless, round-robin reading, the practice of having children take turns reading aloud while the others follow along, is likely to be a halting, listlike rendition of a text that bears little relationship to familiar spoken language and thus obscures rather than clarifies meaning. In the Kamehameha example, the children did silent reading for comprehension and later constructed and co-narrated the story guided by the teacher's questions, which focused on their understanding of the text.

When oral reading in groups is done, teachers will want to keep two standards in mind. The first, which may seem too obvious to mention, is the availability of an authentic audience that has a desire, or at least a willingness, to listen. To assure such an audience, the material being read ought to be worth sharing. If the material is dull, too familiar, or of little interest, nobody can be surprised if some of the students are not paying attention during reading. The second standard is preparation. Durkin (1989) suggests that when oral reading is used, it should be preceded by silent reading of the text. The children will need to have adequate preparation time and assistance in prereading (silently or quietly) the material to be shared.

Another aspect of the oral and silent reading controversy is whether *sustained silent reading* (SSR) or reading to students is more effective. Most reading specialists now agree that silent reading is the most efficient medium for comprehending text. One of the best ways to help children read for meaning and appreciate reading as a valuable experience is to incorporate a sustained silent reading period into the daily schedule. This is a period of five to twenty minutes when children, teacher, and other adults silently read a piece of material of their own choice. The children do not have to be reading in the conventional sense, "decoding and comprehending," to participate. They may "read" the pictures and illustrations. What is important is that there are no interruptions, that no reports or other records are required, that each person selects just one piece of print material for the entire session, and that the teacher participates along with the children.

However, SSR requires a large and varied collection of reading material from which to select, and clear rules must be established. In addition to the classroom collection, children and teacher may want to bring reading materials from home. Children can be encouraged to find a comfortable, quiet place for SSR. Students may choose to sit on rugs in quiet corners, on the floor beside their desks, or simply stay at their desks. They can choose any of these or other locations so long as they understand that reading is done quietly without interrupting anyone or asking any questions. SSR helps children to understand that reading is important enough to be savored in and of itself (Kaisen, 1987).

With respect to SSR's effectiveness in comparison to reading to students, it is important that both occur. Children love to be read to, but the pleasure of independent reading also needs to be developed. When children are interacting around text, when they spontaneously break into playing school where one of them is the teacher and the others the audience, or when children are looking at pictures and constructing their own text, they are performing valuable activities that assist them in becoming literate.

Integrating Languages

As children develop sound literacy skills in their first language, these skills will lay the groundwork for their acquisition and perfection of the second language. From the first day of class, time will be devoted to speaking, listening, reading, and interacting in English. The amount of time allocated for English literacy will depend on the children's proficiency in native literacy and English oral language, and on the program model. (See Chapter 3 for a discussion of program models.) The children's second language will develop when they are provided with a language-rich environment where they can participate in interesting experiences to which the English language is attached.[8] For some children it will also be necessary for the teacher to design experiences that will counteract the distrust that they may have toward English because of previous negative experiences with English language instruction.

Teachers can provide contexts for second language learning by using a variety of strategies requiring the use of language and literacy. The following are some examples of these strategies:

1. Use rich, interesting stories and story-based activities in which children are introduced to English vocabulary and sentence structure in context. Research comparing the teaching of English as a Second Language (ESL) to children using stories, versus traditional oral drill or the total physical response program, has demonstrated that the story-based ESL results in greater overall English language growth (Allen, 1986; Enright & McCloskey, 1985; Elley & Mangubhai, 1983; Urzúa, 1980). Stories that are based on Latino cultural themes, such as *Too Many Tamales* (Soto, 1993) or *The Rooster Who Went to His Uncle's Wedding* (Ada, 1993), will provide anchors for the children's prior knowledge or experiences while they stretch to comprehend and communicate in English.

2. Have children participate in concrete activities, such as cooking or other hands-on activities accompanied by instructional conversations (open-ended questions and comments), to encourage students to use English language in context. Singing songs that have accompanying actions is another way to introduce English in context and for children to practice oral language in a safe environment.

3. As children develop oral expression they can begin dictating language experience stories. A book such as Carmen Lomas Garza's *Family Pictures: Cuadros de familia* (1990) can be used to model the process of dictating personal stories. This leads to the creation of comprehensible text that children can then read (Krashen, 1985b).

4. Children can begin very early using predictable English books in much the same way they used them in Spanish (see previous section). Using materials that are highly predictable (or bilingual books that have first been read, discussed, and studied in Spanish) will increase the reader's ability to read in English successfully. Repetition of language and incident, such as that found in *The Three Little Pigs* and *The Three Bears*, makes these stories examples of predictable reading materials. In addition, many of these materials are available in Spanish and, if the children have read them in Spanish, they will be able to fill in the context for the second language.

5. When texts that the children are not familiar with are introduced, allowing the children to comment or answer questions in their native language will also facilitate their ability to predict and comprehend second language texts (Moll, 1989).

6. For content-area language learning it is crucial that children participate in group context-building activities because each child may have different bits of information and language to contribute. These activities provide the student with the opportunity to learn more content and hear more English.

Teachers must provide an environment that is challenging and one that encourages students to take risks in their language usage. The aim of the second language strategies just described is to help students develop English within varied contexts (environmental print, literature, content-area materials, and real-world print) so that they will be able to meet the literacy demands of school as well as use literacy for their own purposes.

SUMMARY

During the primary school years children develop the ability to read and write by building on their competence in spoken language. Home and community learning form the foundations and are the roots for learning to read and write. The school literacy program suggested in this chapter includes strategies for using teachable moments, classroom routines, students' interests, thematic organization of units, and an integrated biliteracy approach to assure that children have a variety of experiences. Central to this chapter's discussion was the creation of meaningful learning environments that elicit authentic literacy. Strategies and activities for several kinds of integration (i.e., the four language skills, different types of materials, and both languages) were presented.

ACTIVITIES

Journal Activities

1. Did you have a favorite book as a child? What were the qualities (topic, use of language, size of print, illustrations, etc.) that you remember that might have made this your favorite book?

2. Are there still times when you like to be read to or do you always prefer to find a quiet spot to read?

Discussion Activities

1. In small groups, compare your experiences with writing instruction when you were in the primary grades and the writing instruction suggested in this chapter.

2. In the integrated biliteracy lesson (p. 71–73), the expanding knowledge phase invites students to discuss and connect the knowledge produced by the students' common experience. Discuss in a small group what this means by doing a semantic map with a theme such as *calle* (street). One student should record/report the discussion. After the discussion, review the recorder/reporter's notes and discuss what the diverse students' experience with the theme could mean in the context of teaching the expanding knowledge phase of the integrated biliteracy lesson.

3. In a small group, brainstorm ideas for literacy activities using the theme *comunicación* (communication). Develop lesson plans for one or more of the ideas. The lessons can use literature and integrate listening, speaking, reading, and writing.

Field-Based Activities

1. Visit a kindergarten class to observe and record instances of children attending to (a) concepts related to print and reading, (b) vocabulary of reading instruction, and/or (c) concepts related to storybooks. Write about your observations and what insights you have about reading as a result of these observations.

2. Interview two or three kindergarten teachers about their views on emergent literacy and what constitutes a beginning literacy program. How do they differ in views? How do you imagine their literacy programs are set up? How are they similar or different from what is proposed by the authors of this book?

3. Audiotape a conversation of a family group, a group of friends, or a group of children. Bring the audiotape to class and in small groups listen and decide what the central themes of the conversation were, compare the themes identified by various group members, and then decide on a lesson that would center on one of the themes.

4. Using a currently adopted basal reader teacher's guide, contrast the components of a lesson suggested in this chapter with the lesson steps suggested for a basal reader lesson.

NOTES

1. "Reinvent" is used in the Freirian sense, in which students have to reconstruct, recreate, and bring in their own discourses (Freire & Macedo, 1987).

2. This model is an adaptation of the action/reflection/action model of Freire (1970), in which he describes praxis not as verbalism or activism but as both action and reflection and as the integration of theory and practice.

3. This lesson was conducted in a very safe environment and in the context of a larger unit on race relations. As racism is so prevalent in our society, we believe teachers must explore their own internalized attitudes toward race as well as those of the children in their classroom.

4. This is what Freire (1970) calls "hinged themes": "They may either facilitate the connection between two themes in the program unit, filling a possible gap between the two; or they may illustrate the relations between the general program content and the view of the world held by the people" (p. 114).

5. Harste, Woodward, and Burke (1984), among others, interpret writing as an orchestration of multiple cuing systems (graphophonic, syntactic, semantic, pragmatic) to produce a text that has a function in a given context. What this means is that precursors of conventional writing—from scribbling, to forming letters/symbols, to the social or communicative context—is writing. What distinguishes emergent writing from that of older children is that it usually involves nonconventional symbols, that is, scribbles.

6. Ferreiro and Teberosky (1982) studied the writing development of four- to six-year-old Spanish-speaking children and described their progression of invented spellings. They found that the children they studied had developed a syllabic hypothesis—that every syllable should be encoded with one letter. The first, second, and third graders studied by Edelsky (1986) used phonetic features (one letter for one sound), and phonic generalizations followed or were used by those children who were more literate.

7. Edelsky (1986) studied the writing of bilingual children writing in Spanish and English. She analyzed the parts of numerous strategies including spelling, segmentation, punctuation, code-switching, and audience.

8. See Richard-Amato (1988) for a discussion of second language acquisition and for descriptions of and suggestions for different second language approaches, such as Total Physical Response, Natural Approach, Jazz Chants, and so on.

CHAPTER 5

Developing Proficiency in Reading and Writing

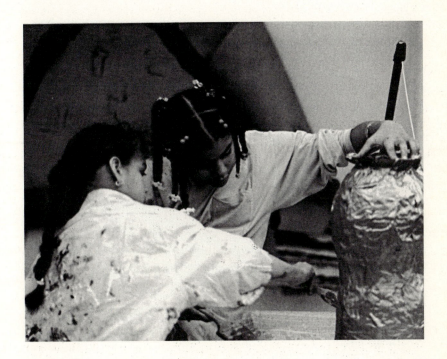

INTRODUCTION

As children reach the middle childhood years (grades three, four, and five) they are beginning to exercise more independence, to participate in formulating and establishing their own rules, and to view experiences from the perspective of others. Most are eager to direct their own learning and to go beyond the limits of their everyday lives. At this stage of development, they are starting to explore more abstract concepts, especially in collaboration with others. They are able to appreciate actual and fanciful interpretations of similar experiences, such as real accounts of space travel and science fiction, and are beginning to develop a sense of history. During this middle childhood period children can develop a sense of autonomy and cooperation as they gain literate proficiency.

By third grade, most children who are receiving Spanish reading/writing instruction will be using their Spanish reading and writing skills with some independence and confidence.[1] The goal of the integrated language arts program in the middle childhood years is to develop and enrich the children's bilingual competency and, in addition to validating their own language and cultural heritage, to broaden their cultural repertoire. Developing language proficiency and literacy in the native language will ensure success in the development of literacy in English (Lambert & Taylor, 1987). Children who develop proficiency in using their native language to communicate, to gain information, to solve problems, and to think can easily learn to use a second language in similar ways (Krashen & Bider, 1988).

This chapter discusses how teachers can help children expand their classroom social roles and interactions so that they may learn more about their world and the world of others, extend their reading and writing to a range of purposes, and explore a variety of literary genres during middle childhood years.

CLASSROOM SOCIAL ROLES FOR LITERACY

Classroom social roles and interactions determine the types of literacy events that children choose to engage in. Literary events are planned or spontaneous situations involving the use of print, where children ask about or observe some aspect of print, discuss reading or writing, or read or write. Vygotskian theory explains how human learning develops through interaction with others. Interpersonal interactions occur during social and cultural processes that involve cultural tools and artifacts such as speech, writing, and drawing. These tools and artifacts are first used to communicate with others and to mediate contact with the outside world; later, they are used for more abstract thinking processes. Thus, from a Vygotskian perspective, one of the teacher's main functions is to create a social context in which these cultural processes and tools will be used in interactions with others. It is through the mastery of these representational and communicative skills (Olson, 1986) that students develop the means for independent thinking. The literacy skills children acquire are directly related to how they interact with others in specific problem-solving environments. Children internalize the kind of help they receive from others and subsequently use what they have learned to direct their own problem-solving behavior.

Teachers and students establish social systems in order to accommodate teaching/learning through social interaction (Vygotsky, 1978). Thus, the ideal classroom social environment will create opportunities for students to collaborate in activities that integrate their interests and experiences with their thinking, listening, speaking, reading, and writing skills.

In the previous chapter we focused on types of lesson organization that would enable students to become literate and open to the process of generating and accessing new knowledge. In this chapter we will focus on grouping strategies for children in the middle childhood years.

Student's Role

Students need a classroom social context that allows them to help create the circumstances of their own learning. They need to feel safe using their home discourses in the classroom to discuss, infer, predict, persuade, and critique their own reading and writing. They also need access to other ways of using language and literacy (folklore, oral traditions, etc.) that are part of their cultural group but unfamiliar to them. As students gain experience in and knowledge of written language, they will begin to examine their homes, classrooms, and other discourses (Harman & Edelsky, 1989).

In reader-writer interactions, just as in conversation, the social context of the situation is systematically related to what children write or say (Couture, 1986; Halliday & Hasan, 1985). Placing students in confined roles as powerless responders will only lead to a narrow use of their reading and writing skills, restricted tests, and limited literacy growth. Discussions, small-group work, and opportunities to share what children are reading and writing will create social interactions that stimulate student interest and lead to diversity in the practice of their literacy skills. As proposed Chapter 4, studies around a theme or issue involving students working in groups can mediate and increase their proficiency in both oral and written language. Children can assume new roles when:

1. they have the opportunity to make choices in selecting what books to read, what topics to study, and what forms of writing to use when presenting their ideas; teachers can supply the environment, activities, positive reinforcement, and opportunity for reading, thinking, and writing, but the motivation and choice should come from the student;

2. they engage in reading and writing processes in a context that allows diverse interpretations and permits them to see themselves and find their own voices;

3. they make metaphorical transactions with authors and discover the joy of reading good literature; talking about books, getting to know authors, and responding to books provide positive support for the development of literacy and self-sufficiency; and

4. their interests and experiences are reflected in classroom materials and activities. For example, children can be encouraged to plan and conduct studies around *insectos* [insects], *la pulga* [the flea market], *el día de los Reyes* [the Epiphany] or other topics of their choice.

Teacher's Role

Researchers studying oral classroom discourse (Cazden, 1986, 1987; Durkin, 1989; Heath, 1986; Mehan, 1979) have documented that teachers tend to rely on the initiation-response-evaluation (IRE) discourse structure as a "default" pattern for conducting lessons. In this three-part structure, the teacher initiates questions (to which there are predetermined answers) in order to check the students' knowledge, a student responds, and the student's response is evaluated with or without teacher feedback. This structure involves the traditional roles played by teacher and student: the teacher initiates and evaluates and the student responds.

Hansen (1987) suggests an alternate concept of response and its effect on students' reading and writing. In this approach, students respond to a written text and the teacher then responds to the students by answering their questions, affirming what they know, clarifying concepts and ideas, and negotiating shared meaning (of teacher, student, and author) based on the text. This is accomplished by asking questions for which neither teacher nor students have a known "right" answer or for which the teacher and students must search for answers. For example, a teacher who has not read the story a child is reading might ask, "You said the prince is a sad person. Why do you say he is a sad person?" If the teacher really wants to know why the student thinks the prince is sad, this question can go beyond factual or inferential information and into a dialogue in which there is no "right" answer.

The roles of teacher and student shift and alternate. Learners are actively constructing meaning all the time; they are "re-creating meaning" (Moll, 1989). They do not just passively absorb information. Harman and Edelsky (1989) suggest teacher/student roles that are flexible and expansive so that students teach and teachers learn. This flexibility of roles encourages multiple interpretations of texts; it honors and uses the language norms or home discourses that students bring to school; it emphasizes language repertoires rather than right answers; and it fosters inquiry, analysis, commentary, and evaluation.

GROUPING STRATEGIES FOR LITERACY

One seldom finds a single pattern of organization in classrooms. Teachers might form groups to work on a common theme or interest, have pairs of students working with the teacher aide or parent volunteer, or be holding student conferences with one or two students. Most teachers will combine whole-class, small-group, pair, and individual instruction. Diversity in grouping is important. While working with the students' progress toward independence, teachers can also help students to expand and explore their potential by organizing the classroom so that collaborative activity is encouraged. A description of one teacher's efforts to foster self-sufficiency and accommodate differences through grouping strategies is described in Table 5.1.

It is important to remember that by the third grade most of the children in your class may have had one or two years of schooling that were very different from the integrated and individualized approach you are planning. Perhaps the only reading they have done in school has been from basal readers. If they have never had the opportunity to pursue the study of a topic independently, it is unlikely that they will

TABLE 5.1. DIVERSE GROUPING STRATEGIES: UNIT ON *CONEJOS* (RABBITS)

Day 1

Whole class	The class watched a film about *conejos* [rabbits]. Afterward, the class discussed the content of the film and their experiences with rabbits.
Pairs	The students select rabbit stories to read, such as *El conejo y el mapurite* [The Rabbit and the Skunk] (Paz Impuana, 1988), *El conejo de chocolate* [The Chocolate Rabbit] (Claret, 1983), *Pedrito conejo, pintor* [Peter Rabbit, the Artist] (Claret 1988), *Historias de conejos* [Rabbit Stories] (Janosch, 1984) and/or *Las liebres blancas* [The White Hares] (Marzot & Marzot, 1987).
Whole class	The teacher and students brainstormed questions to guide and direct the rest of their study on rabbits.

Days 2 and 3

Small groups	Six students who required more assistance with literacy tasks met with the teacher to retell the story in their own words and to begin writing their own rabbit stories.
Individuals and pairs	Eight students, guided by a list of questions selected from the previous day's brainstorming activity, read textbooks or other nonfiction books, such as *Vivía en el bosque* [There lived in the woods] (Ionescu, 1982), to gather more information and prepare oral or written reports on rabbits.
Cooperative groups	Two groups of four students each worked on an analysis of the literary elements (characterization, plot, setting, etc.) of the story read, then combined their work to develop a chart to present to the class. After getting the first group started, the teacher divided her attention between the groups. She posed questions, answered questions, and took advantage of teachable moments.

Day 4

Whole class	The class met together to report on their progress and to review and synthesize what they were learning from various sources.

Rather than promote individual competition among the students or have students bored waiting for each other, the teacher arranged ways in which all were able to contribute to what the class as a whole learned about rabbits.

know how to do so. If the only writing they have ever done was on topics selected by a teacher who emphasized form over content, they may not want to write or know where to start in your class. Regardless of prior experience, it is a good idea to provide the children with a transition period at the beginning of the school year. During the first few weeks of school, get to know the children, help them get to know you and each other, and introduce them to their new classroom organization, routine, and reading/writing program.

The more dissimilar the children's prior experiences, the slower and more careful the transition will need to be. Also, the personality traits and learning styles of individual children will influence the organization and routines you establish. Children who are quite shy or those who have little self-discipline usually need more time working with the teacher or a group before they can become more independent learners. A very good way to begin the year is with a class unit of study (the students study themselves, family histories, interests, etc.) that allows you to provide guidance for those who need it. With your assistance, the students can organize themselves into teams or small groups to identify tasks and information to be gathered, and to select the methods of reporting and the time limit for the unit of study. You may then functionally demonstrate the procedures and routines used in your class.

In this section we will present some alternative classroom grouping patterns. We hope that you will select ideas from those we present and add to them ideas you gather from other classes, conferences, and workshops. The alternatives we present below stem from our own experience and that of other bilingual teachers. We will discuss two strategies for organizing your delivery of instruction: (1) cooperative learning (Kagan, 1985) and (2) organizing for self-sufficiency.

Cooperative Learning

Cooperative learning requires that students working in groups use the classroom social rules, roles, procedures, processing strategies, and protocols as mutually defined and established by students and teacher. An interdependence is established among each group of four or five students as they strive to achieve group or individual objectives. Cooperative learning is composed of a set of conceptual and teaching strategies that develop new ways of thinking and interacting (Slavin, 1983, 1989).

The use of cooperative learning in second language activities leads to functional language practice and diversity in language models (Cohen & De Ávila, 1983; Kagan, 1986). However, Wong Fillmore (1985) cautions that second-language learning students who are not proficient in the target language (English) may not be adequate models for each other; that is, linguistic heterogeneity is important. Moll (1989) reports on the strategy used by an ESL teacher who places students whose proficiency in English is limited with students who know Spanish and English well. Moll proposes that the ESL student will feel more comfortable and enabled in a classroom in which there is access to someone who knows Spanish well. Linguistically integrated cooperative groups can provide comfortable environments in which students can practice language and negotiate for meaning (Long & Porter, 1984; Pica & Doughty, 1985; Porter, 1986).

Cooperative learning can be incorporated very successfully in almost any area of study. In cooperative learning groups, students learn how to communicate and work with others in a full range of social situations. The teacher's role is redefined as mediator of thinking (Cohen, 1987), facilitator, and resource specialist. Kagan (1985) describes five distinct types of cooperative learning, which are summarized below. Note that there are many other versions of these basic types that have evolved for specific purposes and environments. We encourage you to explore, test, and adapt these types to your classroom context.

1. *Peer tutoring*. Teammates teach each other simple concepts.
2. *Jigsaw*. Each member of the group is given the chief responsibility for a specific portion of the learning unit or task. Students have assigned roles and responsibilities for specific assignments within and across groups. Each member must share his "expert" knowledge with others in the group.

3. *Cooperative projects.* The members of the group work together to complete a group project such as a presentation, a composition, or an art project.
4. *Cooperative/individualized projects.* Students work alone on a particular assignment or project. They later share and assist each other in order to achieve the best possible results.
5. *Cooperative interaction.* Students work together to learn a unit that requires a cooperative effort.

The first step in starting cooperative learning is to prepare students. As Vygotsky asserts, learning is a social activity. Most students have had experience in accomplishing cooperative tasks with friends or family members, or in sports. Discuss with students the purpose and function of different types of cooperative groups.[2] Cooperative learning can work if goals and purposes are established cooperatively and students develop responsibility not only for their own behavior but for group behavior and group products. To internalize working in groups, students need to have social rules, roles for interdependence, problems to solve or products to develop, and a process for self-monitoring and debriefing of cooperative strategies. These group interactions may need to be modeled in the beginning and modified as students learn to be more responsive to the needs of the group.

Teaching specific cooperative behaviors and discourse involves practice. The teacher prepares prior to the learning activity, setting up directions for the task, assigning students to teams, and assisting the students in delineating social rules and individual roles. During the activity the teacher observes, learns about the students, studies the process, and reflects on ways of improving the next activity. An important role for the teacher during cooperative learning is monitoring the students and providing feedback, in particular to low-achieving students. Cohen (1987) found that when teachers praise students while they are making an intellectual or creative contribution to the team, the students tend to perform better and gain status within the group.

Some suggestions for establishing effective cooperative learning practices are the following:

1. The teacher overtly, explicitly, and concretely models the discourse and processes in appropriate contexts of cooperative activities.
2. Strategies for working and learning together (helping, accepting, praising, encouraging, listening, and asking for others' opinions) and the range and utility of the strategies (giving reasons for ideas, synthesizing ideas, reaching consensus, etc.) are discussed, and interventions and modifications are attempted by the students.
3. Students' roles are clearly defined for each task. This is important because when roles are not assigned, it is natural for students to turn to the most academically capable student so that the team can get the right answer. Students need to understand that everyone has something special to contribute.
4. Debriefing activities in which thinking processes (metacognition) are discussed in ways that the students and teacher can visualize and learn about

thinking processes are included in each cooperative learning activity. Debriefing is a means of anchoring knowledge after an activity. Debriefing creates "situated meaning" for the learning activity and helps students to remember more. During debriefing discussion, students develop cooperative and social skills as well as metacognitive strategies involving both knowledge and self-control. Learners monitor their attitudes, attention, and engagement in a task.

5. The responsibility for learning to work collaboratively and the debriefing of that process can be transferred to the students as soon as they are able to take charge. Transfer responsibility gradually, working on one cooperative skill at a time until it is internalized.

6. Provide students with continuous feedback on the assigned tasks and also on their cooperative practice improvements.

Organizing for Self-Sufficiency

In classrooms that foster independence and maturity, there is sufficient guidance and structure to create a predictable, secure environment; decision making is valued and children are encouraged to make rational choices. In the beginning of the school year, it is necessary for the teacher to establish, model, and practice the expected routines. As the pupils acquire the desired learning habits, they can accept increased responsibility for their own learning on an individual or group basis in consultation with the teacher. However, dependence and immaturity seem to flourish under two conditions: (1) chaotic situations in which guidelines are few or inconsistent, making predictability impossible (that is, children do not know what to expect), and (2) highly controlled situations that permit little or no choice (that is, children must take their cues from the teacher for everything they do).

To get the best out of cooperative learning, small-group, and individualized instruction, the students need to learn a great deal about the mechanics of the program, what they are supposed to be learning, how they are supposed to learn it, and what their responsibilities are to themselves, their group, and the entire class.

As a new classroom social structure is developed, mediation by the teacher helps children express and obtain knowledge in ways that will enable them to acquire meaning on their own (Pérez, 1993). In these interactive roles, the teacher's major instructional goal is to make classrooms literate environments in which many language experiences can take place and in which students can practice, understand, and learn different types of reading and writing.

READING AND WRITING WITH LITERATURE

The primary goal of studying literature is for children to discover and experience the lives of others, different time periods, places, value systems, and the many world cultures. The rich language and cultural perspectives found in a variety of Spanish literature can expand children's cultural repertoires. Using literature as an integral part of the literacy program provides meaningful social contexts that encourage students to compare and contrast literature with their own experiences and to expand their background and knowledge (Harris, 1992).

TABLE 5.2. LITERATURE TYPES AND EXAMPLES FOR THE MIDDLE CHILDHOOD YEARS

Type of Literature	Examples
Poesía/Poetry	*Margarita* [Margarita] (Darío, 1983)
	Por el mar de las Antillas anda un barco de papel [On the waves of the Caribbean sails a little paper boat] (Guillén, 1978)
Prosa/Prose	
Cuento folklórico/folktale	*Sinfonía de Puerto Rico* [Puerto Rican Symphony] (Mendoza, 1979)
Leyenda/legend	*La montaña del alimento* [The Legend of Food Mountain] (Rohmer, 1982)
Fábula/fable	*Fábulas* [Fables] (Lobel, 1987)
Cuento de hadas/fairy tale	*El patito feo* [The Ugly Duckling] (Andersen, trans. by Garrido, 1982)
Fantasía/fantasy	*Donde viven los monstruos* [Where the Wild Things Are] (Sendak, trans. Gervás, 1984)
Cuento de aventuras/adventure tale	*Una feliz catástrofe* [A Fortunate Catastrophe] (Turin & Bosnia, 1976)
Ciencia ficción/science fiction	*El pizarrón encantado* [The Magic Blackboard] (Carbadillo, n.d.)
Ficción/fiction	*Las liebres blancas* [The White Hares] (Marzot & Marzot, 1987)
Novela/novel	*Abuelita Opalina* [Grandma Opalina] (Puncel, 1983)
Drama/Drama	
Obra de títeres/puppet theater	*¡Respetable público!* [Respectable audience] (Giménez Pastor, 1974)
Obra de teatro/theater	*Teatro para niños* [Children's Theater] (Robleto, 1984)
Informativo/Informative	
Biografía/biography	*Grandes biografías hispánicas* [Great Hispanic Biographies] (León, Spain: Everest, n.d.)
Informativo/informative	*El arte de hacer cometas de papel* [The Art of Making Paper Kites] (Montserrat, 1985)

Literature can not only stimulate students to speak, think, and read, but it also leads them to write with increasing ability. Studying good literature allows students to observe the author's skilled use of language. In addition to learning about others' experiences through good literature, children can develop vocabulary and observe effective models of good writing.

Through exposure to varieties of writing—poetry, prose, drama, and nonfiction-informative—students learn to view experiences and tell their stories in new ways. Table 5.2 lists different types of literature and provides examples for each.

Teaching Literature Units

Teachers can structure literature units by selecting themes around topics of interest, genres, or authors. A literature unit can focus on one genre (poetry, prose, drama, or nonfiction) or it can integrate several genres. For example, the theme of friendship or sibling rivalry could be studied in poems, short stories, and plays. In studying a work of literature, teachers can plan classroom activities that help students get *into* the work, for example, reading a portion of the work aloud or playing a recording to arouse curiosity. To evoke a desire to read, teachers can engage students in instructional conversations (Tharp and Gallimore, 1988) in which they ask provocative questions, provide interesting background information, or organize oral activities. Next, the students can explore the work, understanding their own experiences *through* it and learning about the experiences of others. By enabling students to study the work in depth, asking important questions, and analyzing and critiquing characters and actions, the teacher can connect the meaning of the work to the real world. Ultimately, the students can go *beyond* the text by connecting it to their everyday lives through writing, dramatization, or illustration. Using this process of getting into, gaining insight through, and going beyond the text provides many opportunities to develop critical and creative literacy.

Ada (1990) proposes the Creative Reading Approach, a teacher-student dialogue for the reading/writing lesson that goes through four interrelated and mutually supportive phases: (1) descriptive, (2) personal interpretive, (3) critical, and (4) creative (reading and writing).

In the descriptive phase information is transmitted from the text, and initial comprehension is developed. Often this phase includes questions that begin with *¿quién?* [who], *¿qué?* [what], *¿dónde?* [where], *¿cuándo?* [when], *¿por qué?* [why], and *¿cómo?* [how].

The personal interpretive phase occurs when students interact with the text at an experiential and emotional level, interpreting what they are reading based on their experiences, feelings, and emotions. The role of the text and the teacher during this interpretive stage is to assist students in analyzing new information and to validate the students' individuality, community, and culture. The questions are set up to develop problem-solving skills and to enable learners to relate to the theme presented in the text. Examples of questions asked during this phase are: *¿Te ha sucedido algo parecido?* [Have you experienced something like this?] *¿Has pensado o hecho algo similar?* [Have you ever done or thought about something similar?] *¿Cómo te sentiste?* [How did you feel?] The teacher encourages the dialogue by sharing such experiences with the students.

In the critical phase the student reflects on and analyzes what has been read or written critically. The student draws inferences about the information presented, evaluates significance, and entertains alternatives. Some sample questions are: *¿Cómo podrían haber salido las cosas diferente?* [How could things have turned out differently?] *¿Cuáles son algunas alternativas?* [What are some alternatives?] *¿A quién le beneficia esta situación? ¿Quién sufre?* [Who benefits from or suffers because of this situation?]

The creative phase encourages students to consider how the reading or writing activity enriches their lives or what they learn about themselves in the process of examining others. It also invites the children to imagine new possibilities and to use the information in new and creative ways.

Through the teacher-student dialogue of the creative reading approach, you can assist children in developing critically and creatively as they interact with literature and other texts.

In this section we will look at teaching units whose primary focus or objective is the study of literature. Classroom Activity 5.1 suggests a literature unit study that includes various genres to explore and learn about one theme.

CLASSROOM ACTIVITY 5.1   Life in the Circus

1. Introduce the unit to the class by reading the poem *"Desfile del circo,"* [Circus Parade] by E. Feliciano Mendoza (1985, pp. 25–26):

   DESFILE DEL CIRCO

   Abuelito,
   ¡ha llegado el circo!
   ¡Si vieras la carpa
   como yo la he visto!

   Trabajan payasos,
   caballos, monitos,
   leones y tigres
   y siete perritos.

   Y un elefante
   grande, arrugadito,
   que se hace amigo
   de todos los niños.

   El malabarista,
   juntos, lanza al aire
   platos y bolitas
   con mucho donaire.

   Vuelan como pájaros
   unos trapecistas,
   y hay un guacamayo
   que es motociclista.

   Con los elefantes
   van las bailarinas
   y cinco payasos
   con caras de risa.

   ¡Vamos esta tarde,
   que hoy es domingo,
   a ver maravillas
   del circo, abuelito!

   ¡Abuelito! ¡Al circo
   llévame de prisa!
   ¡Verás qué colores
   tiene este domingo!

2. In small cooperative groups, ask students to brainstorm a semantic map of the different characters and animals found in a circus. Questions you may use to guide them are:

>¿Cuáles son los diferentes personajes del circo? ¿Cuáles son los animales? ¿Puede todo tipo de animal participar en el circo? ¿Cuáles son las características de los animales? [What are the different circus characters? What are some of the animals? Can all kinds of animals participate in the circus? What are the characteristics of the animals?]

3. When the students have shared their group maps, they can decide to concentrate on the different roles of people or the different types of animals found in the circus. Their objective is a dramatization about life in a circus. Using the writing process, each group can write a skit from the perspective of one of the circus characters. You can start them thinking about life in the circus by asking them such questions as:

>¿Qué hacen las personas del circo cuando no están haciendo presentaciones? ¿Adónde duermen? ¿Adónde cocinan? ¿Y qué pasa si se enferman o les da nostalgia de ver a su familia? ¿Cuidarán a los animales apropiadamente? ¿Qué pensarías tú si fueras unos de los animales amarrados o enjaulados? [What do circus people do when they're not performing? Where do they sleep? Where do they cook? What happens if they get sick or homesick? Do they take good care of the animals? What would you think if you were one of the animals that was tied up or caged?]

4. Provide literature that children can read individually, to each other, or that you can read aloud as part of prewriting. On elephants, you can start with the following:

Poetry

>*Elefante* [Elephant], by Nicolás Guillén (1978)
>*¡Adelante el elefante!* [Forward (with) the Elephant], by Nicolás Guillén (1978)

Short Story

>*Una corona para el hermano elefante* [A Crown for the Brotherly Elephant], by Zhu Jiadong (Chinese short story translated into Spanish)
>*Un cuento de elefantes* [A Story of Elephants], by Ester Feliciano Mendoza (1983)
>*Historias de elefantes* [Histories of Elephants], by José Martí (1972)

On lions you can provide:

Poetry

>*Que te corta corta* [It Will Cut Cut], by Nicolás Guillén (1978)

Short Story

>*El león y el ratón* [The Lion and the Mouse], by M. Elalia Valeri and María Ruis
>*La aventura de los leones* [The Adventure of the Lions], by Miguel Cervantes (adaptation by Editorial Ramón Sopena, S.A.)

Information books, videotapes, or films on animals are also important so that students can consider how they are going to cast the characters in their skits.

5. As the children begin to draft, share, and revise their skits, you can expand their information by inviting speakers from the Animal Protection Society, from a local circus, or a veterinarian. The students should prepare questions they may want to ask the speakers.

A short story they or you can read about the circus as a respite during their work is *El circo* [The Circus], by Anita Arroyo, in *El grillo gruñón* [The Grunting Cricket] (Rio Riedras, P.R., 1984).

6. As they finish their skits, ask them questions about their characters, plots, and settings. The students may need to prepare props. Activities can be developed around skit performance needs (e.g., mask making and a discussion of the use of masks in different cultures).

7. In addition to asking them to prepare the skits for publication, you can videotape the dramatizations. The students can then view their skits and critique their presentation. Even if you do not videotape the skits, debriefing, reflection, and critique would still be appropriate. The purpose of debriefing is to give the students a chance to think about the variety of activities, the process, and the different types of information that went into the preparation of the dramatization and the preparation of their publication. It can also help you to think about how you could better guide them in future units. Some of the questions you might ask are:

What worked well?

What would you have done differently?

What are some of the preparatory activities that helped you most?

What would you pay more attention to if you were to do another dramatization?

8. After completing the dramatization, taking the children to a performance can give you the opportunity to explore another type of life, that of the performer. Before the presentation, ask them to think about what kind of preparation they imagine would go into a performance. After the performance debrief on the subject.

Sharing Poetry. The primary value of poetry is to contribute to the development of children's aesthetic sensibilities, to explore the use of language to convey emotions, and to convey the idea that language, besides being communicative, has recreational value. Children will find in poetry a sense of beauty, enjoyment, playfulness, and manipulability that they can treasure and remember. Poetry can also assist children in developing linguistically. The rhyme and rhythm of poetry help children remember new words and linguistic structures with ease. Through poetry children can assimilate and retain images, ideas, and values associated with new words and structures.

In selecting poetry consider the theme of the unit as well as the interest of the students. Poetry is one of the literary forms that abounds in the Spanish language, with some of the greatest Spanish language poets writing especially for children. You can find a wide variety of Spanish poems to integrate into just about any theme of study or you may want to design a whole unit of study on the theme of poetry.

Eight-, nine-, and ten-year-old children enjoy poems with humor, rhythm, and pleasurable, familiar experiences; poems about children and animals; and poems about the ridiculous. Children's appreciation of poetry will grow with the sharing of poems and with the opportunity to explore the meanings expressed in them. One way to get children interested in poetry is by reading aloud a poem on a theme that is of interest to the class. You will need to have good sources of poetry available for reading and studying. Some works to start with are:

Ada, A. F. 1990. *Días, y días de poesía* [Days, and Days of Poetry]. Carmel, CA: Hampton Brown.

Ferrán, J. (Ed.). 1982. *Tarde del circo* [Circus Afternoon]. Valladolid, Spain: Miñón.
Carballo, F. M. (Ed.). 1962. *Los poetas* [The Poets]. México: Fernández, Colección Biblioteca Auriga.
Guillén, N. (Ed.). 1978. *Por el mar de las Antillas anda un barco de papel* [On the Waves of the Caribbean Sails a Little Paper Boat]. Managua, Nicaragua: Editorial Nueva Nicaragua.

Many poems are best appreciated when put in the context of an appropriate background and mood. *Margarita,* by Rubén Darío (1983), can best be understood with an accompanying discussion about its style, mood, context, and the effect of the *cuento* [story] within the poem. After reading the poem, activities can be carried out to identify the words that describe, elicit emotional reactions, move the rhythm along, or give special meaning. Working in groups, children can brainstorm ideas for writing similar poems, writing about the poem, illustrating the poem, or comparing and contrasting several poems. One fourth grader responded to the study of poetry by including verses from her favorite poems in her journal writing (see Figure 5.1).

At times, poetry can be used to take advantage of a teachable moment. Reading *"Canción de la lluvia"* [Song of the Rain] (from *Arroz con leche* [Rice Pudding], by Delacre, 1988) on a cloudy, rainy day after the children have experienced the sight, feel, and smell of a shower will enhance the children's appreciation for the poet's words describing a similar event. The children may even be inspired or the teacher can encourage them to write their own poems about rain.

Many of children's favorite poems come from the oral folk tradition and from the chanted street games of today as well as yesteryear. Children at this age are also interested in contemporary songs, for example, rap music, which may be used as part of a unit of study. Many Latino poets in the United States are exploring the confluence of the two languages. You can find bilingual poems and poems employing and exploring code-switching that capture the lived experience of Latinos.

Students can begin to write in poetry form through group poetry experiences in which they are given a theme and each one contributes a line. They can then edit the poem in a group. Figure 5.2 contains two poems from a collection published by bilingual classes in a New York City public school.

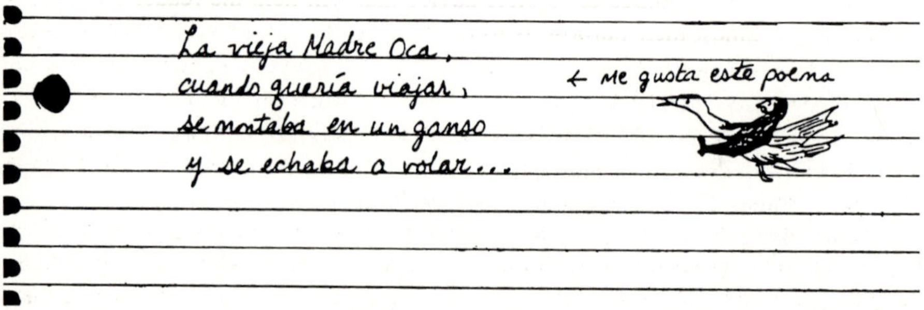

[When old "Mother Oca" wishes to travel, she climbs on a goose and takes flight . . .] [I like this poem.]

Figure 5.1. Poetry in a Journal Entry

VAMOS A

correr una silla como una bicicleta,
caminar una bicicleta como un perro,
saltar un perro como una soga,
columpiar una soga como una cadena,
jugar una cadena como un balón,
hablar a un balón como a un ratón,
escribir a un ratón como a una madre,
leer una madre como un mapa.

PELEA

Las cucarachas de Caracas
y las hormigas amigas
son enemigas.
Las cucarachas son
chacharachas
quo quiere decir
feas y gorbachevascas.
Las hormigas son
chusmozas y mimimigas
porque les gusta
pellizcar a la gente.

Las hormigas y las cucarachas
se pelean mordiéndose
como donuts. Las cucarachas
comen a las hormigas,
y las hormigas comen
a las cucarachas desde dentro.
Y sigue igual hasta que
tienen que ir al baño
a lavarse las manos
para comer de nuevo.

Figure 5.2. Two Poems from P.S. 84

Working with Stories. Good prose may convey shreds of history or experience, common everyday or unusual anecdotes, amusing or scary happenings. At times, their intention is to moralize or to offer advice that will help the reader meet life's difficulties; at times, their purpose is to offer an escape from the routine, to entertain and delight. Many children's stories have as their protagonists animals or objects with human characteristics and attributes. Often the protagonists triumph over force and power using their cleverness, goodness, or other redeeming qualities. The most common forms of prose appropriate for children in third, fourth, and fifth grade are fairy tales, myths, fables, short stories, diaries, and novels.

In designing a unit using stories, keep in mind that by the third grade children have had lots of experience with stories, and because most of what has been read to them and what they have read themselves has been written in a story format, they have an implicit understanding of story structure. Thus the tasks are to provide experiences that stimulate the children's imagination and interpretative and critical skills, and to provide opportunities for them to write. Children can be encouraged to react to books they have read in imaginative and critical ways. Some activities that can be suggested are to rewrite the ending; to design a book jacket and compose an insert about the book for the front and back flaps; to compose a letter to the author of the book with questions about style, characters, and so forth; to create a dramatic spoof of the book; or to write a commercial advertising the book. Use the writing process discussed in the previous section and, if available, a word-processing package and a computer in order to improve the quality of the children's work.

To assist children in developing the interpretive and critical skills that they can use to compose a book of their own, you may wish to develop a unit that identifies distinctive artistic features used by different authors or in different genres. A unit that helps children understand the structure of different literary models can be the basis for organizing their own writing. Younger children can identify and write simple statements in response to stories by identifying their elements as illustrated in Classroom Activity 5.2.

As children develop more experience working with literature, other elements of stories can be added. Since setting, mood, point of view, theme, and plot affect

---

CLASSROOM ACTIVITY 5.2   *Elementos de un cuento* [Elements of a story]

1. Select a story that has definite events, problems, and a solution, e.g., *Santiago* [Santiago] (Belpré, 1969), *La piedra del Zamuro: Un cuento del Tío Nicolás* [Zamuro's (vulture) Stone: A Story by Tío Nicolás] (Rivero Oramas, 1981), *Chispa de luz* [Spark of Light] (Robles Boza, 1984).

2. Read one story at a time to the children or have the children read the story on their own in preparation for the activity.

3. In a small group or class activity have different children write the name of the story, the names of the characters, the event(s), problem(s), and the solution on a chart. A chart like the one shown will assist children in comparing and contrasting how stories use different elements.

El cuento [story]	*Los personajes* [characters]	*El (los) evento(s)* [event(s)]	*El (los) problema(s)* [problem(s)]	*La solución* [solution]
1.				
2.				
3.				

4. Select, read, and analyze two or three other stories.

5. Compare and contrast (orally and in writing) how the elements of a story were used in the different stories read.

6. Have children write their own story using one of the stories as a model.

7. Dramatize one of the stories read or one of the children's stories.

TABLE 5.3 A SENSE OF STORY

Question?	Literary Term	Ideas/Elements
Who?	Characters	Protagonist/antagonist
Where?/when?	Setting	Place/location/time/mood
What?/why?	Plot	Sequence/problem/theme/ point of view/transition/climax
How?	Conclusion	Solution

the outcome of stories and the way that students interpret them, they need to study these elements. The character development of the antagonist and protagonist provides insight into humankind. If there is an anticlimax in the story, can students discover its purpose? Developing a chart, such as the one illustrated in Table 5.3, will help students identify, define, and note the elements of any given piece as they are reading and studying.

As children begin to identify the sense and elements of a story, they can also begin to work with "point of view." Most stories can be written from several different angles. Working with point of view, the teacher can check students' comprehension of stories, situations, or activities. Students can begin to study point of view by reading and discussing first-person narratives. As students identify the point of view of the narrator, the author's attitudes, prejudices, opinions, values, and judgments can be listed and categorized. Students can thus define the author's viewpoint. As children master identifying the point of view of the narrator, they can begin to interpret stories from the point of view of different characters, for example, *Caperucita Roja* [Little Red Riding Hood] (Grimm, 1980) can be told from the point of view of the *lobo* [wolf]. To study and understand writing from a "point of view" the children can read *La verdadera historia de los tres cerditos* [The True Story of the Three Little Pigs] (Scieszka, 1991). As they retell or rewrite an event from a different point of view, students not only clarify facts and information about a given subject, but become aware of their own feelings, opinions, and insights. Having students tell or write stories, individually or in groups, using opposing points of view helps develop empathy and assists children in evaluating the validity of what they read.

Studying Novels. As children's abilities and interests develop they become ready for the study of more sophisticated works. By fourth or fifth grade, students can begin to study novels as well as other longer pieces of prose. Publishers in Spain and Latin America are publishing more and more juvenile novels and works for older children. In selecting which novels to study, it is important to know whether the novel was originally written in Spanish for Spanish-speaking children or is a translation. Some examples of works originally written in Spanish are *Citlalli en las estrellas* [Citlalli among the Stars], by C. Aguilera (1982), and *Abuelita Opalina* [Grandma Opalina], by M. Puncel (1983). Some good Spanish adaptations or translations to consider are *Las telarañas de Carlota* [Charlotte's Web], by E. B. White (1988); *El Principito* [The Little Prince], by A. de Saint Exupéry (1989); and *La isla de los delfines azules* [Island of the Blue Dolphins], by S. O'Dell (1964).

In composing a unit on a novel, the teacher can plan and prepare as follows:

1. Read the novel and identify major and minor themes.
2. Develop a strong context-grounded activity that reflects a theme(s) developed in the book and relates to students' previous learning, experience, or interest.
3. Develop strategies for directing children's attention to any special or stylistic cue systems (graphophonic, semantic, pragmatic) employed by the author.
4. Design discussion questions that reflect the author's intentions and techniques, elements of literature, and major and minor themes.
5. Identify possible writing domains that the children can explore (as a group or individually) through the novel.
6. Find other works of literature with similar major and minor themes to include as part of your total unit. This literature can be the basis for additional reading/writing.

Studying Authors. Each literature unit should include an investigation of the author(s) and illustrator(s). When studying authors and illustrators focus on their personal background, find other titles related to them, and compare the titles to find connections among the topics. The students can discover how authors and illustrators use their personal experiences, develop a style of writing or illustrating, and organize ideas and other elements in similar ways across different books. For Spanish-speaking children to see themselves as future authors, it is essential that they relate to the themes developed in the books and lives of the authors and illustrators. Selecting Latino authors who reflect the experience of Spanish-speaking people in the United States will provide more possibilities for children to find their experiences reflected. Although there are still too few U.S. Latino authors and illustrators creating for children, and even fewer writing in Spanish, a small number stand out as meriting study. Some authors that can be studied include Pura Belpre and Nicholasa Mohr, who write from their Puerto Rican experience; Pat Mora, Gary Soto, and Sandra Cisneros, who are beginning to develop a collection based on the Mexican-American experience; and Alma Flor Ada, who is of Cuban heritage and whose many children's titles reflect various Latino traditions.

Working with Drama. Reading, writing, and acting out dramatic material offer children many advantages by providing a real purpose for reading aloud, for memorizing lines, for interpreting and expressing oneself, for studying dialogue forms, and for entertaining others. Plays for children depicting stories from everyday life at home or in school, historical episodes, traditional fiestas or holidays, characterizations of plants, animals, and objects, and many other themes can stimulate children's language development. The works can be serious or humorous and can be performed as skit comedy, dialogue tragedy, parody, readers theater, mime, or puppetry.

Studying Nonfiction-Informative Writing. This type of literature is just as important for young readers as poetry, prose, and drama. It offers a different experience

and opportunity to reinforce language concepts and learn different writing styles for different purposes. This literature, unlike fiction, has as its purpose the conveying of knowledge about real objects, events, and processes. Although this is the style of writing most used in classrooms, here we are referring to nonfiction-informative materials other than those found in school textbooks. This can include books on the sciences, social studies, art, and music, as well as biographies, autobiographies, essays, articles, and other journalistic materials.

The challenge for teachers is to plan classroom activities so that all of the students move into, through, and beyond the literary work to a new understanding of themselves and the world around them. An inviting book corner, shelf, or classroom library that provides a rich variety of books on assorted reading levels will encourage children to browse and read. Students will usually select books on their own that are of interest and on an understandable reading level. Teacher and students can explore literary concepts and forms together through book sharing, book talks, reading logs, and writing. The love of books, with the promise of becoming a life-long reader of literature, is one of the greatest gifts that a teacher can give to a student.

STRATEGIES FOR READING AND WRITING

Proficiency in reading and writing will develop as children use their Spanish literacy for numerous purposes: reading individually; reading to others; reading to prepare an oral report; reading and writing for pleasure; reading to prepare for a written test; reading and writing to prepare a project; reading for text editing; writing in journals and logs; and reading and writing to assist in the management of the classroom social system.

In successful literacy programs, both readers and writers make meaning and have real purposes and audiences. Helping students to understand the processes of making meaning and communicating with diverse audiences may require some learning activities that model this process. As teachers organize and suggest a variety of reading and writing activities to their students, knowing about the reading and writing process will give them and their students options. Next we will discuss reading and writing processes and their interacting commonalities.

The Reading Cycle

Prereading. How students and teachers prepare for reading activities can have a positive impact on attaining meaning. Teachers and students can prepare for reading by (1) activating prior knowledge of the text subject, (2) knowing or inquiring about the genre to be read, and (3) establishing a goal for reading or a hypothesis about the text.

As emphasized earlier, in Chapters 2 and 4, the reader needs to have the background knowledge (experience) that is required for comprehending a particular piece of text and also an awareness of possessing this background knowledge. Conscious awareness is important because it fosters the use of relevant knowledge during the reading process. Activating prior knowledge thus constitutes one component of "making plans to read." Teachers can help students examine the strategies that convey meaning: how we filter and interpret what we read through our own experience; how we feel about the characters and why; how we interpret illustrations and other graphic text; how we form predictions and guesses about what is going to happen; and how writers manipulate words, phrases, descriptions, or dialogue to influence readers.

Awareness of the genre to be read is another important part of reading planning. The genre suggests the author's structure, and knowing the genre and structure helps readers select their purpose for reading. Certain genres and purposes go hand in hand, such as novels for relaxing and newspapers for current information. Appropriate planning helps students invoke different mental frameworks for reading a factual description of butterflies versus the fanciful legend of *La mariposa dorada* [The Golden Butterfly] (Osorio, 1985). (See Chapter 6 for a sample passage.) Forming predictions or having purposes in mind before reading keeps a person from wandering aimlessly through a piece of text not knowing for sure what is most important, what is fairly important, or what is least important. Reading is a purposeful pursuit that is most likely to succeed when prereading planning occurs.

Hypotheses and predictions lead the reading process to focus on creating meaning. Having a goal or hypothesis at the outset helps to establish a hierarchy for what is important that, in turn, helps the reader select and organize anticipated content. The reader's original purpose may be altered in the process of reading, with new hypotheses and predictions being formed along the way.

Reading. The behavior of the successful, strategic reader is characterized by an active, purposeful effort to understand. The proficient reader's prior knowledge is being called on at appropriate times. This may help the reader to integrate parts into wholes and may also raise questions about the message being constructed. The level

of understanding may depend on the reader's background knowledge and purpose for reading.

At times, questions about comprehension may be so frequent or important that the reader feels the need to slow down or even interrupt the cycle of reading. Stopping allows corrective strategies to be employed—rereading a sentence or a paragraph, or finding the meaning of key words. Based on what is learned, the reader may revise or reaffirm the already constructed message. For actively engaged readers, this cycle continues until the end of the text is reached.

Postreading. Postreading discussions give readers the opportunity to assess their construction of meaning and its relationship to the author's intended message. Most texts allow for different interpretations. Therefore, one reason for postreading classroom discussions is to give students a chance to share their divergent interpretations and assess how and why they differed. A second important reason is that readers should have an opportunity to reflect on how they went about constructing meaning.

Postreading reflection and discussion may reveal the need to reread. Rereading one or more segments of a text may be necessary to understand the meaning of the whole piece, to assess others' interpretations, or to confirm one's own interpretation. For classroom teachers this suggests that if a text is worth reading, rereading all or parts of it for specific reasons that are clear to students will not be uncommon. Thus, purposeful rereading would not be viewed as solely for remedial or corrective reasons.

Just as instruction can help students become aware of the reading process, so instruction can have a positive effect on students' ability to write. Conversely, if students can create a written text, they can also read it.

The Process Approach to Teaching Writing

One important assumption underlying integrated language approaches is that children learn to read or refine their reading skills by writing (Goodman, 1986; Graves, 1983; Lundsteen, 1976). Much discussion has taken place in the last decade concerning the purpose and authenticity of school writing tasks. Harman and Edelsky (1989) contend that most school writing tasks are not real writing but are writing exercises because even though the students may select the topic and genre, the only real audience is the teacher and the only real purpose for writing is the fulfillment of an assignment. Delpit (1986) raises the issue of the need for minority students to learn about the forms and functions of the language of "power." She contends that in order to do this students must be directed and instructed in these new forms and functions. Delpit suggests that the relationship of culture and power between teacher and student mediates the potential success of the literacy process. We feel that in addition to providing authentic purposes and audiences for writing, students need exposure to forms and functions that may not be in their repertoires.

The process approach to teaching writing described in this section shows one way that children can explore a variety of writing, forms and functions, for, as Delpit points out, much needs to be made explicit about the process. Figure 5.3 illustrates the cyclical nature of the writing process.

Prewriting. Thinking/planning prewriting efforts should focus on creating, clarifying, and expanding the students' understanding of purpose. The first stage in the writing process includes any experience, activity, or exercise that motivates a person to write, generate material and ideas for writing, or focus on a particular subject. The child is stimulated to move from the stage of thinking about a topic to the act of writing. Relevant prewriting strategies have been associated with higher writing achievement (Applebee & Langer, 1984). The following are a few suggestions for engaging students and stimulating ideas for writing.

Concrete experience	Pictures	Brainstorming
Listening to a story	Reading	Interviewing
Listing ideas	Doodling	Conversations
Poetry, music, art	Movies/videos	Field trips
Outlining, mapping	Daydreaming	Guest speakers
Dramatic activities	Surveys	Show and tell

Writers must have adequate knowledge of the topic about which they have chosen to write. Because activating and organizing what is commonly known reveals what is unknown but essential, it is not unusual for a writer's early plans to include attempts to learn more about a topic.

Selecting a topic as well as a purpose are decisions directly related to the intended audience. The audience also figures in the writer's choice of genre. A story, for instance, may be a more effective medium than an essay for conveying a certain message to a certain audience. Prewriting decisions about topic, audience, purpose, and genre are interrelated and essential to the development of meaningful text.

Drafting. The mental activity that goes into composing occurs at a very conscious level. Linking together different ideas in a way that produces a well-integrated whole, even when the whole is no more than a note or paragraph, requires intent. During this stage the writer composes; ideas and images are translated into words, phrases, and sentences. For children who have clarified their ideas during the thinking/planning prewriting stage, writing the first draft may proceed smoothly. They may write, sequence, and organize a paragraph or piece in one sitting. At other times, the same

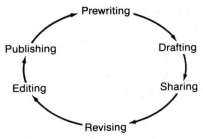

Figure 5.3. The Writing Process

child or other children may struggle back and forth with prewriting, writing, and rewriting. Teacher support during drafting includes providing uninterrupted time, a variety of writing materials, and the opportunity to write and talk or to write quietly. Giving children the choices of topic and audience, accepting the child's invented and other spelling strategies, and focusing on communication and the development of their voices rather than mechanics will assist the drafting cycle.

Sharing. Writers may also find it necessary to step back from their efforts so that the constructed meaning can be examined somewhat objectively. Decisions to revise may then be made for the purpose of improving organization, incorporating unplanned content, deleting what was originally thought essential, elaborating ideas, or building smooth transitions from one idea to the next. If writers keep the audience in mind, they are anxious to make sure that both the message and construction are clear and appropriate. Sharing writing in progress will help the writer clarify purposes and meaning. Thus, it is important that children have the opportunity to share their drafts for the purpose of receiving reactions, advice, suggestions, affirmation of strengths, and ideas for change. Children can learn to give each other feedback as they read or share first drafts. The teacher can provide demonstrations or role play how to respond in the sharing stage. As students make suggestions about others' writing, they themselves gain a better understanding of the writing process. Some methods of response can be rereading (writer responds to self), whole-class response, small-group response, peer or team response, writing conferences with the teacher, or response sheets or forms from the teacher or students.

Revising. In this stage, the children consider the feedback from sharing and make decisions about their writing. As children develop confidence in writing, they can be encouraged to focus on how effectively the material communicates their intent. For writers, the revising, or self-editing, that makes a difference usually starts with a reconsideration of their purpose. The purpose—to inform, to express feelings or opinions, to entertain—provides different mindsets for the revision. The ability to be objective is very important. In other words, writers must step outside of themselves to evaluate what they have written from the perspective of the intended audience (reader). The effective writer goes over the whole text to see if the purpose has been achieved in a way appropriate for the intended audience. During the revision stage children refine content, change emphasis, add or change words, add description or detail, delete information, and reorganize for clarity. Some children will choose not to rethink or rewrite, and they may have this option, especially at first, when they need to be encouraged to develop fluency rather than to revise for correctness. Not all writing needs to be taken through the revision stage. Part of learning to revise is deciding which pieces of writing deserve or are ready for revision.

Editing. This is the refinement stage of the writing process in which students learn to edit a piece of writing. Beginning writers may confine editing to one or two areas at a time, for example, the use of capitals and punctuation. As children develop more experience they can edit for spelling, diction (appropriate, effective, and precise word choices), syntax (changing sentence structure, correcting awkward construction, adding transitions), and accuracy. Students can be taught to do the editing themselves. Figure 5.4 illustrates a model that a teacher posted for a group of third graders as an illustration of the self-editing process.

Publishing. When children are satisfied that their stories, poems, reports, or letters are finished, the works should be published (in class books, school newsletters, com-

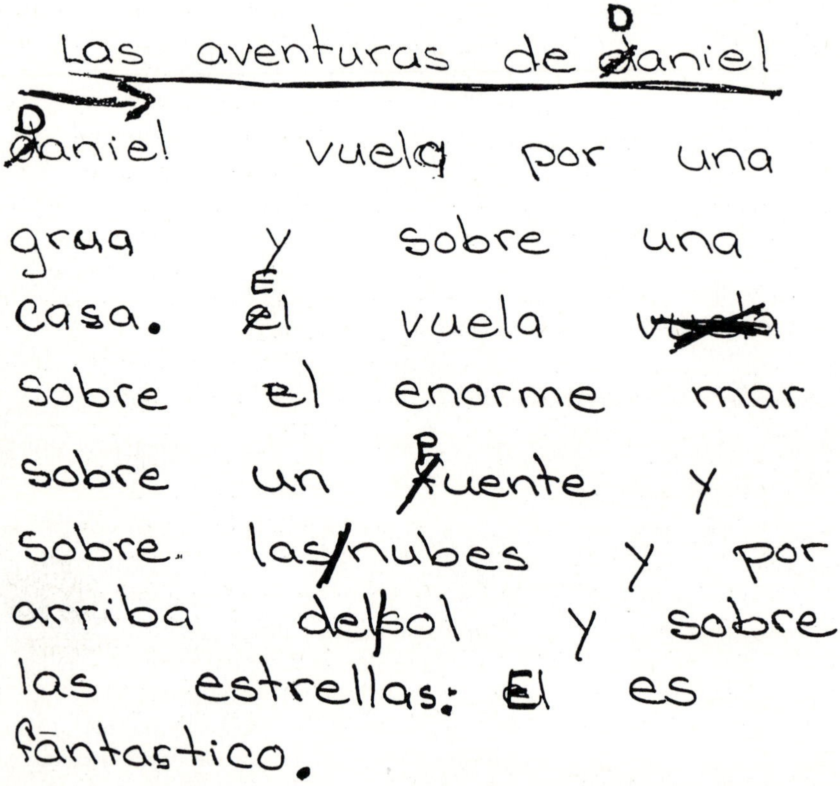

[Daniel's adventures. Daniel flies over a tow truck and a house. He flies over the enormous sea, over a fountain and over the clouds and over the top of the sun and over the stars. He is fantastic.]

Figure 5.4. Editing Sample

munity newspapers), mailed, or posted (on a school or classroom bulletin board devoted to writers or authors). Publishing, mailing, and posting create a real need and purpose for children to use conventional spelling, punctuation, and grammar (Edelsky, 1986). A collection of one person's work or the class's work on a theme can be bound using a variety of bookbinding techniques. See bookbinding suggestions in Figure 5.5 (pp. 120–121).

ENGLISH LITERACY INSTRUCTION

Researchers (Krashen & Bider, 1988; Cummins, 1979) have estimated that children participating in properly designed bilingual education programs, in which they have acquired literacy skills in their native language, acquire English rapidly and typically achieve at grade level norms for English after three to five years. Lambert and Taylor (1987) propose that the native language be maintained in school until it becomes secure as a foundation for the acquisition of the English language: "Only then (after three or four years of elementary education) can a switch to a primarily English language program safely take place" (p. 81). Teachers need to build on what students know and can do in their native language in order to help them increase their control over what they need to do in English (Jiménez, 1994).

Moll and Díaz (1985) demonstrate that by allowing children to read in the second language and to have follow-up discussions bilingually, their ability to demonstrate comprehension of what is read is heightened. In classrooms that use a strategic mix of social resources, activities, and tasks to teach different aspects of literacy, fluent native-language readers will be able to use what they know about literacy and about the purposes of literacy in their developing second language (Reyes et al., 1993). Once a student becomes literate in the first language, the knowledge and rules of reading and writing are adapted for the other languages that the student acquires. Krashen (1982) argues that second language learners rely on and use first language rules and knowledge when their repertoires do not include the appropriate second language rules. Rather than being prevented from acquiring a rule in the second language because they already have one in the first language, they use the rule from the first language until they acquire the rule in the second.

Moll (1989) studied teachers who grouped students by interests or activities and frequently changed the composition of the groups. The teachers experimented with grouping children by language in order to create bilingual groups that ensured that the students participated in tasks at an appropriate intellectual level while monitoring and assisting the children's English development. Moll gives the example of Sylvia, an ESL student, and Gloria and Ana, both fluent bilinguals, who work collaboratively on an assignment to write the dialogue for a *Peanuts* cartoon.

> Initially, the bilingual girls took the lead and dominated the assignment. They created the dialogue, gave names to the characters, and told Sylvia what to write. Progressively, however, Sylvia became more active, offering bits of dialogue . . .
> SYLVIA: (almost leaping from her seat) "*¡O, ya sé! Esta bola de* (inaudible) *se hace más grande y más pesada.*" [Oh, I know! I know! This (inaudible) ball is get-

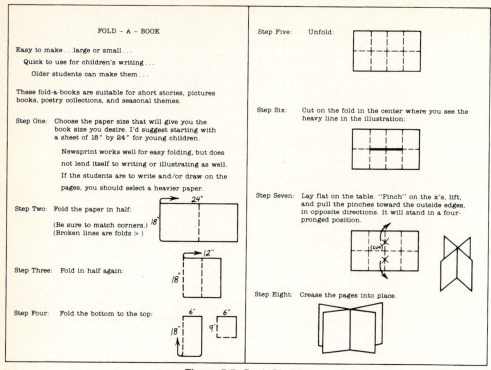

Figure 5.5. Book Binding

ting bigger and heavier.] ANA: "Oh, yea, that's very good." GLORIA: "*De veras . . . wait, look, boy is this hard work. O . . . este, este es trabajo muy duro.*" [Oh this, this is very hard work.] . . . SYLVIA: (asserting herself) "*No, mejor le deberíamos de poner, esta bola de nieve está muy pesada.*" [No, we should write, this snowball is very heavy.] (pp. 65–66)

Moll goes on to describe how Gloria attempts to reword Sylvia's dialogue, but Sylvia prevails. He points out that by working collaboratively and being allowed to use her total language system, Sylvia demonstrated that she understood the assignment and had the necessary writing competence in Spanish to participate in the activity. Moll (1989, p. 66) suggests: "In such a bilingual arrangement, the teacher assured that the ESL children participated in tasks at the same intellectual level as the rest of the class while monitoring and assisting the children's English development." Teachers need to take a more global look at what second language learners can do, particularly in the context of more supportive and linguistically rich settings.

Reading material in English that relates to the life and experience of the Latino children will also assist them in becoming literate in English as they begin to see their realities and experiences reflected and validated in English literature. Works like *My Name is María Isabel* (Ada, 1993), *The Skirt* (Soto, 1992), and *Tomás and the Library Lady* (Mora, 1993) are good examples of contemporary stories that depict varied experiences, struggles, and triumphs of everyday life of Latino children.

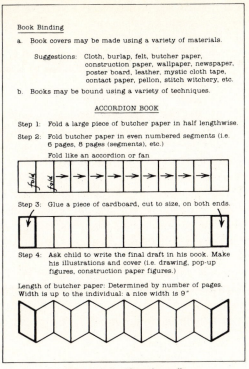

Book Binding

a.   Book covers may be made using a variety of materials.

   Suggestions: Cloth, burlap, felt, butcher paper,
                  construction paper, wallpaper, newspaper,
                  poster board, leather, mystic cloth tape,
                  contact paper, pellon, stitch witchery, etc.

b.   Books may be bound using a variety of techniques.

ACCORDION BOOK

Step 1:   Fold a large piece of butcher paper in half lengthwise.

Step 2:   Fold butcher paper in even numbered segments (i.e.
          6 pages, 8 pages (segments), etc.)

          Fold like an accordion or fan

Step 3:   Glue a piece of cardboard, cut to size, on both ends.

Step 4:   Ask child to write the final draft in his book. Make
          his illustrations and cover (i.e. drawing, pop-up
          figures, construction paper figures.)

Length of butcher paper: Determined by number of pages.
Width is up to the individual: a nice width is 9″

Figure 5.5. (Continued)

The children can relate to situations that are familiar or perhaps even similar to theirs. The use of Spanish words and phrases to describe particular experiences provides continuity for the transition from Spanish literature to English literature. Seeing a literary form that incorporates and validates the language style that is common in most Latino communities affirms the child's home discourse. For example, Galarza (1971) in *Barrio Boy* describes one young boy's recollections of his immigration from Mexico, his life in the *vecindad* [neighborhood], the role of the young as translators for the family, the cultural encounters experienced when the family moves across town to a white middle-class neighborhood, the death of his mother, and working as an agricultural worker in the fields in the summer. After reading different passages from *Barrio Boy*, the children can write about their own similar or very different experiences. Several passages offer opportunities for fourth and fifth graders to study and discuss metalinguistic and sociolinguistic concepts. For example, reading and discussing the passage (Galarza, 1971) that follows can lead to a study of the use of questions in the two languages and cultures.

I had fallen into the habit of asking our landlady questions as I did my mother and my uncles. One day she did not answer a question but said scowling, *'Qué muchachito tan preguntón'* . . . [what an inquisitive little boy] I told my mother what the landlady had said, and asked: 'Am I?' She explained, *'Preguntón* [inquisitive] means nosy and minding other people's business. *Preguntar* [to ask] means just to ask about things you don't understand. It is not good to be nosy. It is good to ask.

Just be careful who you ask and what you ask' . . . There was a certain way to deal with the problem of questions and answers, which I discovered. If there were people around to hear me I was to be quiet, look and listen, and ask later. Adults were queer. They were offended if they heard me ask why they had a wooden leg or why they were bald or why they had such black warts. Keeping to this rule I looked and listened and waited, . . . (p. 95)

Heath (1986) points out that there is a universe of ways to use language but that each cultural group transmits and reinforces only a few. Although researchers have found differences in the ways cultural groups approach second language use and learning (Au, 1995; Heath, 1986; Wong-Fillmore, 1986), individual differences also exist among students (Hudelson, 1989; Kitagawa, 1989). Each student's experience with English reading and writing differs. The students' cultural experiences, background knowledge, linguistic repertoires, and personalities all shape their engagement in second language proficiency. Their status as an experienced or inexperienced language user for a defined task in a specified situation comes from both personal and social experience. Recognizing this, we need to set goals and create learning environments that expand the range of second language literacy. At the same time we must not devalue students' other intellectual abilities while learning the second language. Further, we must always be mindful of all they may want to accomplish through literacy in the future in any of their several languages.

SUMMARY

In this chapter we suggested ways that teachers may help students continue literacy development in Spanish and English, gain experience and knowledge through the study of literature, and direct their own learning. We discussed the kinds of interactive contexts needed in order to promote intellectual growth, collaboration among learners, authentic use of written communication, and the input and interaction needed for continued second language development. The processes for reading and writing were also presented.

ACTIVITIES

Journal Writing

1. When working on a task that requires study and/or creativity, do you prefer working independently or in a group? What implications does this have for the type of student grouping and social roles you will create in your classroom?
2. Do you have a favorite poet or author? What qualities attract you to this poet or author?

Discussion Activities

1. Working in pairs, select a children's short story or short novel. Discuss how a teacher-student dialogue using the creative reading approach can be used. Develop some sample questions to illustrate your discussion.

2. In a small group, select a theme and brainstorm ideas for a literature study unit. Develop plans for one or more of the ideas. The activities can utilize literature and integrate listening, speaking, reading, and writing.

Field-Based Activities

1. Interview three or four children of the same age but in different classrooms about their favorite kind of reading (e.g., "What do you like to read?"). Do not use the word *book* in your question. Repeat the interview with older or younger children and compare and contrast the children's responses.
2. Visit a book store and a library (school, public, college) to determine what the most popular recent trade books are that children are reading. Select one or two of them, read them, and develop hunches about why they are popular. In sharing your ideas with the children in the class, pay attention to your assumptions about the children's interests.
3. Visit a classroom for at least a week. Keep a log of the writing activities and processes you observe. Categorize these activities according to function and purpose. Compare your findings to those of other teachers.

NOTES

1. This assumes a maintenance and/or enrichment bilingual program model and the continuous and consistent participation of students in Spanish literacy instruction.
2. Kagan (1985) describes a highly structured cooperative learning system consisting of team building, management techniques, and rewards based on a fairly complex system of points. Much of the discussion is on cooperative learning centers and the evaluation of the performance of groups or individuals. We prefer to downplay behavioristic goals (points and other extrinsic motivational devices) and feel that cooperative learning can work by concentrating on social interaction goals (sense of group accomplishment and respect for others).

CHAPTER 6
Literacy in the Content Areas

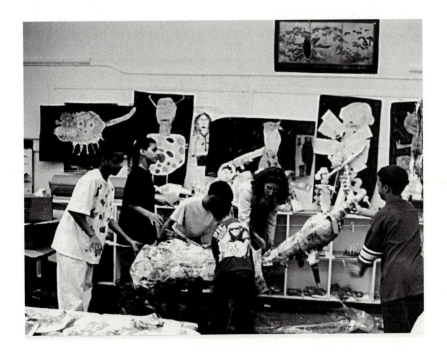

Chapter Overview

The Content Areas
Comprehension Strategies in the Content Areas
Study Skills as a Theme

INTRODUCTION

Reading, writing, and thinking are the basic processes of learning and cannot be limited to the reading or language arts class. As mentioned previously, teachers can contribute to the development of literacy in all subject areas. Reading, writing, and thinking are essential at all stages of our lives. Access to information and knowledge requires different forms of literacy. Using reading, writing, and thinking to enhance learning across the curriculum not only makes sense, it is essential. Reading/writing processes and content can be integrated using a thematic approach that provides contexts in which students learn important content in purposeful ways. It is important to consider how this can occur in the social studies, math, and science curricula.

Trends within content areas are moving in the direction of creating learning environments that promote purposeful activity. Based on the concept of situated cognition (Brown, Collins & Duguid, 1989) and the Deweyan tradition of theme-based learning, a multidisciplinary team at the Learning Technology Center at Vanderbilt University is developing what they call the "anchored instruction" approach. The goal is to create environments that permit sustained exploration and enable learners to explore the different kinds of knowledge that make sense in situations that resemble "ordinary practices of the culture" (Brown, Collins & Duguid, 1989:34). In this way, students can "experience the value of exploring the same setting from multiple perspectives" (Cognition and Technology Group at Vanderbilt, 1990:3). This approach is used in a social studies curriculum called the Young Sherlock Holmes project. The movies *The Young Sherlock Holmes* and *Oliver Twist* are the context for teaching. The results of this instruction have been very favorable. In comparison with a control group receiving high-quality social studies instruction, the Sherlock group developed more complex story structures, used more complex language skills, demonstrated greater historical accuracy, used historical information in inferences about characters in new movies, and were more likely to direct their own learning by finding and defining issues to explore. Other approaches also aim to create similar purposeful learning environments for children: the inquiry approach, guided discovery approach (Burns, Haywood & Delclos, 1987), cooperative investigation (Lansdown, Blackwood & Brandwein, 1971), and language through science approaches as well as the cognitively guided instruction approach (Carpenter & Moser, 1983; Carpenter el al., 1989), constructivist teaching approach (Cobb, Yachel & Wood, 1988), mathematical argument approach (Lambert, 1988), and authentic instruction in the content areas (Newmann & Wehlage, 1993). In addition to providing a richer context for developing students' understanding of the content areas, these approaches create environments for the use of more complex language skills. They create situations in which different literacy skills are used for different purposes and a variety of content-area materials are utilized.

Whatever the approach, teachers must face the reality that content-area texts usually present factual information in expository form. Many texts are written from the perspective that knowledge is an accumulated body of facts, information, and skills that needs to be conveyed. Much rarer are content-area texts developed from the perspective that knowledge is constructed through the act of knowing and that classrooms can be organized so that students can actively construct knowledge about a subject area or theme. Frequently, significant amounts of information are presented in a relatively short selection. This results in considerable density of text and a heavy concept load. Authors often convey at least part of their information through the use of illustrations, diagrams, charts, graphs, bold-faced headings, and subheadings. These factors result in texts that require teachers to reconceptualize the teaching of the content area and use special learning/instructional techniques so that students will effectively interact with existing texts and learn the information, facts, and technologies that become part of the construction of knowledge and enhance their language skills.

Academic expository texts, with their use of language and concept load, present comprehension problems. For children who possess a limited proficiency in English and who are in the process of transferring to English language instruction, the problem is exacerbated (Chamot & O'Malley, 1987). Thus it is crucial that the approach used for developing literacy through the content areas include concrete experiences for concept development. It is equally important that the approach include exposure to skills for reading and writing expository texts in the native language prior to the children being transferred to an all-English language instructional approach (De Avila, et al., 1987; Secada & Carey, 1990). Through concept development and the use of Spanish expository texts, students can develop strategies for constructing meaning and building the type of knowledge found in content-area materials.

In this chapter we will look at (1) reading and writing in content subjects, (2) uses of expository discourse, and (3) study skills.

THE CONTENT AREAS

Schools have been organized around subject matter such as mathematics, science, and social studies. The student is faced with having to acquire appropriate skills for the cognitive and literacy demands in these areas. Students have many informal experiences that can help them understand the subject matter (Lave & Wenger, 1991), but it is necessary that teachers make explicit connections between the knowledge students bring in and the content area. Imagination and creativity are necessary, but the expository writing and reading skills required for the content area are more reality based.

With respect to the literacy context of content areas, teachers need to help students develop a variety of strategies for accessing information found in print. It has been proposed that proficient readers use different strategies (e.g., they speed up and slow down the rate at which they read) depending on the difficulty of the text and their purpose for reading the text (Rankin, 1970). Good readers do not engage in the same reading process for every text and for every purpose (Samuels & Dahl, 1975); they skim, scan, read, strive for understanding, evaluate, and memorize. Students need to be taught how and when to engage in these different processes when encountering expository text. Developing a repertoire of strategies for reading is an important goal.

Reading and writing expository material necessarily involves the integration of prior knowledge or experience. Material of which children have more prior knowledge will be more easily understood than material of which they have little or no prior knowledge or background. But sometimes, even when they have prior knowledge, the connections are not made between informal, experientially based knowledge and formal learning activity and knowledge building (Scardamalia, Bereiter & Lamon, 1994; Bereiter, 1994). Children need to have a frame of reference for what they read, and teachers must help them consciously bring this frame of reference (see the discussion on schemata in Chapter 2) to their interaction with expository text. In this way, their learning emphasizes connections and relationships among ideas and builds on existing knowledge, but also goes beyond it.

Creating literacy environments in content areas can be viewed from the perspective of the process, how the skills are acquired and refined, and its purpose, what needs to be accomplished. First, constructing knowledge in subject areas by being able to use appropriate reading and writing strategies to access knowledge is usually referred to as developing literacy in the content areas. The focus is on the goal of constructing knowledge. The process, using a variety of oral and written skills to access knowledge, is equally important. The process of learning how to use literacy skills as tools for expanding subject matter concepts is consciously explored. The activity of bringing the learning process to a conscious level helps students focus attention on the development of appropriate study skills. In the following sections, we will examine content areas as contexts for developing literacy and the use of reading and writing to enhance the construction of knowledge in content areas.

Literacy and Social Studies

Learning skills and concepts in the social studies curriculum can provide a natural environment for the practice of reading and writing. For example, if the concepts include change, citizenship, culture, environment, identity, interdependence, and technology, and the skills to be used include the gathering of information from a variety of sources, learning how to use the information and present it to others, and participating in groups, then it is necessary to listen to others, talk with them, read about the subject, and make sense of the information. Literacy skills play a critical role in information gathering, and teachers will find ample opportunities to enhance them.

When students read about the past, think about its meaning, and write to clarify thinking, the study of the past becomes alive in their imagination. For example, following the anchored instruction approach and using a visual medium to introduce the topic, the video *Seguín*[1] can serve to explore identity, culture, the history of land grant titles, the role of Tejanos in the relationship between Mexico and the United States, the legal issues involved in the Treaty of Guadalupe-Hidalgo, and many more themes. The use of this approach stimulates thinking and provides many opportunities for reading and writing.

Much of the Spanish social studies series has been adapted from English series. Most series are composed of textbooks (and teacher's manuals) sequenced by grade level from kindergarten to sixth grade. Each level deals with a theme. In grade

five, for example, social studies units prepared for use in the United States focus on U.S. history and geography.

Generally, by about third grade, teachers are expected to use the textbook for the grade level, and most teachers assume that the textbook should be covered one chapter at a time. However, the chapter is not always the best unit to use. The teacher, after taking into account factors like students' interest, abilities, and the nature of the text, must decide on the best organization and use of content textbooks.

The next section of this chapter will describe teaching procedures as illustrations of practices that may be appropriate for much of the social studies curriculum as well. Specific suggestions on vocabulary, previewing a chapter, outlining, and examining text structure may be applied to social studies, although the timing of the activities or the sequence of the suggested practices may need to be altered. There is no reason for teachers to adhere to a particular sequence, that is, always dealing with vocabulary before previewing a chapter. For example, in a civil rights lesson, when the teacher decided to ask Latino students how they would explain concepts such as racism, stereotyping, and discrimination before going on to the written passage in the text, Torres-Guzmán (1989; 1994) found that the teacher was, in effect, altering the relationship of the students to the text. Because the students had experienced racism and discrimination, they could describe events in their community. The utilization of this prior knowledge helped the students read the passage in the text more critically and permitted them to go beyond existing knowledge. Student experience, text structure, and different concepts presented in the text will help the teacher decide on the sequence of instruction.

After the study of geography, lifestyle, economics, politics, and daily life in a country, students can create their own fictional country, presenting written as well as visual material. Maps of various types might display land forms, bodies of water, and other geographical characteristics. Illustrations of shelters, clothes, and ceremonies can be included. A written description of the people and their social rules is important. Creating a new country also promotes group projects and interdependence so that these issues can become items for class discussion.

Literacy and Math

Our lives are rich in experiences that include informal knowledge about mathematics (Lave & Wenger, 1991), but these experiences are rarely encountered in classroom settings (Stigler 1990). Most of us who have struggled with the formal, symbolic math taught in school are well aware that identifying numbers or being able to read a formula does not necessarily mean that we understand the underlying logic of such symbols. Furthermore, understanding a word problem does not necessarily mean we know how to translate it into the appropriate calculations or know when to apply the mathematical reasoning to our everyday problem solving.

Reading and thinking logically are extremely important in solving word problems. Both monolingual and bilingual students have been found to apply reasoning skills to mathematical problems beyond addition and subtraction; they focus on problem structures such as elements that join two parts, elements that separate parts, the relationships among more than one part and the whole, and the comparison of quantities. Their strategies for solving mathematical problems are associated with the structures they identify (Carpenter & Moser, 1983; Secada, cited in Secada & Carey, 1990).

Thinking about literacy in the context of math has led to an emphasis on the relationship between the ability to read and the ability to solve written problems (Tiedt et al., 1989). Students are encouraged to use context clues, find the main idea, understand key words in context, make inferences, and understand the underlying logic of math symbols and formulas. Although this is insufficient for a better understanding of mathematics because students need to understand the logic of the operations themselves (Secada & Carey, 1990), they are the skills needed for unlocking meaning and finding solutions to word problems.

It is in the context of understanding problem structures and identifying effective strategies for solving them that language becomes the key to instruction. The basic decision the mathematician makes is what determines the process employed to solve a problem. No matter how well students add or subtract, if they use these functions at the wrong time, the answer will be incorrect. One way to help students is to provide them with concrete experiences. A teacher who was concerned about her first graders' understanding of the concept *one more* used Cuisenaire® rods to test their understanding. There had been some confusion apparent in the paper and pencil exercise she had given them previously. But when the students worked with the Cuisenaire® rods, the teacher realized they understood more math than she had thought (Berkey et al., 1990). However, she still needed to deal with the pedagogical question of how to help students show their math competency in print. Secada & Carey (1990), based on cognitively guided instructional techniques, identify various options teachers have when students do not solve problems correctly: (a) pose a similar problem, (b) simplify the language of the problem, (c) add a familiar context, (d) translate, if not in the child's dominant language, and (e) if all else fails, try a simpler problem.

Teachers should engage students in talking about possible solutions and in sharing ideas about problem structures, strategies, and the vocabulary of word problems.

CLASSROOM ACTIVITY 6.1   Math Word Problem Activity

1. In the context of thematic units, create the need for students to use mathematical operations to solve problems. For example, within the unit on water suggested in Figure 6.1, the students might encounter some activities that require being able to calculate volume.

2. Pose word problems within the context of the unit of study. Students working in pairs can analyze the problem structure, identify words or phrases that provide clues, and discuss possible strategies for their solutions.
   a. Have the students write a description of the context of the problem.
   b. Ask students to list the words that are key to the problem. Tell students that getting the right mathematical answer is not the objective at this time.
   c. Ask students to guess what the problem structure may be and the strategies and mathematical process(es) needed to solve the problem.
   d. Ask them to put their responses in their own words first; then ask them to use words they learned when they were deciphering the problem.

3. Share the work of one team with another to see if the students agree on the context, the problem structure, and mathematical strategies and process(es).

Within the context of a thematic unit, take some time to have students identify the problem structure and discuss strategies for their solutions. Have them underline or make note of words that give clues to the identification of problem structures and strategies they have identified. The teacher can model this process by asking students to think through their problems and solutions while helping them clarify misunderstandings. The next step before calculation might be for students to write the problem using different words and exchange the paraphrasing with their peers. Students can evaluate each other's analysis of the problem. Classroom Activity 6.1 describes an activity that can be used to help students with word problems.

Another useful activity might be to ask students to rewrite a problem for other students, thus clarifying their own understanding of the word problem. They will think logically about the problem and practice using synonyms and other context clues in math. Also, you can ask the students to write their own story problems based on their own experiences and what is relevant to the world around them (Davison & Reyhner, 1992). Ask the students to record in their journals or keep math logs describing the math processes they are using. In this way, the students may become aware of accurate and inaccurate patterns of thought. If students can identify how and why they have used a process, the chances of greater understanding are improved.

Songs and rhymes can be integrated into thematic units to help children learn addition, subtraction, and multiplication facts. Have students adapt traditional songs such as *La muñeca vestida de azul* [The doll dressed in blue] using their math facts while attempting to maintain the rhyme. In this type of activity they are using mathematical concepts as themes for a literacy activity; they are both playing with language and clarifying math concepts.

Literacy and Science

Doing science is a dynamic process. Engaging in science "appeals to the basic curiosity that youngsters feel about the natural and manmade world around them" (Newman, 1994:29). Beyond the exposure to a body of knowledge that serves to explain and understand natural phenomena, students are involved in thinking, feeling, experiencing, and talking about ideas concerning natural phenomena. When students are doing science, they hypothesize or connect ideas, gather data, look for confirmation of their ideas, and reach conclusions that may lead them in new directions. This is the process used by scientists. The student clarifies thinking that is based on data gathered from observations, reading materials, and so forth.

Hedegaard (1988) describes the use of a method similar to that used by scientists for integrating subjects and "also of allowing us to stress the internal connection between society and nature" (p. 36). Third through fifth graders worked with integrated activities to acquire the basic concepts of biology, geography, and history and then related these concepts to their concrete surroundings. Through their learning, the pupils acquired a general conceptual model system for the subject based on the teacher's model system. Hedegaard's integrated activities were organized as themes and subthemes. The conceptual structure of the theme teaching was aimed at the development of the children's theoretical thinking. Hedegaard (1988) cautions that the use of theme teaching must have a scientific conceptual foundation: "The teacher's knowledge must be theoretically anchored so that the pupils are neither drowned in facts nor led into social interaction, pure and simple, in which there is no 'red thread' running through the content of the teaching . . . (p. 36)."

Finding Out/Descubrimiento (De Avila, Duncan & Navarrete, 1987) is an inquiry-based curriculum that integrates science, math, and language (both Spanish and English) around three basic principles: (a) that children like to engage in activity that gives them a "sense of mastery over their environment" (p. 1); (b) that a purpose of education is to provide children with a repertoire of "generalizable strategies" that help them engage successfully in mastery activities, and (c) that pyschosocial access requires that the language of instruction—both receptive and productive aspects—be in a language in which the student has greater opportunities to learn (Valdez-Pierce, 1987). This program calls for the teacher to assume a facilitator role, for cooperative groups, for assigned student roles, and for the organization of a work space that will facilitate deepening the first language and learning the second.

Figure 6.1 (pp. 134–135) is a semantic map of a water theme that could be developed by teachers and students for a semester or yearlong unit. (Figure 6.1a is in Spanish and Figure 6.1b is in English.) Using the theme and subthemes as a rough, general plan, the children can work in a research fashion like scientists. A wall chart can record the goals and results achieved in the study of the cycle and uses of water. The teacher's job will be to direct the children's research activity. It is important to stress, though, that the teacher only directs the activity and does not formulate it concretely or expect particular results. In order to interest the children in the subject, use their interest in the "big questions of life": Where does rain come from? Has there always been water? How much of my body is made up of water? What would happen if there was no more water? Maintain interest through research procedures, model building, and generating/testing hypotheses, and bring up areas of contrast and conflict. For example, discuss the contrasts between the uses of water and the symbols for water in different cultures, or the conflict in a drought year over water allocation to cities (so we can flush the toilet and water our lawns) as opposed to farms.

It is possible to organize teaching around central generative concepts that integrate the different subthemes as part of exploring the general problems and concepts of the content area. The children can integrate their knowledge into a general model and use this model in new and unfamiliar areas of study.

COMPREHENSION STRATEGIES
IN THE CONTENT AREAS

What children are expected to do with the information they access in the content areas is different from the goals of reading, communication arts, or language arts classes. Learning in subject areas requires different comprehension strategies. In particular, the technical vocabulary and limited contextual cues of the texts pose a unique challenge. Accuracy in time periods and sequences is demanded, and the presence of formulas, symbols, calculations, and other abstractions necessitate special attention. Central to our discussion of comprehension in the content areas is that it can be taught.

Children may find reading and comprehending expository material difficult because the concepts may be too technical or complex; the level of reading difficulty of many content area textbooks is higher than their grade-level designation (e.g., a third-grade social studies textbook may actually be written at a fourth- or fifth-grade reading level); or the format of such expository material is quite different from the style and structure of stories with which children are more familiar.

One way children can learn about the purpose and style of expository writing is by comparing its structure to that of a story. Passages on the same topic, one written as a story and the other as exposition, can be selected for the theme under study. After the students have been exposed to the different types of texts, take the opportunity to read aloud the different passages. Figure 6.2 (p. 136) is an example of these two types of text.

You can discuss and illustrate the style and structure of stories (e.g., characterization, plot, and setting) and contrast this with the techniques used in expository writing (e.g., listing, cause and effect, and comparison and contrast). Ask the children to write about an event—for example, what occurred on a recent trip. Suggest that they first write in expository form, focusing on sequencing the events or providing a straightforward guide. Later they can write about their experience as a story. Compare and contrast the modes of narrative and expository writing used by the children in recounting the event. Through the experience of writing different types of texts, they will become more aware of how to negotiate the information, facts, and technologies offered in expository texts and will learn strategies for approaching different types of writing.

There are several things you can do to assist children who are reading in this new mode. Once you have observed and assessed the children's strengths and weak-

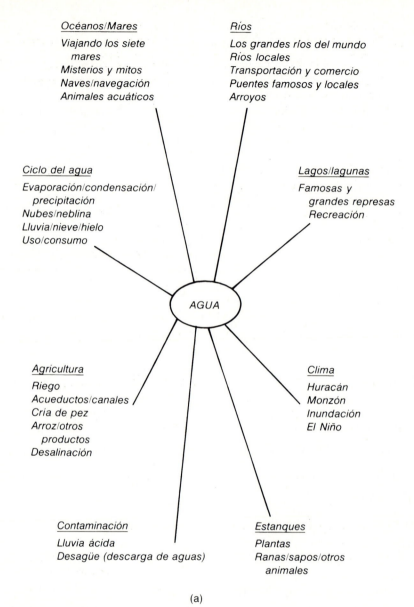

Océanos/Mares

Viajando los siete
  mares
Misterios y mitos
Naves/navegación
Animales acuáticos

Ríos

Los grandes ríos del mundo
Ríos locales
Transportación y comercio
Puentes famosos y locales
Arroyos

Ciclo del agua

Evaporación/condensación/
  precipitación
Nubes/neblina
Lluvia/nieve/hielo
Uso/consumo

Lagos/lagunas

Famosas y
  grandes represas
Recreación

AGUA

Agricultura

Riego
Acueductos/canales
Cría de pez
Arroz/otros
  productos
Desalinación

Clima

Huracán
Monzón
Inundación
El Niño

Contaminación

Lluvia ácida
Desagüe (descarga de aguas)

Estanques

Plantas
Ranas/sapos/otros
  animales

(a)

Figure 6.1. *Unidad sobre el tema del agua* [An integrated theme on the subject of water]

nesses as they attempt to interact with content area textbooks or trade books, provide them with different media for gaining knowledge. Second, provide them with concrete background experiences that they can draw on in order to understand what is being taught, particularly if you find that a child's difficulty with a book is on the conceptual level. Through teacher/student conferences or in-group instruction (using an experiential or problem-posing method), you can help by discussing con-

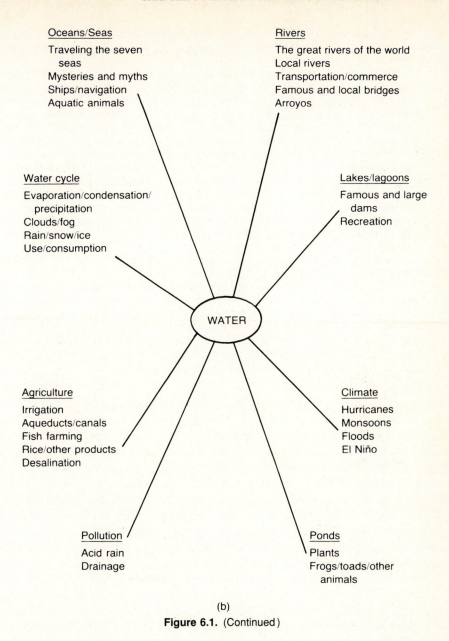

Oceans/Seas
Traveling the seven
   seas
Mysteries and myths
Ships/navigation
Aquatic animals

Rivers
The great rivers of the world
Local rivers
Transportation/commerce
Famous and local bridges
Arroyos

Water cycle
Evaporation/condensation/
   precipitation
Clouds/fog
Rain/snow/ice
Use/consumption

Lakes/lagoons
Famous and large
   dams
Recreation

WATER

Agriculture
Irrigation
Aqueducts/canals
Fish farming
Rice/other products
Desalination

Climate
Hurricanes
Monsoons
Floods
El Niño

Pollution
Acid rain
Drainage

Ponds
Plants
Frogs/toads/other
   animals

(b)

Figure 6.1. (Continued)

cepts and previous experiences or simplifying ideas and clarifying the material. You can guide their reading by giving them direction and purpose through questioning and problem posing. Scrutinize the content area textbooks and other informational trade books available to your class in order to calculate a more accurate index of your students' reading levels. The informal and formal techniques for this purpose described in Chapter 7 will be useful here. Finally, you can provide the student with

Both passages are about the moment when a butterfly emerges from its cocoon. The first passage is from *La mariposa dorada* [The Golden Butterfly], by M. Osorio (1985), and is written in narrative form:

. . . *Primero asomó una cabecita brillante con dos largas antenas, después el cuerpecillo suave. Cuando ya estuvo fuera, pudo abrir y extender las dos grandes alas en las que tanto había trabajado. —Jamás te hubiera conocido—dijo el rayo de sol, contemplándolo entusiasmado. —¿Crees que será bastante este cambio?—le preguntó el gusano con inseguridad—He hecho todo lo que he podido. —Tu trabajo no ha podido ser mejor. Ya sí que puedes salir. Aunque espera, antes quiero darte algo . . . Y el rayo de sol derramó su polvillo dorado sobre las alas del gusano [mariposa] para que brillara aún más . . .* [The first thing to show were its two long antennas, then its soft body. Out came the two great big wings it had worked on. —I might have never recognized you—said the ray of sun, watching him with glee. —Do you think I changed sufficiently?—asked the caterpillar a bit unsure of himself—I did all I could. —You could have done no better work. You can come out now. But wait, I want to give you something. . . And the ray of sun spread a golden powder on the butterfly's wings so it would also glow. . .](p. 17; our translation)

The second passage is from *Cómo y por qué de los insectos* [The How and Why of Insects], by R. Rood (1973), and is written in expository form:

. . . *en la primavera, el envoltorio ninfático se rompe y sale arrastrándose el insecto, que ya no es una oruga, sino una polilla o una mariposa de alas brillantes. La mariposa extiende sus alas para secarse al sol, luego se aleja volando, dejando tras sí el envoltorio ninfático.* [. . . in the spring, the cocoon breaks and the insect crawls out, not as a caterpillar, but as a butterfly with wings. The butterfly extends its wings to dry in the sun, flaps its wings and flies away, leaving the cocoon behind.] (p. 25; our translation)

Figure 6.2. Comparing Narrative and Expository Text

specific strategies to use when reading content-area materials, for example, guiding, simulating, debriefing (Moore & Readence, 1986), and examining text structure and critical inquiry. Let us look at each of these suggestions and strategies.

To assist children in reading material that may be beyond their reading level you can tape-record selected passages that they can then listen to while reading along in the text, or you or an aide can read the text aloud to those who are unable to read it by themselves. Another way to approach the problem is to pair children off in their content-area reading in a tutor-tutee arrangement. In this way both children learn, and the children who are apt to have difficulties have a ready source of assistance available. Your aim, to borrow from the computer field, is to make the texts user friendly.

Of course, providing the children with concrete background experience prior to reading will help them understand new concepts and deepen their understanding of others. Organizing instruction around basic concepts using the integrated biliteracy instructional approach described in Chapter 4 is also helpful. Rayner and Pollatsek (1989) indicate that in order to comprehend a text "broader pragmatic real-world knowledge must be used, which includes plans and intentions and causation" (p. 123). In other words, real-world knowledge has to actively intervene for comprehension to take place. Comprehension is the act of associating new information with prior knowledge or experience.

Directing children to read for certain purposes is also helpful, but they are frequently not told how they might acquire the information to fulfill those purposes.

A number of strategies that revolve around questioning and teacher guidance will help create the scaffolding effect they need to move beyond what they know and can do independently. Some form of study guide is typically used to accomplish this. For instance, if the material to be learned uses a compare-contrast organizational pattern, then the children might be provided with a guide reflecting that comprehension skill. The guide should be designed to lead children toward the information desired and improve their comprehension abilities by showing them the processes one would use to identify main ideas and details. It is not necessarily true that children will acquire the learning habits the guide intends them to acquire; that is, children may not become aware of the processes they are using in searching for meaning. It may be necessary to use metacognitive strategies (talking about the process) to bring this to a conscious awareness. Children will learn best and acquire skills and information when their attention is focused directly on the phenomena to be learned.

Incorporating the simulating, debriefing, and fading methods of Moore and Readence (1986) into the biliteracy integrated lesson can provide both direct skills instruction in and guidance to selected text information in context. That is, the text information is stressed alongside the process of learning the skills needed to acquire that information. And it is done in context. For instance, in a unit whose theme is the evolution of the life of a chick, learning about the various stages of development can be organized so that students are observing, reading, viewing, drawing, discussing, and writing about the various stages. See Figure 6.3 for a fourth grader's writing and illustration of such a cycle.

One skill children may need is that of organizing information into a main idea/detail format while attending to accuracy of factual information. After viewing a film, you can ask the students to write about the first twenty-five days in the life of a chick. Provide them with information books and other materials. Ask them to do two things: write what they remembered about the film and confirm their facts. They may consult with classmates, but they must also consult printed matter. The teacher can model both types of behavior. Thus attention to the process of learning is provided while attending to content. Once students have done this, the teacher can ask them to talk through the process of confirmation. The teacher can take the students' ideas and simulate the process with them, going beyond behavior into the thinking process that accompanied the behavior while paying attention to both process and content. In a concurrent approach to comprehension instruction the teacher explicitly points out how to learn from the text, doing so by modeling the processes necessary to comprehend and by providing feedback in a debriefing session after the content has been learned. Debriefing is a reflective activity that includes self-reporting, introspection, and hindsight. Such feedback entails discussing with children the processes they used to comprehend the material in relation to what was modeled for them.

In addition, clarifying the text structure, or the patterns in which text may be organized, can be useful in helping students to comprehend and recall a text selection. Knowledge of how the ideas in a text are bound together to form a whole enables a child to understand the overall text better than if the text is perceived as a

[How chicks grow]

Figure 6.3. The Development of a Chick

series of discrete information or facts. A number of types of text structure are common in content text material. A brief description of each follows:

1. *Cause-effect*. This text structure links reasons with results, or actions with their consequences. It is often cued by words such as *porque* or *a causa de* [because]; *por esto* or *por lo tanto* [therefore]; and *puesto que* [since]. These words serve as signal devices to cue the reader to the structure of the text, as in the example below (Seymour, 1986):

   La luna brilla porque refleja la luz del sol. Durante un eclipse de luna, la luz re-flejada desaparece porque la tierra se interpone entre la luna y el sol. Cuando es la luna la que bloquea la luz solar, se produce un eclipse de sol. [The moon shines because it reflects the light of the sun. During a lunar eclipse, the reflected light dis-

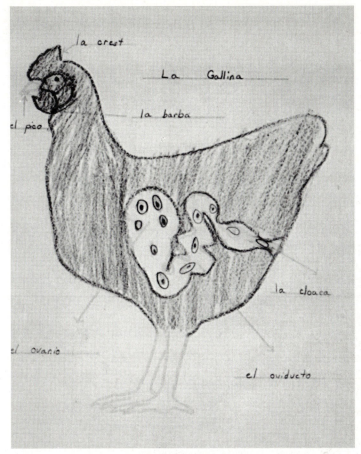

[The hen: the crest, the beak, the chin, the ovary, the conduit, the oviduct]
Figure 6.3. (Continued)

appears because the earth moves between the moon and the sun. When the moon blocks solar light, an eclipse of the sun is produced.] (p. 4; our translation)

2. *Compare-contrast.* This text pattern examines the likenesses and differences between at least two people, objects, or concepts. Cue words typical of this text structure include *pero* [but], *además* [also/in addition], and *sin embargo* [nevertheless].

   El tigre es el felino más grande. También es el más fuerte. Sin embargo, necesita ayuda. Necesita un lugar donde vivir. [The tiger is the biggest feline. It is also the strongest. Nevertheless, it needs help. It needs a place to live.] (p. 10; our translation)

3. *Time order.* This text structure is exemplified by a sequential relationship of ideas over the passage of time and is typically cued by such words as *antes* [before], *despues* [after], *luego* [then], *enseguida* [follow/following],

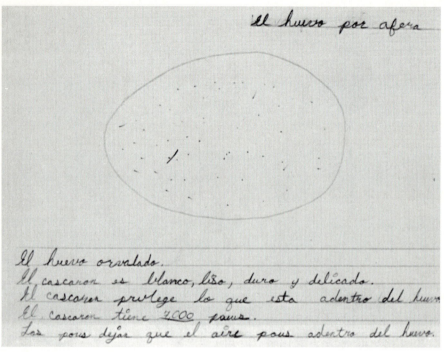

el huevo por afera

El huevo ovalado.
El cascaron es blanco, liso, duro y delicado.
El cascaron protege lo que esta adentro del huevo
El cascaron tiene 7000 poros.
Los poros dejan que el aire pous adentro del huevo.

[Title: The outside of the egg
The egg is an oval.
The shell is white, smooth, hard, and delicate.
The shell protects the insides.
The shell has 7,000 pores.
The pores permit the air to go through to the inside of the egg.]

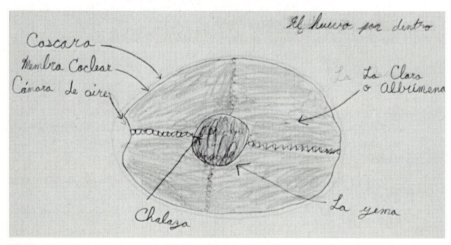

[The inside of the egg
Shell, membrane cavity, air chamber, the white, the chalaza, the yolk]

Figure 6.3. (Continued)

140

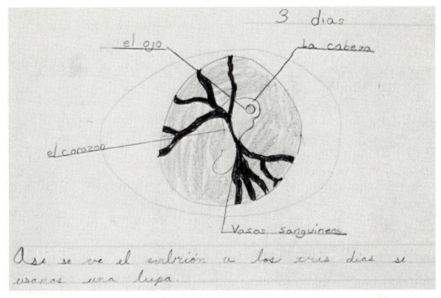

[The third day
   The eye, the head, the heart
   This is what the third day looks like, if you use a magnifying glass to look.]

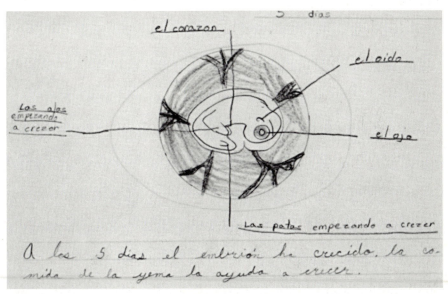

[The fifth day
   The heart, the ears, the eyes, the wings starting to grow
   By the fifth day, the embryo has grown. The nourishment from the yolk makes it grow.]

Figure 6.3. (Continued)

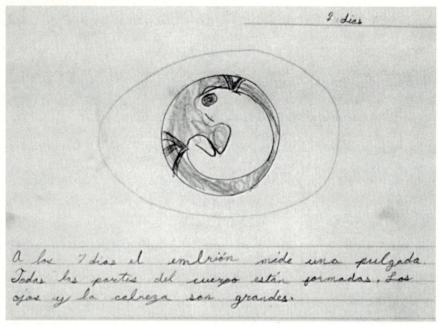

[The seventh day
   On the seventh day, the embryo measures an inch. The parts of the body are formed.
     The eyes and the head are big.]

[The tenth day
   By the tenth day, the embryo looks like a bird. It still doesn't have feathers.]

Figure 6.3. (Continued)

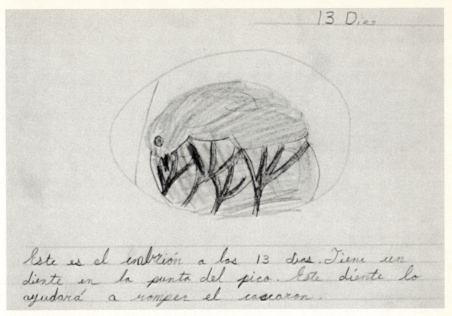

[The thirteenth day
    This is what the embryo looks like on the thirteenth day. It has a tooth at the end point of
    its beak. This tooth will help it break the egg shell.]

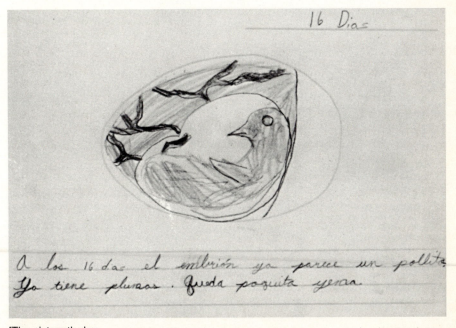

[The sixteenth day
    By the sixteenth day, the embryo looks like a chick. It has feathers. Very little yolk is left.]
Figure 6.3. (Continued)

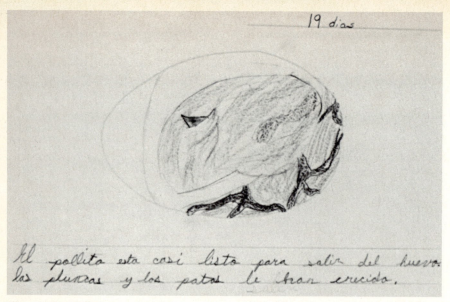

19 días

El pollito esta casi listo para salir del huevo. Las plumas y las patas le han crecido.

[The nineteenth day
   The chick is almost ready to come out. Its feathers and its feet have grown.]

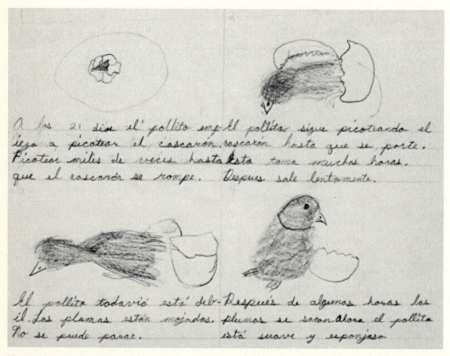

A los 21 días el pollito emp- El pollito sigue picoteando el
ieza a picotear el cascarón. cascarón hasta que se parte.
Picotea miles de veces hasta Esta toma muchas horas.
que el cascarón se rompe. Despues sale lentamente.

El pollito todavía está deb- Despues de algunas horas las
il. Las plumas están mojadas. plumas se secan ahora el pollito
No se puede parar. está suave y esponjoso

[By the twenty-first day
   The chick starts to peck at the shell. It will do so thousands of times until the shell breaks.
   The chick will continue pecking until it breaks. This takes hours. Then it slowly comes out.
   The chick is still weak. Its feathers are wet. It cannot stand up.
   After a few hours, the feathers dry. Now the chick is soft and fluffy.]

Figure 6.3. (Continued)

Figure 6.3. (Continued)

and *por fin* [at last]. The following paragraph (Sund et al., 1987) is an example of the time order text structure:

> *Las plantas de semillas cambian. Primero, las semillas germinan, luego las plán-*
> *tulas crecen y se convierten en plantas adultas que producen semillas . . .* [The
> plants that come from seeds change. First, the seeds germinate, later the shoots grow
> and become adult plants that produce seeds . . .] (p. 27; our translation)

4. *Simple listing.* As it implies, this text structure is a listing of events or facts
   where order is not significant. Typical of the structure is the following paragraph (Webster, 1986):

> *La energía eléctrica se puede cambiar en calor de una plancha, en luz de una lám-*
> *para y en energía mecánica (movimiento) en un ventilador.* [Electrical energy can
> change into the heat of an iron, the light of a lamp, and the mechanical energy
> (movement) in a fan.] (p. 33; our translation)

Working with Content Vocabulary

A heavy load of new vocabulary is one of the greatest challenges in content area
reading. Simpson (1987) suggests that in the content areas "vocabulary load im-
pedes the students' ability to comprehend" (p. 632). The question of why vocabulary knowledge is so closely related to reading comprehension ability is another
reading issue that is often debated. Psychologists have studied the relationship between word knowledge and thought in an attempt to use word knowledge as a measure of intelligence. Vygotsky (1986) has noted that the relationship between thought
and word is an "immense and complex problem" (p. 153). It is no wonder then that
there is no clear, easy definition of what it means to "know a word."

Given the profound implications of the relationships among word knowledge,
reading comprehension, and thought, and given the rich variability of connotation,
denotation, historical change, local variation, and creative use of language, it is no
wonder that there is no definitive way of teaching vocabulary.

There are a number of ways to enrich children's storehouse of concepts and vocabulary. The most significant way is through direct, concrete experience; rich experiences yield rich vocabulary. Teaching measurement and science vocabulary within the context of a cooking activity will give the children concrete concepts and experiences to use as referents for the words. After the children have had direct, firsthand experiences, you may supplement this with visual vicarious experiences, such as films, videotapes, and pictures, that associate words with contexts.

Perhaps the most significant clue to the understanding of vocabulary in print is the context in which it appears. People use words in particular contexts to denote only part of the usual meaning of the word; sarcasm, irony, and humor prompt people to use words to mean the opposite of what they usually mean. Meanings of words change over time and change within cultural or generational groups; for example, slang ("cool," "rad," "dope") is deliberately invented so that outsiders (in this case, adults) will not know what is being said among members of the in-group (that is, youth).

Teaching vocabulary in the content areas often means teaching the content area plus word recognition. All the word recognition skills—whole word, phonics, structure, and context—come into play.

Another way to expand children's vocabulary is through direct word study. This may include the development of dictionaries, word banks with words grouped by categories, semantic maps (Johnson & Pearson, 1978), and word webs (listing words associated with the target word; see Figure 6.4 for an example), as well as the study of words based on morpheme features such as prefixes, suffixes, and roots. (See Figure 6.5 for some examples.)

Finally, consult the teacher's guides to content-area textbooks for suggested strategies concerning the designated subject matter vocabulary for each chapter or lesson. Lists of technical words and terms in Spanish are also useful aids in preparing vocabulary activities in the content areas.

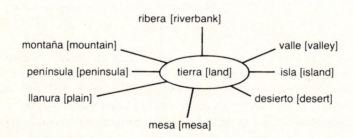

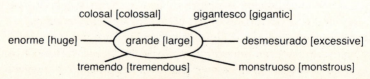

Figure 6.4. Word Webs

Prefijos	Significado	Ejemplos
anti-	contra [opposed]	antiséptico [antiseptic]
co- [co- or con-]	junto con [with]	cooperar [cooperate]
re-	de nuevo [repetition]	reajustar [readjust]
sub-	debajo [under]	subterráneo [subterraneous]
Sufijos		
-able, -ible	digno de o se puede	demostrable [demonstrable]
-ción, -sión, -xión	[worthy to or able to]	invención [invention]
-iento	acción o efecto [action or effect]	crecimiento [increase or
-oso	parecido o tendencia	increment]
	[resemblance; tendency to]	luminoso [luminous, shining]
	lleno de [full of]	
Raíces		
bio	vida [of living things, life]	anfibio, biología
geo	tierra [earth]	[amphibious, biology]
cracia	gobierno [government]	geografía, geología
hidro	agua, líquido [water, liquid]	[geography, geology]
		democracia [democracy]
		hidrosfera [hydrosphere]

Figure 6.5. *Prefijos, sufijos, y raíces* [Prefixes, suffixes, and roots]

Maps, Graphs, Diagrams, and Pictures

There are many ways to present information in graphic, diagrammatic, and pictorial form in print media. With the addition of audiovisual media, particularly the combination of interactive computers, easily accessible multimedia packets, and television displays, the possibilities seem endless.

In print media, one finds bar graphs, line graphs, tables, time lines, flow charts, diagrams of hierarchical relationships, pictorial step-by-step directions, political cartoons, timetables, and maps. Of course, this list does not exhaust the possibilities. Furthermore, each of these categories has many variations, for example, different maps may show political boundaries, roads, air routes, distribution of crops, rainfall, minerals, and so on.

In preparing to teach any text, the teacher needs to consider its graphic format and be aware that the information that is easily, almost unconsciously obtained from graphs by an experienced reader may be inaccessible to some students. Teaching students to interpret such material can occur during the question and discussion phase of the lesson. Modeling the metacognitive processes used in reading graphic representations will assist students in developing this skill. Creating class charts, graphs of the growth of the children in class, and maps of the school or community are but a few of the ways that children can learn to read and interpret graphic material. The teacher's guides that accompany content-area textbooks often offer suggestions as to when and how to teach students to interpret graphic materials in the text.

The use of highly interactive computer programs in which students can take fantasy trips and choose, from among many options, where to go, what to do, and so forth, can guide students in the interpretation of visual and graphic information.

There are interfacing programs in which students can hear prerecorded messages, view segments of a videocassette, and interact with the computer by pressing particular keys or touching certain areas of the screen.

STUDY SKILLS AS A THEME

Traditionally, study skills have been taught in isolation. However, a number of studies (Askov & Kamm, 1989; Stoodt & Balboa, 1979; Wolf, 1978) concluded that students performed better in the content areas when study skills were integrated into the students' system of study of a given content. Students do not need study skills for isolated activities; rather, they need to use them within the context of a reading/learning assignment in a content lesson. Focusing on the tasks to be achieved rather than on the skills to be mastered will also enhance the learning/teaching of study skills.

Students are faced with numerous tasks that require them to read, comprehend, remember, and express what they have read. The creative reading lesson (Ada, 1988) described in Chapter 5 can assist you in guiding the students through these tasks. Requiring students to answer questions, discuss content, or express their feelings about a text immediately after reading will encourage them to develop critical reading skills as well as assist them in comprehension.

However, many tasks require students to remember and express ideas from expository texts, many of which call on students to solve problems or answer questions that were not directly addressed in the material that was read. They are asked to analyze ideas and discuss the ways in which these ideas are related, or to read several sources and synthesize what they have read in answering a question or presenting an argument. They may also be asked to compare and evaluate materials they have read. These tasks have two ingredients that the typical reading lesson does not: the students' performance demonstrates that they have remembered over a period of time what they have read and that they have the ability to select and organize what they have read for a coherent presentation. Comprehending content-area texts and preparing oral or written expository reports require specific study skills.

Although teaching study skills is often presented as something that comes after teaching comprehension, you must not get the idea that the processes of reading, comprehending, remembering, and organizing are separate processes performed in that order.

Organizing for Thinking

In order to think about a subject, children may need to be receptive to collecting information for a while. When children do not have enough knowledge to know how to integrate information, they may need a data collection period, much as they have a silent period in language development. In the thinking process, children need to relate separate facts and see interrelationships in order to process the information and then be able to reintegrate the whole.

Study Techniques. Children need to know how to organize the information they find and connect it with what they already know. You can help them develop good study techniques by guiding them through the process of reading and retrieving information from selected passages in a given content area. Children generate hypotheses, and as new information is extracted from further reading, these hypotheses are continually refined. Thus, children pose questions or make predictions about a text; test these questions by reading; confirm, reject, or refine them; and generate new questions as their reading progresses.

The essential difference between the creative reading approach and the teacher-directed reading lesson (found in most textbooks) is that the creative reading approach encourages children to develop their own reading and thinking processes by setting their own purposes for reading. In the creative reading approach the teacher, through questioning, helps the children enter into a dialogue with text material.

Expectation Outline. Still another study technique is an expectation outline (Cunningham et al., 1983). Because an expository text usually consists of one or more central ideas that are embellished with related details, this overall structure can be reflected in outlines and also in the headings and subheadings that some authors provide. To get outlines started, the students conduct an initial survey of a passage and skim all of the special features that give clues to its content—title, headings and subheadings, words or phrases printed in a special typeface, illustrations, diagrams or photographs, maps, tables, and charts, and questions within and at the end of the text. The children make predictions and tell you questions they think will be answered by the text, and you organize the questions into a rough outline form on the chalkboard. The passages you use for this ought to be relatively short and simple so that the children will be able to anticipate the content with some accuracy. Next, the children read sample text passages silently to verify their predictions and to determine which of their questions are actually answered. Finally, they read the section of the passage that answers each question; oral rereading may be used to highlight particular pieces of evidence. Previous predictions are evaluated in light of whatever information the children have acquired, and new predictions are generated as the outline is filled in.

The teacher should encourage the children to discuss and evaluate suggestions. The processes of surveying and making predictions are in themselves strategies for making meaning of text. To illustrate, let's say that a chapter in a fourth grade text deals with *minerales* [minerals]. After surveying the chapter, the children predict the major questions or topics of information, and the teacher lists these as the major headings of the outline and allows space for subtopics and details to be filled in later (see Figure 6.6).

Once they understand the survey, prediction, reading, and evaluation procedures of the expectation outline, the children can outline passages or articles in groups or individually.

It should be noted that if children encounter any new vocabulary as they outline using this cycle, they can be encouraged to use context to figure out the word. If unknown words are encountered, children are expected to try to make informed

I.   ¿Cuáles son las propiedades de los minerales? [What are the properties of minerals?]
    A.
    B.
II.   ¿En qúe se parecen o diferencian los minerales, las plantas, y los animales? [How are minerals, plants and animals alike or different?]
    A.
    B.
III.   ¿Donde se encuentran? [Where are they found?]
    A.
    B.
IV.   ¿Cómo podemos usar los minerales? [How can we use minerals?]
    A.
    B.

Figure 6.6. Example of Expectation Outline

guesses about the word. This can be accomplished by having them read to the end of the sentence in which the word occurs. This gives children access to available syntactic and semantic cues as well as any graphophonic cues provided by the word itself. If children require help from the teacher, they are first encouraged to suggest what the word might mean and explain how they arrived at that guess. Older students can be encouraged to consult the dictionary. Before providing the word, the teacher can also model thinking processes and the interpretation of contextual clues. The accent is always placed on reading for meaning.

Organization facilitates thinking, recall, and the linking of new learning to old. Some second and third graders may not be ready for elaborate schemes for organizing information, such as outlining what they have read, but they can profit from simple ideas that help them to organize the information they are collecting. Building a semantic map is another way to organize ideas because of its focus on the connections and relationships between ideas and its relatively loose structure (Hennings, 1984).

Semantic Mapping. Although this technique has been presented in previous chapters, we would like to discuss it in more detail here as a strategy for assisting students in organizing thinking and knowledge in the content areas. When the information the children are collecting as part of their class unit of study begins to mount, they will see the need for a simple and efficient way to organize it. This is the time to introduce semantic mapping. Write the title of the topic or a word that refers to the unit of study on the board (for example, farm animals), draw a circle around it, and ask the students, "What do you know about farm animals?"

The children respond by naming some farm animals and describing what they eat, what they look like, the sounds they make, and the like. The teacher suggests categories and writes the categories on spokes radiating from the encircled theme. As students volunteer more information about farm animals, the teacher adds words and phrases under the appropriate categories. As information that fits into new categories is suggested, the teacher creates new categories on the board. Soon a semantic map begins to appear on the board.

Form cooperative project groups to study subtopics: kinds of animals, feeding, habitats, benefit to humankind. These main divisions are written in boxes or circles around the center with lines running to the center. Finally, the children in each group give the main points for their assigned subdivision (see Figure 6.7a and Figure 6.7b).

One of the advantages of this kind of pictorial representation is that it ties the work of the several groups together and illustrates the cohesion of the theme. Because it shows how the findings of some groups are parallel, it may suggest further modifications in organization. For instance, in this example both the animal-feeding and the animal-care committees discovered that adaptation to the animal's needs is an important consideration. Perhaps as a result of creating this semantic map, these two groups, or members of the groups, might want to collaborate on further investigation of this point. Semantic maps can be drawn at strategic moments in the course of an investigation. If you transfer each map to paper and date it, the children will have an interesting way of tracking their progress.

Fifth grade teachers using a similar technique can ask students to use the titles and section headings in a text to identify main ideas and categories and supporting details to create postreading semantic maps such as the ones in Figure 6.7a and Figure 6.7b. Such maps can easily be turned into outlines and are a good first step

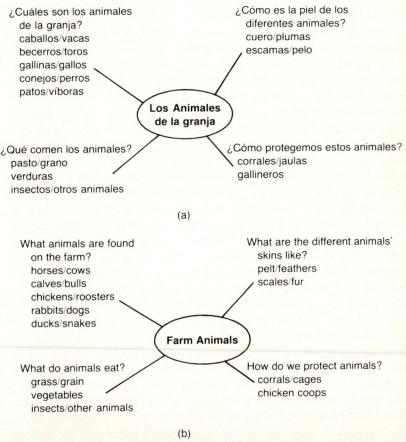

Figure 6.7. Semantic Map: *Los animales de la granja* [Farm animals]

to beginning writing. Other useful ways of organizing information are underlining, taking notes, and summarizing. Students need to learn different techniques and when each is appropriate.

Writing and Reporting Information

One of the corollaries of children's intensive and extended investigations in the later primary grades and beyond is the preparation of both oral and written reports. As students accumulate more and more information when studying a unit, they will see the need for an efficient and coherent way of organizing it. In addition, children's increased sense of audience coincides with the excitement of knowing and natural inclination to share what has been learned with classmates and others, which reinforces the need for a report that is both attractive and intelligible. When children have enough knowledge and information, their voices find expression in their reports. The writing process described in Chapter 5 can be used for written reports.

Although some children are comfortable drafting reports from notes, there are several reasons why it is generally a good idea for oral reporting to precede written reporting. Children need to have many firsthand experiences with a topic before they are ready to gather new material from books. If children are familiar with a topic before they read more about it, they will be less prone to copy masses of information verbatim. In addition, sharing findings with classmates requires that the children synthesize the material so they can report it in their own words. If the oral report is a group project, the children's interactions provide an excellent opportunity for them to learn about meeting an audience's needs. When you confer with either an individual child or a small group, you can help them to work out strategies for handling the sequence of a report. You might suggest they create a simple prop—a set of pictures arranged in the order of the report—as a sequential guide. Or they can write the major points of the report on strips of chart paper. The strips can be pinned up as each point is raised in the report; you may also need to model how to use these strips.

For written reports, children can be encouraged to make notes about what they have learned; then, after writing down notes and sharing, they can go back in groups or in pairs to formulate paragraphs with expository structures. For elementary students, learning to write a well-organized expository paragraph acts as a bridge to understanding difficult expository material. Also, if children are exposed to good models of informative and expository writing, they will be able to observe and integrate this genre of writing into their own texts. Flood (1986) suggests that composing and comprehending expository text are interrelated activities and can be taught as such.

With the teacher's guidance, the children can take their organized information gathered from the study of a theme and draft a class-generated expository paragraph. The teacher can focus the students' attention on the information and assist them in recording it in charts or outlines. The students can formulate a sentence for each of the ideas on the chart and record their sentences on the chalkboard. Teacher and students can read the sentences back while making suggestions for revision. When the children are satisfied with the paragraph, they can give it a title and rewrite it on clean chart paper. If the children compose several paragraphs in this manner for a unit of study, they will soon be able to draft their own paragraphs using similar strategies.

As children learn to write well-organized paragraphs, they can also learn how to organize them into a report. Work with the children on arranging several class-generated paragraphs into a logical order for a composite report. Asking students what should come first, what is most important, or what happened first will get them started in ordering the paragraphs using their own system of sequence and logic. Once the paragraphs are rearranged, the parts that are still needed—summarizing and transitional sentences, introductory and concluding paragraphs—can be called to the students' attention. You can again work with the entire class on these parts or with smaller groups that have been assigned to tackle particular parts. It is a good idea to keep a record of each step of this entire procedure from brainstorming to final report. It can be recorded as the "story of the group" or arranged as a "flow chart of the activity" on a bulletin board and will serve as a useful reminder to the children of the steps involved in organizing information.

When are children ready to compose extensive and detailed written reports? Some educators believe that most children are not ready until they are in the middle grades, but the most accurate answer must come from your own assessment of the individual children in your class. Students' knowledge about a topic can be reported in a variety of ways. Regardless of their level of sophistication, all the children in the class can participate in written reporting in a way that is individually appropriate and rewarding. For a few, this might mean reports consisting mostly of illustrative material, with much of the writing confined to labels and captions. Even without extensive writing, these reports can reveal intensive investigation and careful analysis. For example, a third-grade table and bulletin board display on a unit study of plants had (1) a chart and an experiment that illustrated *el proceso de fotosíntesis* [the photosynthesis process]; (2) a class collection of plants labeled with *raíces, tallos, hojas,* and *pétalos* [roots, stems, leaves, and petals]; (3) individual student's poems and stories with illustrations about plants in stories, such as *el fríjol que crece hasta el cielo* [the bean stalk that grows to the sky], *la rosa del amor* [the rose of love], and *el olivo de la paz* [the olive of peace]; (4) a chart that illustrates the life cycle of plants; and (5) a chart with tidbits of interesting information the children have found, such as *hay muchas plantas medicinales* [there are many medicinal plants], *hay unas plantas que son carnívoras* [there are some carnivorous plants], and *la cuerda de brincar es una fibra de una planta* [the jump rope is made from a plant fiber]. This kind of report would have been the pride of many a fifth grade class.

You can encourage those children who are ready to report more extensively in writing to get their ideas down on paper by having them write everything they can think of concerning one aspect of their investigation on a single sheet of paper labeled with that subtopic. When they have written all they can think of about this one subtopic, they can write about a different aspect on another sheet of paper. The separate sheets are also handy for making revisions and can be rearranged easily when the children are working on the sequence of their report. If they have access to computers, the process of composing and editing their work can become easier.

Regardless of their writing proficiency or their access to sophisticated writing tools, what is important is that children have the chance to work on a topic of their own choosing, pursue the investigation over weeks or even months, and draw their findings together in a careful and polished report that is shared and gives them a sense of personal accomplishment.

SUMMARY

The skills a student must master in reading and writing about the content areas are numerous and differ from those of the language arts areas. Familiarity with the content area through the lens of reading and writing capability will help you see the many opportunities for addressing listening, speaking, reading, and writing skills while teaching other subjects and content area skills.

All the strategies for teaching comprehension can and should be used in teaching reading in the content areas. However, reading in each of the content areas presents its own challenges to the reader. Content areas have specialized vocabularies. Information is often presented in graphic, diagrammatic, and pictorial forms. Students must learn to "read" these graphic displays just as they must learn to read printed texts.

The content areas place special demands on the student's study skills, particularly in the upper grades. Literacy development must be integrated in the teaching of subject matter. Study skills include learning how to locate and record information in order to retrieve it in useful ways. Outlining, note taking, semantic mapping, and summarizing are some of the retrieval options available.

ACTIVITIES

Journal Writing

1. Keep a log for a week of your interactions with print in a content area (biology, natural science, history, and so forth) that you may be taking. Answer the questions, What is the new vocabulary? How do you study for this subject? Compare your answers to those of your classmates.

2. As you think about the content area you have kept a log for, what are the main concepts? Can you write these in your own words? What if an extraterrestrial being were to ask you what you mean? How would you explain the most basic elements and the relationships you are studying? Write a story about such an encounter.

3. Write a math story about some economic exchange you engage in regularly—supermarket shopping, mall shopping, pricing and quality comparisons, or football averaging, for example. In the story, include a problem you encounter frequently. Write about strategies you use to solve these problems. Then translate into mathematical terms. Share the stories with classmates. This can also be translated into an in-class group activity.

Discussion Activities

1. Form several small groups.
   a. Brainstorm (five minutes) a list of topics that are commonly taught in science, math, and social studies. Select one topic and construct a theme map, listing as many concepts and skills that can be studied in relation to the chosen theme as possible. Share and critique the results of each group's efforts.
   b. Ask each group to seek out a variety (four or five per group) of children's literature in Spanish that could be used with their theme map. Bring samples to class and share.
2. Review content texts and find examples of expository writing. Think about how you could teach text structures or modify the text to assist children in comprehending.

NOTE

1. The video *Seguín*, produced by the Public Broadcasting System, is available through KLRN, Austin, Texas.

PART III
Asesoramiento y recursos

CHAPTER 7

Assessment

Chapter Overview

The Purpose of Assessment

Portfolio Assessment System

An Array of Classroom Assessment Strategies

Observation

INTRODUCTION

Assessment is a natural human activity. You engage in both self-appraisal and the judgment of others as you go through the day. For example, in the morning as you open your eyes and look at the clock you make a judgment about your timing. Did you wake up on time? Will you have enough time to read the newspaper or will you have to rush out of the house? Are you healthy enough to go to work today or are you ill? Can you afford to be ill or must you push yourself to engage in the planned activities for the day? How hungry are you and do you have the necessary staples and culinary needs that will fulfill that hunger? For each of these decisions there are internal conscious or unconscious standards by which you assess what your next step is likely to be and judge yourself once you have accomplished it. Did you miss the bus because you stopped to read the sports section even when you knew you did not have enough time to do so? Did the friend you car pool with leave you behind today? The standards for judgment of self and others as to the appropriateness of attitudes, values, and behaviors are likely to be related to the internalized standards you hold and share with others.

Teachers and students are engaged in assessing each other's needs and the merit and value of their actions on a daily basis. In planning and organizing instruction, in selecting books and materials to use, and in deciding which students will be included in an activity, teachers are assessing the potential of the available instructional tools at their disposal and the instructional possibilities of the students in their classroom. When they state that "the class went really well today," they are appraising the value and worth of their organization and of the interaction of the students during the lesson.

Students are also part of the process of assessing needs and making judgments about the appropriateness and value of classroom activities. They assess their own abilities and those of their peers when they take the floor and respond to a teacher's question, when they take their turn reading aloud, or when they select a library book. Students also monitor and assess the teacher's expectations (McDermott & Gospodinoff, 1981) as a way of helping them to determine how they should behave for a given activity or at a given moment. In other words, assessment and appraisal occur as natural activities in classrooms and schools.

Today, the natural assessment occurring in classrooms is coupled with a move toward national standards for instruction and assessment (Weiss, 1994). As the nation moves toward defining such standards (see Figure 7.1), educators are cautioned about the purpose and use of assessments in general.

> Assessment must serve, not harm, each and every student. This means that each individual's intellectual, social, and emotional well-being must be considered . . . We must recognize that assessment experiences, formal or informal, have consequences for students . . . Assessment procedures have profound effects on students' lives. Assessments may alter their educational opportunities, increase or decrease their motivation to learn, elicit positive or negative feelings about themselves and others, and influence their understanding of what it means to be literate, educated, or successful. (International Reading Association & National Council of Teachers of English, 1994, p. 13)

1. The interests of the student are paramount in assessment.
2. The primary purpose of assessment is to improve teaching and learning.
3. Assessment must reflect and allow for critical inquiry into curriculum and instruction.
4. Assessments must recognize and reflect the intellectually and socially complex nature of reading and writing and the important roles of school, home, and society in literacy development.
5. Assessment must be fair and equitable.
6. The consequences of an assessment procedure are the first, and most important, consideration in establishing the validity of the assessment.
7. The teacher is the most important agent of assessment.
8. The assessment process should involve multiple perspectives and sources of data.
9. Assessment must be based in the school community.
10. All members of the educational community—students, parents, teachers, administrators, policy makers, and the public—must have a voice in the development, interpretation, and reporting of assessment.
11. Parents must be involved as active, essential participants in the assessment process.

Figure 7.1. Standards for the Assessment of Reading and Writing (Source: International Reading Association and National Council of Teachers of English, 1994.)

THE PURPOSE OF ASSESSMENT

The national standards movement and the performance assessment of those standards have been critiqued (Linn, 1994; Nieto, 1994), in general, and for what the movement may mean for the education of language minority students (Torres-Guzmán, 1994) in particular. In this chapter, however, our focus is less on the national assessment movement than on how teachers engage in natural assessment and evaluation of student learning in the classroom. Often the natural assessment and evaluation occurring in classrooms are impressionistic, unconscious, and coupled with inadequate formal assessments.

Carrasco (1981) documents some of the dangers of these types of assessments for children. In working with a teacher in a bilingual kindergarten classroom, he describes how Lupita, a student who had recently come from Mexico, was written off as a student who could not make sufficient progress to go on to the first grade. Lupita had been assessed as incompetent in various school tasks based on a placement test administered by the teacher in Spanish. Lupita's behavior in the classroom did not counter the placement test results. Lupita made herself invisible by behaving in an "attentive, quiet, well-mannered" fashion. When given the opportunity to perform in group tasks, Lupita behaved in ways that "weeded" her into the "preschool group." For children in the preschool group, the teacher planned a strong preschool experience that year. By systematically observing the teacher-directed activity, Carrasco (1981) found that "the teacher rarely called on her [Lupita] to participate, although a few times she [Lupita] was recognized for her appropriate behavior" (p. 166). He also observed that she "sat away from the teacher and on the edge of the group" (p. 166) when the group sat on the rug. He decided to observe Lupita in a non-teacher-directed activity. The first day of observing her Carrasco found that Lupita was able to perform the visual discrimination tasks of identifying and matching the spatial configurations of puzzles. Moreover, he found that Lupita was perceived as a leader and teacher by other students who required her assistance when they found a task difficult. Capturing Lupita's behavior on videotape permitted the teacher to view and think about what she saw and reconsider the assumptions, methods, and findings on which she had based her initial assessment of Lupita and other students in her class. The teacher had been consciously not calling on Lupita to participate in class. She felt that given the lack of school competency, Lupita would be humiliated and embarrassed if called on to display her incompetence in front of her peers. This genuine concern for Lupita led the teacher to work minimally with her and to expect very little progress. The teacher even stopped assessing Lupita's progress after a few months.

The awareness the teacher experienced as a result of systematically viewing the videotape and reflecting constructively on her teaching practices had various results. First, she became aware of the limitations of some assessments, such as the placement test. Second, Lupita became more visible. Third, the teacher reassessed and adjusted her classroom interactions. Lupita responded accordingly, participated more actively, and in May, scored high enough in the posttest to progress to the first grade. The other effect of the videotape was that the teacher began to self-evaluate. Lupita's progress became more visible with observation over time and with a change in teaching strategies. Furthermore, she acknowledged the need to remain open to the diversity of needs of the children in her classroom and to the multiple purposes of assessments.

Because classroom literacy assessments are used for multiple purposes (Cole, 1988; Haney, 1991; Pearson & Valencia, 1989; Salinger & Chittenden, 1994) and there are different information needs for each, the first thing you need to determine is what you want to know.

Harman (1992) differentiates between *self-referenced* and *theory-referenced* measures. In the self-referenced assessment, the teacher collects information that allows for each child's work to be compared to his/her own earlier work; the purpose of assessment is to evaluate the child's growth and not to compare the child's work to other children's work. For example, a child's oral or written narrative about a favorite pet, collected in October, can be compared to a narrative on the same topic collected in March. The theory-referenced assessment collects information that allows children's growth to be assessed in relation to theories of literacy acquisition and child developmental benchmarks. For example, a young child who is writing words or stories using a letter or symbol for each syllable can be said to be exploring the syllabic principle (i.e., theory reference); an older child who continuously retells descriptive or expository texts in the narrative form can be said to still be operating in a concrete, child-centered stage and may not be able to decenter or interpret ideas in the abstract. Assessment practices that are self- and theory-referenced focus the purposes of assessment on documenting individual growth and providing instructionally useful information (Harman, 1992).

In addition to the purpose, the context of the assessment will contribute to its authenticity. Newmann and Wehlage (1993) suggest criteria for authentic achievement as the following: "(1) students construct meaning and produce knowledge, (2) students use disciplined inquiry to construct meaning, and (3) students aim their work toward production of discourse, products, and performance that have value or meaning beyond success in school" (p. 8).

Using these criteria, you can plan to gather evidence from multiple sources such as work in progress, observation, self-evaluation, peer evaluation, and collaboration that documents students' progress in the construction of meaning, disciplined inquiry, and performance. You may also want to rely on the many voices of the learning community, such as other teachers, students, peers, parents, and other observers. The emphasis should be on the students' strengths and performance as well as the appropriateness of the instructional practices to students' developing abilities. A way to collect and manage the evidence of progress in developing literacy processes and products from these multiple sources and voices systematically is through a portfolio assessment system.

PORTFOLIO ASSESSMENT SYSTEM

Portfolios can serve as a management or recordkeeping system for the collection of reading and writing products to be assessed periodically by the student, teacher, and parent. Its central purpose is to systematize a process for assessing students' growth and progress in relation to classroom instruction (Canales, 1993; Salinger & Chittenden, 1994). Portfolios can also be used to plan for future work based on the student's progress (Wolf, 1989). Student and teacher must jointly determine what constitutes performance evidence, how to collect it, and how the information collected will be used.

An example of a successful portfolio experience is that of the South Brunswick Early Literacy Portfolio project. This project demonstrated that the portfolio could be used in place of traditional teacher measures, such as tests, checklists, or grades. The project leaders developed a "theory referenced" scale of early literacy development "referenced directly to contemporary research and practice" (Salinger & Chittenden, 1994, p. 447) to assist the teachers in end-of-year evaluation of the contents of students' portfolios and report student progress to the district in a format that met the local and state evaluation requirements. In addition to providing a systematic measurement of student performance that would satisfy administrators and parents, the teachers reported that it helped them better understand what was going on in the classroom. One teacher in the project commented, "At the beginning of the year, it helps me to get to know the kids. At midyear with some children, it forces *them* to show *me* strategies I otherwise didn't know they have . . . [It] makes me shut up and listen. And that's hard for a teacher to do" (Salinger & Chittenden, 1994, p. 450).

Another important value of the use of portfolios reported by the South Brunswick teachers was the use of the portfolio material during teacher-parent conferences. Parent-teacher discussions were based on concrete pieces of evidence of students' work, "instead of the teacher's reported impressions or summaries" (p. 450).

Organizing and Introducing Portfolios

An important factor is to distinguish between student work folders and a portfolio system. Although some teachers like to include all the children's written products in a portfolio, it is preferable to include representative samples (both the best and the developing) of the students' work over time, or a selection of pieces based on some previously established criteria. Keep in mind that if the portfolio is just a col-

Written Work
1. Examples of initial and final drafts of writing assignments or student-initiated writing
2. Examples of student's literature response logs
3. Plans for thematic unit studies
4. Other illustrations, graphic organizers, charts, graphs, and the like that may demonstrate student's planning and organization of learning

Audio or Video Tapes—For Performance Pieces
1. Examples of student's oral reading
2. Retelling, discussions, or reflections of literature read
3. Role-playing, readers theater, or other productions based on literature or classroom study themes

Other Data and Evidence
1. Student self-analysis and reflection
2. Teacher observations and running logs
3. Running records or informal reading inventories (IRI) of oral reading
4. Critiques of items from peers
5. Parent's analysis and reflections

Figure 7.2 Suggested Data or Evidence for Starting a Portfolio System

lection of teacher-initiated assignments, students will not be motivated to exert the effort and reflection necessary to make portfolios an authentic assessment system that will inform instruction.

When you have decided on a portfolio system, students ought to be brought into the planning and the process of selecting materials to be included, if they are to take ownership of the portfolio. It is important for teachers and students to prepare a list of the basic categories of work samples to be included in each student's portfolio. The list will delineate what data the teacher will collect and what samples students may themselves select. Work samples and performance evidence should be included, such as tapes of oral readings, illustrations and drawings, transcriptions of interviews and conferences, and other indicators of students' growth based on preestablished goals. The accumulated documentation (see Figure 7.2 for suggested data or evidence to consider when starting a portfolio system) is kept in a folder for each child. It is important for the portfolio to be considered the child's property, with the child having full access and primary responsibility for its maintenance. It is also important to establish and respect procedures for sharing information in the folder. For example, will other students or teachers also be evaluating portfolios? When and how will the portfolios be shared with parents?

Student Reflection and Evaluating Portfolios

When students are encouraged to select, organize, and explain a range of items in a portfolio, the process can add richness to their literary experiences, provide connections to self and others, and afford opportunities to reflect on their questions and concerns about learning (Smith, 1989). For each evaluation period, students can write a self-assessing reflective piece (explanation, letter, poem, etc.) that provides insight as to why particular products in the portfolio demonstrate growth and understanding. Ideally, the portfolio evaluation culminates in a teacher-student conference in which they each can explain their assessment and together analyze and understand the reading, writing, and thinking strategies the student is using successfully and those that are developing and need to be mastered.

In addition to student reflection, teachers can include students in making decisions as to the evaluation of the products contained in the portfolio. Evaluation of specific items can be referenced to a list of objectives or skills that must be demonstrated; that is, these items can be considered "criterion-referenced" to certain objectives and activities. For example, some items—such as story retelling, informal reading inventories of oral reading, or written assignments—can be said to be criterion-referenced if they are evaluated using specific rubrics. (These and other assessment strategies are discussed in following sections in this chapter.) Other items can be evaluated more holistically, that is, in terms of students' growth in more global areas of development (e.g., creativity, inquiry). Any set of questions or checklists used to evaluate portfolio pieces ought to be shared with students before they are used in the evaluation process and should also be re-explained during teacher-student portfolio conferences.

In addition, the purpose of the portfolio will to some extent dictate the selection of items and their evaluation. For example, if the portfolio is to be used as a cumulative record to be passed along to subsequent teachers, the items included must provide information about the student's literacy growth in specific areas, and the content as a whole must communicate a balanced record of the student's capabilities. Artifacts collected and systematically evaluated throughout the school year can document the progress and effort that children have made over time, and such portfolios can serve as cumulative records of the student's literacy development.

Teacher-Student Conferences

The teacher-student portfolio conference should be a process that focuses on constructing meaning from the items in the portfolio. You can decide the frequency of the teacher-student portfolio conferences, but at a minimum they should be held two to three times each reporting period. You can establish procedures for holding conferences on a regular basis by putting up a chart or writing on the chalkboard the

times available for conference appointments. The students can be scheduled by the teacher or they can volunteer for conferences when they are ready. Preparing for the conference may include having the student write down a list of questions, concerns, or plans. Some general guidelines for helping students prepare for the teacher-student conferences are provided by Siu-Runyan (1991).

1. Students may select samples of their drafts as well as their best writing and arrange them in a way that is meaningful to them.
2. In preparation for teacher/student conferences, encourage students to think about why they selected the pieces they did, and what they want to say about them. You might suggest they think about:
   a. What parts of a particular piece do they really like and why?
   b. What they were trying to accomplish in this piece and were they successful?
3. Ask the student to examine all the pieces selected for their portfolio and think about what they learned about themselves as a reader and writer by putting together their portfolio.
4. Ask the student to think about what next steps should be taken as they develop as readers and writers. What goals [do] they have for themselves as a reader and writer? (Siu-Runyan, 1991, pp. 124–25)

Other similar questions and guidelines can be established for illustrations, graphic organizers, and audio items in the portfolio. Systematic collection of portfolio data occurs best when scheduled times, every week or every other week, are set aside for students to select and organize items to be included in the portfolio. Students can choose their own works, have time for planning and reflection, make revisions, and, in some instances, choose representative samples of what they consider to be their best work, as well as drafts leading up to their best work. It is often helpful for students to work in pairs during these times, discussing, comparing, critiquing, and possibly defending their individual choices.

During the conference, the teacher and student discuss the samples in the portfolio. Both can question and offer opinions: the student may ask for assistance in writing ideas, revising, and editing; the teacher and child can engage in a conversation about books; the teacher may ask questions for clarification of the child's writing; the teacher may listen to the child read from a book or from his or her writing; the teacher may read aloud the child's writing as the student listens; the teacher may ask comprehension, vocabulary, or skills questions; the student may ask for assistance in understanding words, passages, idioms, and the like. The conference can also include questions to which neither the teacher nor the student knows the "right" answers—questions that lead the child to an increased awareness of the reading or writing process itself and to self-assessment. Conferences should end with teacher and child setting goals for further reading, writing, or study, and with a suggested time for the next conference.

The teacher can keep simple records on a form designed for such a purpose or notes on files cards, or can tape the conference. Part of the record can include the strategies the child is using (e.g., context clues, whole words, sounding out, visual skills, incorporation of classroom print in writing, writing of own ideas, invented spelling), the progress the child has made since the last conference, and the changing interests of the child. The transcribed notes of teacher-student conferences can become a part of the portfolio for future conferences.

Teachers must be willing to discuss observations and evidence about strengths and weaknesses and support these discussions with concrete suggestions for improvement in specific areas of development. By being involved in meaningful ways in the assessment process, students are given insights into their own learning and become aware of their own responsibility in the learning process. When these evaluations are conducted in a respectful, constructive, positive atmosphere that allows students to provide valued input, such discussions can encourage students to take risks, assume responsibility, and generally become more independent.

AN ARRAY OF CLASSROOM ASSESSMENT STRATEGIES

Different assessment measures give you distinct information (García & Verville, 1994). Informal reading inventories, miscue analysis procedures, and cloze tests, for example, disclose different strategies used in reading. Scoring rubrics for written samples and graphic organizers, as well as benchmarks for writing development, can be used to assess strategies used in writing. It is important to understand what you want to know in order to determine what strategy is most appropriate. Let's take a look at some strategies, their purposes, and appropriate use.

Reading Strategies

Reading Miscues. Goodman (1969), Goodman and Burke (1972), and Goodman, Watson, and Burke (1987) developed a procedure for analyzing the oral reading and retelling of an unfamiliar story. Students' "errors" were referred to as miscues, which, when analyzed, would provide information as to the strategies the individual was using in the reading process. The term *error* was avoided because of its negative connotations. Goodman emphasized that reading is not naming words but is instead a meaning-making process achieved only when a reader uses both the words on the page and what he or she knows to construct something meaningful. Prior to Goodman's investigations, children's reading errors were perceived as reflecting what the children did not know. Goodman's analysis of children's miscues was aimed at identifying the graphophonic strategies, the processes of comprehension, memory, and retrieval of information used by the reader, and attempted to recognize what children knew about reading.

Researchers (Barrera, 1978; Flores, 1981; Goodman, Goodman, and Flores, 1979; Hudelson, 1981, 1987; Silva, 1979, 1983) have examined miscues children produce when reading in Spanish. Barrera (1978, 1981) examined the reading miscues and retelling of Spanish-speaking third graders. Barrera found that children's miscues in Spanish reading commonly had the same syntactical characteristics and functions as the text. Miscues involving inflectional or intonational changes in some words caused inflectional changes in the words that followed. Miscues involving omissions did not affect the meaning of the text. Omissions often created a more natural spoken language than appeared in the formal written text. Readers substituted words from their own experiences that did not change the meaning of the text; they corrected miscues that disrupted the meaning, which indicates a continuous interaction between meaning and print. Children reading in Spanish produced many miscues that were semantically acceptable. Barrera found that the number of miscues had little or no effect on comprehension. Figure 7.3 is a sample of Spanish miscue analysis (Barrera, 1978). Barrera explains that in the first two examples, the children predicted words that had no graphophonic relationship with the words in the text. The substitute words made sense in the first part of the sentence, but as the students read on they realized that the substitution no longer made sense and self-corrected.

This type of miscue suggests that readers predict, infer, evaluate, and correct as they are reading. In the third example, *su mano* [his hand] makes more sense or is more logical than having a ball on one's head in terms of one's everyday experience with balls. In the fourth example, the informal *tus* [your] is more common when a person's name is used in a sentence. In the last example, the use of the definite article *los* [the] in place of the indefinite article *unos* [some] is more common in many Spanish language communities in the United States. In the last three examples the reader did not make corrections because the substitution did not interfere with the meaning or understanding of the sentence (Barrera, 1978; Freeman, 1988).

The children in Barrera's study (1978) were also observed using strategies developed in Spanish while attempting to read in English. Her subjects received initial instruction in Spanish reading until the beginning of the third grade, when English reading was introduced. The children read the same passage in Spanish and different passages in English. The children used the Spanish phonological system, which caused the children to deviate from the printed text and alter pronunciation

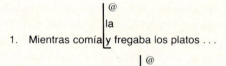

1.   Mientras comía**|**y fregaba los platos . . .   (above: @ / la)

2.   Protegieron las plantas**|**que pudieran helarse . . .   (above: @ / y)

3.   Tiene una pelota en la cabeza.   (above: su mano)

4.   Gracias, Pedro, pero no quiero sus zapatos.   (above: tus)

5.   Tengo unos pies muy chiquitos.   (above: los)

Figure 7.3. Miscues in Spanish

and grammatical features but had insignificant effect on meaning. Children who used strategies (predicting, confirming, and rejecting information) in Spanish reading also used these strategies when reading English. Barrera concluded that the miscues produced indicate that children do not process information in a precise, letter-by-letter or word-by-word manner, but rather use all their language experiences to help them confirm and anticipate information as they read Spanish and English print.

Hudelson-Lopez (1975) examined how children used context and prediction when they read Spanish print. Second and third grade students were asked to read isolated words in a list, followed by the reading of a passage containing these words. A significant number of words missed in the list were read correctly in the passage; some words that were read correctly in the list, however, were missed in the passage. Hudelson concluded that the children were using their phonic skills when they were asked to read the word list and their contextual strategies when they were reading the passage. They were then asked to read a "cloze" passage in which every seventh word was missing. Students predicted the missing words correctly or substituted a semantically equivalent word 50 percent of the time. Hudelson concluded that this finding illustrates that children read for meaning and anticipate information.

Silva (1979) studied first graders reading unfamiliar Spanish passages. She found that the children used their knowledge of language systems and semantics as they attempted to read. Children would attempt to correct by backtracking when something did not make sense or when it did not retain the structure of the language with which they were more familiar.

These studies suggest that the miscues children make can be analyzed for the types of strategies children use when attempting to obtain meaning from text. While observing and working with children, teachers might keep the following in mind:

1. Given time, children who make errors when reading may self-correct or reread when they find that what they are reading does not make sense to them.
2. Beginning readers tend to transform print into their spoken dialect. Children seldom correct miscues that shift languages into their own dialect because these miscues make sense to them. Most of the time, such dialectic miscues do not change the author's meaning. Miscues involving dialect appear to be a positive way for children to transform the author's language into their own, creating a transaction between author and reader.

The Cloze Procedure.   Another informal way to estimate children's functional reading levels is the cloze procedure. The cloze procedure is another technique in which the reader derives meaning from a passage by using its semantic and syntactic cues. The cloze procedure is an extension of the principle of closure, which is the tendency to perceive incomplete objects as whole entities by filling in the gaps of the actual sensory input. Applying this principle to reading, the cloze procedure requires the child to fill in, by use of contextual clues, words that have been deleted at regular intervals from a selected passage. The cloze procedure helps to identify students who are either frustrated or not challenged by the text (Hudelson-Lopez, 1975;

Readence, Bean & Baldwin, 1985) and is recommended for use when the teacher introduces a new text.

The cloze procedure is simply a passage-completion task. The first and last sentences are left untouched; all other sentences have words that have been systematically (typical range is from fifth to tenth word) deleted from the text and replaced with blank lines of uniform length. A typical example of a cloze passage consists of approximately 250 words at a level appropriate for the students. Children read the text silently and try to fill in the blank spaces with the exact words used by the author. The student must use contextual and grammatical clues to fill in the blanks. The extent to which children successfully replace the original or an appropriate word within the context is believed to be an indication of their ability to cope with the text material. Since the cloze test involves rather complex mental operations it is best used with older children (third or fourth grade and above).

Although there is some research to indicate that accepting only the exact word for deletions makes the cloze procedure a more effective diagnostic tool (Henk, 1981), teachers find it useful to accept good synonyms as correct responses because they do not alter the meaning of the passage significantly. Perhaps the major advantage of the cloze procedure is its measure of the process of reading as the communication process takes place. The child must acquire a feel for the author's language structure, use of vocabulary (style), and communicative intent. Inferential reasoning must be employed to fill in the gaps. Children are forced to deal with language at a syntactic and semantic level, rather than at the graphophonic level only. Because the blank space does not offer visual clues to the identity of the missing words, children must think in terms of sentence patterns and meaning. The procedure allows readers to be observed as they are reading, predicting, inferring, evaluating, and correcting.

Informal Reading Inventories. The purpose of the informal reading inventory (IRI) is to determine the level at which the child can read comfortably with good comprehension and word identification (Cunningham et al., 1983). It determines three functional reading levels based on the number of correct responses made by the child in word identification and comprehension: the independent level, at which reading for enjoyment and reading in the content areas should occur; the instructional level, at which the teaching of reading should occur; and the frustration level, which indicates that the reading material is difficult for the child.

A set of graded passages and accompanying questions is used to estimate children's reading levels. The student reads from a passage while the teacher records what is being observed. Figure 7.4 illustrates the symbols used to record oral reading errors. The passages can either be those preselected and included in a commercial IRI or they can be selected from the reading series being used. Each word the child substitutes for another word, repeats, omits, or inserts is counted as an error.

After the child reads a passage, comprehension questions are asked. Figure 7.5 shows a sample of the comprehension questions used in the administration of an IRI. The child continues reading at successively higher levels until the three functional reading levels are determined.

Type of Errors	Symbol (inserted into text)

Reversal   Cada mañana a͜las 8:15, la puerta de Maxie se abría con un chirrido.

Omission   Maxie bajaba los ⟨cuatro⟩ pisos hasta la puerta ⟨de⟩la calle. Golpeteaba

Addition repetition   con <u>sus</u> viejas pantuflas de <u>cuero</u> los escalones sin alfombra. Afuera, al

Substitution   lado de͟l͟a puerta, estaban las botellas de leche en *su* u̶n̶ cajón. Maxie

siempre trataba de mantener la puerta abierta con el pie izquierdo,

Self-correction   mientras aǧarraba la leche. Pero las botellas estaban demasiado lějos.

La puerta se cerraba de golpe dejándola en la calle.

Figure 7.4. Symbols Used to Record Oral-Reading Errors

The following chart shows the percentage of correct responses required in word identification and comprehension for each of the three levels:

Level	Word Identification (%)	Comprehension (%)
Independent	99	90
Instructional	95	75
Frustration	90	50

These criterion levels, however, have been contested over the years; the percentages have been challenged as being arbitrary, too stringent, or simply inaccurate. Probably the most sensible solution is to use the informal reading inventory methods without rigidly adhering to the numerical standards and by using the criterion levels only as general guidelines.

To prepare an informal reading inventory, randomly select a passage of approximately a hundred words from each level of a graded series of basal readers or content-area textbooks. (These have been found to be more difficult to read than their grade-level designations indicate.) Type or copy each passage onto a separate sheet of paper for use in recording your observations. Prepare four comprehension

Text

Cada mañana a las 8:15, la puerta de Maxie se abría con un chirrido. Maxie bajaba los cuatro pisos hasta la puerta de la calle. Golpeteaba con sus viejas pantuflas de cuero los escalones sin alfombra. Afuera, al lado de la puerta, estaban las botellas de leche en un cajón. Maxie siempre trataba de mantener la puerta abierta con el pie izquierdo, mientras agarraba la leche. Pero las botellas estaban demasiado lejos. La puerta se cerraba de golpe dejándola en la calle.

Questions

1. ¿Qué quiere decir *golpeteaba*?
2. ¿Por qué tenía que bajar Maxie cada mañana?
3. ¿Por qué estaban las botellas de leche afuera?
4. ¿Quién le abrirá la puerta a Maxie?

Note. The text is from *La pájara pinta* (p. 104) by J. Flores et al., 1987, New York: Macmillan.

Figure 7.5. Sample Comprehension Questions

questions for each passage: two literal comprehension, one interpretation, and one critical evaluation.

The IRI is an assessment of the interaction of the student with written passages and can help determine the level of reading that the student is capable of undertaking independently (although, when children are interested in a subject, they tend to read far above this measure). It is also an assessment that enables the teacher to use a structured format when observing a child reading orally. In addition to supplying quantitative data, the IRI context offers the opportunity to examine qualitative aspects of a child's performance. By analyzing the types of errors the child makes, the teacher gets a better idea of the strategies being used to interpret text.

Bilingual Communication Strategies. A different approach is possible and preferable in certain circumstances. Vygotsky's (1978) concept of proximal development proposes that children display qualitatively different abilities when they work alone as opposed to when they work in cooperation with others. When Lupita (Carrasco, 1981) was helping other children, she was displaying leadership as well as demonstrating that she possessed school-related abilities. Upon viewing the videotape of the puzzle scene, the teacher reassessed Lupita's standing within the class. The assessment of students' abilities based solely on measures of independent performance, such as that measured by the IRI or the placement test, is insufficient to determine levels of proficiency and instruction. As a means of assessing and maximizing students' potential, the strategies such as probing questions, explicit connections between languages and scaffolding have been used (Cazden, 1983; Jiménez, et al. 1995; Langer et al., 1990; Moll & Díaz, 1985).

Scaffolding is a question-answer pattern used after the reading of a passage. It consists of adjusting the difficulty level of questions until students begin to respond. As students exhibit more competence at answering more difficult and abstract questions, the adult's help, through scaffolding, is removed. Such questioning focuses on comprehension, thinking, and inference, thus pushing students beyond the mere regurgitation of facts. In this sense, it is both an assessment and an instructional strategy.

Moll and Díaz (1987) propose a corollary to the use of scaffolding in the context of biliteracy: "Children differ in their abilities in ways that cannot be assessed solely by techniques that analyze performance in one language" (p. 305). Thus, while the passage may be read in English, the scaffolding begins in Spanish and focuses on making sense and establishing meaning rather than on oral language and decoding skills in English. In this way, the teacher taps the students' receptive knowledge of English while helping them develop vocabulary.

By using bilingual communication strategies to assess language and literacy the teacher preserves and respects students' individuality at the same time that students are empowered to self-assess how to be responsible and responsive members of linguistic and learning communities. In other words, we must respect their right to their own interpretations of language, including the texts they read and hear. As students learn to negotiate meaning with other members of the learning communities, including the teacher, they assess their understanding and mastery of the language practices and means of negotiation of the cultures and contexts in which they live and work.

Assessing Home/School Discourse. Heath (1983) reports on teachers who turn assessment around and focus on what children know rather than on the areas in which they are deficient. By systematically comparing the retelling of read stories to the recounting of unsolicited stories generated by the children themselves, the teachers realized that the school's convention, school discourse patterns, and expectations for storytelling were different from those of the community or home discourse patterns. In several classrooms, the children were asked to tell stories into a tape recorder. The teacher then typed the stories, and the students were asked to edit the typed stories before sharing them with the rest of the class. By using this method the teachers not only became more familiar with the ways of storytelling in the community, but were gradually able to observe how the children began to integrate school conventions in their stories. Similar to the scaffolding and bilingual communication strategies, this is both an assessment and an instructional strategy. Oral language and print material were utilized to further literacy production by using what was already known to the child. In this case, however, the process went from oral production to print and from familiar ways of the community to school conventions.

Writing Assessment Strategies

In Edelsky's (1986) study of children's writing in a bilingual program, she concludes that most "errors" in writing are sensible. In other words, children are often trying "to make sense of or connect various ideas or systems" (p. 60). Young writers develop through a process of hypothesis building whereby they test ideas about how something should be written. They use invented spelling, invented punctuation, and unconventional segmentation. Yet they are likely to abandon these hypotheses for others, frequently the more conventional and acceptable ones. Most "errors" are not random, and the strategies children use are multiple in nature. Children use phonetic categorizations, phono-grapheme information, local norms, experiences with basals, and the like. By understanding children's errors, adults can help children deepen their understanding of what factors to consider as they are experimenting with language. Changes in children's strategies can be linked to reorganizations that occur because of a change in purpose, hypothesis, or context. Thus, while there may be general patterns of development, Edelsky (1986) stresses the need to acknowledge "tremendous intra-individual variation" (p. 86) as well as the process of self-correction.

Teachers can use students' writing to assess linguistic development. Figure 7.6 seems at first glance to be an example of the alphabetic stage (isolated letters) of writing. It was produced by a student who was placed in a second grade classroom in the middle of the year. The teacher asked the student to read what he had written. While he read, she transcribed his reading of the text. It was through this analysis of the child's reading of his writing that the teacher could assess the child's thinking processes and use of language strategies.

Journal Writing. Flores et al. (1985), for example, propose a method of assessing student writing by using journals. They suggest the use of an evaluation form that helps teachers assess the quality and mechanics of children's written languages

YU .Qlludo a mi PaPa a Coι ɾaι
Chιρῖ,esτa d vei τι ɾ Oιamimegu
Sτd, Parce Pue des, a semaSca
a S ιeSma Sme Gc V ι Sυda mucho
ιluego corτa mo Selhι lеι lυeg o
lo deGamos ce cese ɾeι lυegocuan
do S;cSece loca lg a m c Sι lo mo ga
m c Sι lo c o S ι n a m c S

[I help my father cut chilies and it is fun and I like it because you can do other things and it is best if you sweat a lot and then we cut the string and then we let it (chilies) dry and then when it is dry we hang it up and (later) we wet it and cook it.]
Figure 7.6. Alphabetic Writing

across time and space. The teacher evaluates the child's performance in various categories, such as audience, hypothesis construction, and self-correction. If the child demonstrates a consistent use of any category (90 percent of the time), the teacher records such performance by checking the appropriate column. If the child does not show consistent use, does not demonstrate evidence of any use of a category, or if the category is not applicable, there are corresponding columns that can be checked. In other words, the evaluation forms are record-keeping devices that can help teachers understand and assess their students' literacy development.

Morrissey (1989) adapted Flores' evaluation form to use for her students' journal entries, stories, and letters. Figure 7.7 shows the uses of this form to assess a student's growth through two Spanish writing samples and one English sample.

Rubrics for Holistic Scoring of Writing.   Holistic scoring of writing samples is another assessment method. It is based on the idea that the whole composition is greater than its components, that all components should be judged simultaneously, and that the overall effectiveness of a piece of writing depends on its communicative value. It involves scoring a paper based on its total effect. Using a holistic method for evaluating compositions introduces both teachers and students to a set of criteria for establishing scores (grades) for student writing performance. The criteria set the standards by which the paper will be evaluated. Instead of evaluating student writing

Name _AZUCENA_

Writing Quality:	Date 9/4 C	D	NE	Date 10/28 C	D	NE	Date 1/88 C	D	NE
Self-selected topics	L1			L2			L1		
Uses expansive vocabulary	L1			L2			L1		
Uses complex sentences	L1				L2		L1		
Experiments with different styles		L1		L2			L1		
Revision strategies		L1		L2			L1		
Writing Mechanics:									
Handwriting	L1			L2			L1		
Uses periods	L1				L2		L1		
Uses quotation marks		L1			L2				L1
Uses exclamation point		L1			L2				L1
Uses question marks		L1		L2			L1		
Uses capitalization	L1			L2			L1		
Grammar usage	L1			L2			L1		
Ratio and % invented spelling	2/17 (12%)			3/14 (21%)			22/182 (12%)		
Ratio and % conventional spelling	15/17 (88%)			11/14 (79%)			160/182 (88%)		

C = controls this   Primary language _Spanish_

D = developing this

NE = no evidence of this   Secondary language _English_

Comments: _Capitals after periods ~ Sept. Cursive Oct._
English in diary ~ Oct. Question Marks¿? Jan.
No sign of accents ~ Jan.

Figure 7.7. Evaluation Form for Azucena

with red pencil in hand, teachers respond to the entire piece with one score, and that is the only mark they make on the paper. Although holistic scoring does not provide for the correction of errors or the writing of comments about the work, its use of sets of criteria and scales does give young writers more information than simple grades. Students and teachers become more aware of what constitutes good writing. Stress is placed on content and organization, not just the conventions of writing or usage. Tiedt et al. (1989) suggests a rubric (set of criteria) scoring system. An example of Tiedt's 1–7 rubric scoring system is illustrated in Figure 7.8. The rubric is a simple list that describes the expected performance for each level:

1. The student follows directions and addresses the topic.
2. The student uses appropriate capitalization and punctuation.
3. A paragraph is developed with a topic sentence and supporting sentences.
4. The student uses interesting vocabulary and detail.
5. The student demonstrates organizational skills.

Score of 1—Weak
Writer does all or most of the following:
1. Minimal description.

2. Poor spelling.

3. Confusing use of mechanics.
4. Poor use of capitalization.

5. Vocabulary limited with errors in agreement.
6. Little or no organization.

7. Not legible.
8. No paragraphing.

Score of 3—Fair
Writer does all or most of the following:
1. Some details, but writing is colorless, flat.
2. Some common words and homonyms misspelled.
3. Frequent mechanical errors.
4. Generally correct use of capitalization and periods.
5. Limited vocabulary with some errors in agreement. Some use of slang.
6. Some organization, but tends to be mechanical.
7. Legible, possibly messy.
8. Little or some paragraphing.

Score of 5—Good
Writer does all or more of the following:
1. General details, adjectives and adverbs in use.
2. Adequate mechanics. Some errors that do not interfere with meaning.
3. Adequate vocabulary with few errors in agreement, person, or number.
4. Clear sense of organization with beginning, middle and end. May deviate from topic but returns.
5. Spelling adequate, possible misspelled homonyms or difficult words.
6. Proper paragraphing.
7. Varied sentence structure.

Score of 7—Excellent
Writer does all or most of the following:
1. Vivid details and images.

2. Few mechanical errors. Internal punctuation correct.
3. Excellent vocabulary with good use of agreement and tenses.
4. Clear control of structure. Natural flow and unity. Moves toward completion and conclusion.
5. Few spelling errors.

6. Proper paragraphing.
7. Obvious use of style.

Figure 7.8. 1-7 Rubric Scoring System

The limitation of the holistic scoring system is the highly judgmental approach to evaluation that implicitly assumes a hierarchy in the development of writing skills. For example, some children have vivid details and imagery in their writing even though they have not mastered spelling or paragraphing. This scoring is particularly troublesome when working in bilingual/bicultural settings in which children are still trying to develop vocabulary in English and are spelling words using Spanish orthography. Another judgment you must keep in mind is that holistic scoring assumes a finished product rather than a process. Nonetheless, some teachers find the holistic scoring system useful in understanding weaknesses and establishing goals for students' writing.

Peer Group and Self-Assessment. When students work independently and in small groups, the teacher can also observe how the learning process works: what the students say, do, read, and write. Peer response groups are an important element of assessment because they take advantage of the social aspects of the classroom and the purposeful use of literacy by encouraging listening, reading, and responding to one another's work. The teacher can observe how the children in groups discuss and elaborate on their own conclusions, how they develop themes for study and writing, how they make their own decisions, how they select materials for group use versus independent use, how they resolve problems among themselves, how they take risks, how they combine independent work with collaborative group work, and many other possibilities (Guthrie et al., 1994). The focus is on how the students resolve cognitive conflicts for themselves while participating in a group by revising, confronting, comparing, and reconstructing their knowledge. The students are the actors, the creators of the learning; the teacher is the facilitator and observer of the process.

Peer writing groups can be set up as a way of providing students with a safe environment for self-assessment among peers. The groups should be no larger than four or five students and be heterogeneous with respect to language proficiency and ability. Students can stay in the same groups for several weeks. Once students are placed in a group, they should be given the rules for peer editing:

1. Students are to give each member of the group a copy of their writing on a weekly basis. The authors are to indicate to the readers the areas in which they need help.
2. The readers review the entire work. Initially all comments, suggestions, and so forth should be in writing. When students are able to provide more concrete suggestions and the author is able to take criticism better, they can move on to providing suggestions, comments, or criticisms orally.
3. Turn taking is very important, especially at the beginning. The readers provide comments without interruption; the author listens carefully and is the last to speak. The author is free to accept or reject suggestions, provide information for clarification, or request clarification from the readers. The turn taking is employed so that the young authors do not feel obliged to accept or reject the suggestions of the readers under the pressure of the moment; it gives the authors time to think about the suggestions and to choose those

to which they would like to respond. Furthermore, they can decide what information to provide or request from the readers.

4. The way comments and suggestions are provided is also important. The readers are to begin with a positive statement about the writing. Questions of clarification, suggestions for changes, or other criticism follow. The readers are encouraged to comment on what the author has asked them to focus on. Initially, you may want to demonstrate how to do this. It is important to remind students that structure, organization, and clarity of expression are the aspects they need to attend to in the early stages of writing. Ask them to resist focusing on choice of words, grammar, and misspellings in early drafts, as these issues will later surface for the young authors when they are clearer about how they want to present their ideas.

One of the goals of the peer group is for students to help each other and in the process become conscious of and comfortable with the process of writing. When the teacher facilitates an environment in which children feel comfortable taking risks, making decisions, and expressing varying opinions, the "errors" children make are seen as necessary elements in the process of development. You can study these errors for information regarding the strategies, hypotheses, and strengths of the children's metacognition or metalinguistic processes. Analyzing these errors can help you develop students' awareness and guide them in self-assessment processes. The final goal is the development of an environment in which errors are valued as an important step in risk taking and learning. This creates an atmosphere in which children develop positive personal and social attitudes toward reading, writing, and learning.

OBSERVATION

While videotaping, as in the case of Lupita (Carrasco, 1981), may not be available to all teachers, observation is always available and is a critical tool that teachers must learn to use appropriately. Almost any behavior that you observe contains important information. Suppose you observe that Tomás only selects materials about animals to read; that Patricia's independent writing consists of copying charts and other written materials from around the room; that Lisa edits her stories several times before she meets with you in conference; and that Rafael has no problem answering questions about what he has read, but stumbles over many words when he reads aloud. These are observations that can guide you in assessing children's needs.

Durkin (1989) and Moore (1986) call this naturalistic assessment or "diagnosing by observing" and suggest, as we have, that naturalistic assessment occurs—or should occur—daily. Teachers routinely look for evidence of what is being learned and what still needs to be taught, retaught, or reviewed. They diagnose the needs of students through observation. For example, Cándido may need to learn to use graphophonic and contextual cues in a more balanced way; Marta may need to learn to select meanings offered in a dictionary that fit specified contexts; and Edna may need to adapt her rate of reading to suit the purpose of the reading. You need to view the whole spectrum of the children's behavior and attempt to detect patterns that signal the onset of difficulty. These patterns are used to interpret the children's development and to reach conclusions regarding their strengths and weaknesses.

This is not an easy task. It requires the ability to separate the important from the unimportant and facts from interpretation. This ability usually comes with experience. Recording observational data can be difficult at first because it is hard to see how our own subjectivities or biases affect what we observe. In trying to help teachers find ways of becoming conscious of their biases, Torres-Guzmán tried a "situational frames" (Erickson, 1971) activity that required teachers to keep a running log of events on 3 by 5 index cards for a certain period of time. One of the teachers noted her observation of "a mother and a daughter walking down the street." Torres-Guzmán asked her how she could tell what the relationship was between the woman and the girl. The teacher's eyes opened wide in amazement and she flushed with embarrassment; she had assumed rather than observed what she had written. At this point, while acknowledging the need to examine assumptions as part of the process of observation, Torres-Guzmán also acknowledged that the teacher may have been correct in assuming the relationship between the woman and the child, but she needed to present more convincing evidence. Keeping facts separate from judgments is not easy and requires some attention.

Turbill (in Berglund, 1989–1990)[1] proposes the concept of markers as a means of determining teachers' assumptions and individual progress in whole language classrooms.

> Teachers have certain mental markers that tell them when children have attained a skill or ability . . . In general, markers are evidence of "some kind of linguistic knowledge, skill, or attitude" . . . They come from the values and knowledge that teachers and the community hold about language and language use, and they are used to make informed judgments about a child's language development. The markers that teachers should use vary according to: a) the purpose and audience in the language situation being observed, b) teachers' values and understanding of "good" language use . . . markers are embedded in every language situation and educators just need to learn to see them. Teachers must structure situations that will show the presence or absence of certain markers. (p. 7)

Teachers need to identify and recognize internalized markers and openly question some of the assumptions of reading and writing curricula. In a staff development/research project one of us worked on, one of the teachers never questioned what actually occurred when she asked the children to read in a round-robin fashion. Furthermore, she assumed that she created safe, nonthreatening environments in her classroom. After observing five students in the lowest reading group in her classroom, however, one of the researchers wrote (Berkey et al., 1990), "The turn at reading aloud when you have trouble decoding seems so frustrating. You have to show others that you're stuck—it's a scene for the public display of incompetence" (p. 222). This observation led the teacher to question both her assumption about how reading instruction should occur in her classroom and her assumption about the safety of the learning environment she had created. Her willingness to look critically at what she was doing led her to create a better learning environment for her students.

Child or Group:	Date:
Language/Behavior	Context

Figure 7.9. Observation Card

Running notes of observations can give you valuable information about relationships, roles, and statuses established among children (as was possible with the
videotape of Lupita or the researcher's journal entry in the preceding example). They
can also give you information about the segmentation of conversation and activity
according to the rules established by the children in groups. After a period of observing the children, it will become clear whether grouping patterns and situations
are appropriate or inappropriate for stimulating language development.

Although running notes are preferable for the purposes of discovering new organizational patterns and self-discovery, some teachers find it useful to have a beginning structure. Figure 7.9 is a sample observation card.

The form shown in Figure 7.9 allows for both flexible and instantaneous use.
To illustrate, the teacher records what the child says and does on the lefthand side
and the context within which the child is working, reading, or discussing on the
right. Notes should be brief and descriptive of student behavior. After a number of
observations are conducted, the teacher has enough data to analyze. In the context
provided, the teacher can then assess the types of strategies the child is using, what
the child is attending to or is interested in, which children work well together, and
so on.

Teacher observation can be a valid means of reading and writing assessments
when: 1) the observation occurs as a natural part of classroom procedures; 2) children's responses are viewed as a response to lessons/environments structured by the
teacher and students; and 3) the assessments are conducted in the context of real literacy events (Moore, 1986). Teachers can avoid the problem of inconsistency when
their conclusions are based on numerous, systematic observations over a period
of time.

It is important that the classroom furnish a broad range of opportunities and
experiences that will provide the student and teacher with many opportunities for
assessing the students' learning. Berglund (1989–1990) suggests that teachers observe the following when assessing children's growth as language users:

- Sense of audience when communicating (oral and written)
- Convention control appropriate to the language context
- Vocabulary acquisition and use appropriate to the context
- Control of grammatical options

- Confidence in using language in different contexts
- Comprehension of what has been heard or read. (p. 3)

There are many other classroom events that can help you organize systematic observation. Teacher-student conferences and peer groups are also useful.

Teacher Reflective Journal

An important tool for assessing student progress, instructional activities, and teacher growth is the reflective teaching journal kept by the teacher. Aside from the aforementioned formal or informal observations conducted about student growth, consistently keeping an ongoing journal (recorded biweekly or weekly) in which you can reflect on your feelings about your teaching, about the organization of your environment, about the frustrations and successes in your classroom, about the growth of particular students, and about encounters with parents will provide valuable data for reflection. Periodic rereading and reflection can inform the teacher about her teaching practices and about the growth of the students in the classroom. During the periodic rereading, repeated frustrations and concerns can be identified and can help you focus on the need for adjusting some aspect of classroom activity, the teaching, or the learning environment, or something else. It can also give you a sense of your own progress over time. The teacher reflective journal, together with students' portfolios or other students' observations, can be a powerful tool for the assessment of student and teacher literacy growth and development.

SUMMARY

Assessment must be approached not as a product, but as a process and natural event. There are many types of assessment: formal and informal, one-time occurrence and ongoing. For instructional purposes, we recommend informal and ongoing assessment because the teacher's interpretations will be more contextual and because growth and change in individual students as well as the context of the reading or writing activity are more likely to enter into the teacher's judgment. As with Lupita's teacher, judgments are frequently made impressionistically.

In this chapter, we presented information on the purpose and standards for assessment, methods for the informal assessment of various literacy activities, a portfolio management system, and systematic ways of integrating assessment activities into the everyday life of the classroom. However, the bulk of the assessment information you collect will come from daily informal observations of the children, conferences, and interaction with your students. Children are effective communicators for the most part. What literacy programs should aim for is to make them more effective language users so that they can gain control of the language in a variety of contexts. What you need are ways of heightening your awareness of the children's potential through observing them and assessing their development as they engage in a variety of print-related and oral activities. Furthermore, children can help each other as well as assess their own progress. Actively involving students in assessing their own learning creates another learning experience and promotes an understanding of self and the outside world.

ACTIVITIES

Journal Writing

1. In order to implement the portfolio assessment system the teacher must have very good organizational skills. Assess and reflect on your organizational skills. If you do not consider yourself very organized, could you still implement the portfolio system?
2. Reflect on the type of feedback that is most useful to you when you are trying to learn a new task. Is the preferred feedback in an area that you feel fairly competent with different from feedback in an area in which you feel less competent? How can this reflection inform the type of feedback you give your students?

Discussion Activities

1. Discuss in groups whether teacher observation can be objective and fair in the assessment of learning. What are some factors that might influence the usefulness of observations?
2. Work with groups to select and prepare a passage for an informal reading inventory. Write comprehension questions for the chosen passage. Share with the class your passage and questions and the criteria used in creating the questions. The class as a whole can critique the passages and questions written by each group.

Field-Based Activities

1. Arrange to do observations in an elementary classroom. Select one child or a group of children working together to observe for a minimum of four or five sessions. Take notes on the child's or group's use of and purposes for using literacy, the child's or group's awareness of audience, and the use of other human resources (teacher, aide, peers, etc.) to accomplish literacy tasks. Write your notes. Discuss your observations with the group.
2. Collect some writing samples from fourth or fifth graders, or have three or four students from a class write a paragraph in their second language. Assess the writing samples in groups using the holistic scoring system. Compare scores and discuss difficulties and areas of disagreement.
3. Interview a teacher who is using a portfolio assessment system. Inquire about the process for involving students, collecting evidence, evaluating materials, conferencing, and reporting to parents. Discuss concerns that you might have about the implementation of a portfolio assessment system.

NOTE

1. Turbill, J. (University of Wollongong, New Zealand) as paraphrased in R. L. Berglund, "Convention sessions address whole language evaluation," *Reading Today*, 7, 3, December 1989/January 1990.

CHAPTER 8
Resources

Chapter Overview

The Relationship of Physical Environment and Literacy
Community Resources
Evaluating and Selecting Literature
Children's Literature for Primary Grades
Children's Literature for Intermediate Grades
Content-Area Children's Books

INTRODUCTION

Many different kinds of materials have been suggested throughout this book. Most of them have been materials that we have seen in use in bilingual classrooms. It is not the purpose of this chapter to advocate specific books or materials. Rather, the chapter will describe the creation of a physical environment that encourages literacy and will emphasize considerations that must be taken into account when making decisions concerning books and materials. It will discuss community resources, suggest criteria for evaluating children's literature and software, offer information on distributors of Spanish books and software, and provide lists of recommended literature for primary (K–2) grade and intermediate (3–6) grade students.

Because resource lists of English materials are readily available from numerous sources, we have concentrated on providing lists of materials in Spanish or those dealing with the Latino perspective. The literature recommended represents genres that we think should be emphasized in contemporary bilingual classrooms. No list is exhaustive; you will also need to read journals that review books and other instructional materials.

THE RELATIONSHIP OF PHYSICAL ENVIRONMENT AND LITERACY

Classroom environments provide strong messages to students about the use and importance of print and literacy. Classroom design suggests the type of language and behavior expected in that environment. Some settings are more likely than others to encourage collaboration and peer group interaction. If the teacher is interested in encouraging children to use human and physical resources, then the room itself must be arranged to make these resources readily available and functional.

Space for Collaboration and Social Interaction

The integrated biliteracy approach requires an environment that allows students to work on concrete projects or experiences (e.g., cooking, constructing, creating a book, etc.) in a variety of social groupings. The environment should be organized so that there is space available for children to work in large groups, small groups, individually, or in pairs. The use of a variety of social groupings encourages the use of language for real purposes (informing, mediating, persuading, and controlling). Grouping strategies will vary based on the purpose of the specific learning activity.

To begin creating such an environment, arrange your own desk and the children's tables and chairs to allow for maximum interaction and collaborative group work. If there are individual desks for the children rather than tables, group these together into sets of four or six. The layout of the classroom and the amount of space available are fixed factors that often limit the ways in which a class can be organized. If space is allocated for a large-group meeting area, that limits the amount of space that may be allocated for small-group and individual work. Extending space (creating reading lofts) or utilizing space for multiple purposes (rotating centers) must be considered. First and second grade teachers might look to kindergarten or early childhood settings for environments where children are encouraged to be active learners through maximum interaction with materials, other students, and the teacher. Block building, woodworking, easels, and dramatic play are used in some schools throughout the primary grades to encourage language development and concrete learning experiences. In primary grades youngsters delight in integrating print in the form of signs and directions with woodworking and blocks. Such materials and media are excellent stimuli for developing literacy skills. It should not be the basic design of a classroom that changes as children progress through the primary grades. What should distinguish the upper elementary grades from the early grades is the sophistication of resources.

Heterogeneous Linguistic Grouping Strategies

Once the environment is organized so that space is available for children to work in a variety of social groupings, the teacher must facilitate interaction among children who have diverse linguistic competencies. Heterogeneous linguistic interactions should be the guiding principle for assigning student seating and forming groups. Through working in pairs and small groups, children with diverse linguistic and literacy competencies (both within a language and across languages) have the benefit of using peers as resources as well as drawing on them for support. For some children it is easier to take risks in front of a friend or one or two other persons than in front of an entire class. The power of heterogeneous interaction in learning has been documented by the work of various researchers (Vygotsky, 1988; Bruner, 1978; Halliday, 1988) who suggest that students learn more or can do more with the support of others than on their own.

Begin with a definite plan for the physical environment and social groupings on the first day of school. This establishes the ambiance of the class. A careful introduction to the room will encourage students to discuss and describe the purpose, function, and use of areas and materials, and will establish some ground rules for the classroom community. Evaluate the environment and the types of collaboration and interaction required for specific tasks. Make students responsible for helping to organize the environment to meet their needs. Student collaboration in establishing guidelines for the use of space is important. They need to understand the "traffic flow" and dynamics of the room and share responsibility for keeping their classroom a lively and orderly learning environment. Through this process, the children will develop a sense of ownership and comfort in a place where they live, play, and work.

Spanish/English Print Environment

The teacher must organize a print environment that will create varied relationships between children and print. If a variety of environmental print—books, newspapers, and other materials in both languages—is available and become an integral part of the classroom, the children will interact with print on a daily basis.

The print environment can include a wide range of children's literature and trade books, school texts, newspapers, magazines, advertisements, self- and class-generated materials, and other environmental print (e.g., Spanish and English bus schedules, health information, and product labels). Children's interests and developing literacy needs become the criteria for selecting materials for the classroom.

Equity of Language. The teacher must be aware of the messages children get from the display of classroom print. Therefore, the issue of equity in the selection and display of Spanish and English print is important. For example, the display of the Spanish alphabet and the English alphabet should be equally prominent. If books in both languages are to share a library stand, be careful not to place English books on the top shelves and Spanish books on the bottom shelves or vice versa. Calendars, charts, graphs, and books should be of similar quality (paper, printing, color, illustrations, etc.) in both languages. This does not mean that a "literal" translation of all classroom environmental print is necessary or desirable but that the overall quality and prominence of Spanish/English print should be equitable.

Language Models. The print environment should include an area displaying children's literature and trade books in both languages. The splendid diversity of children's literature now obtainable in Spanish makes it possible to give the Spanish-speaking child beautiful books to read (see guidelines for selecting literature and lists of distributors that follow). Children should have access to the best literature the world has to offer in the form of works in their native language, good adaptations/translations of works in other languages, works from their own culture, and works from other cultures and places in the world. For Latino children living in the United States, children's literature can open paths to the valuing and appreciation of their first language and culture, and to a better understanding of the new English language and American culture.

By creating the opportunity for children to interact with a wide variety of published children's literature and trade books, you are providing models of different genres, uses of grammar, standard spelling, and so on. It is through a "wide exposure to literature . . . [that] children expand their world of literacy" (Edelsky, 1986, p. 45). The available books must reflect a wide range of reading difficulty. Children will select books based on their interests, peer pressure, developing literacy skills, and perceived teacher expectations.

In addition to literature and trade books, the classroom should also prominently display reference materials in both languages, for example, encyclopedias, dictionaries, atlases, directories, cookbooks, and songbooks. By using these materials, children will learn that they can consult specific books for specific information.

Print Production as Artifact/Instrument

Growth toward literacy requires the opportunity to experiment and practice with written symbols in a multisensory environment. Through the use of multisensory materials, children learn from concrete experiences and relate new learning to previous learning. Remember, learning has cognitive, affective, and physical components. Elementary schoolchildren need to experience the world and tend to need learning experiences that are concrete. These concrete experiences provide the prior knowledge and referents for literacy. As children interact with each other and with the kinesthetic, auditory, visual, and technological media in the environment, more authentic opportunities for the use of language and literacy skills can be created and recreated.

Learning Kinesthetically.   To hold water in your hands is to feel its liquidity; it is to know something about the characteristics of the substance. Children need this kind of experience. Children can experience the tactile configurations of letters and words by writing and working with sand, salt, clay, felt, wooden letters, letters in the shapes of people, and so forth. Puzzles in the shapes of letters or puzzles with an object/action picture on one piece and the name on the other provide opportunities for children to discover or practice the meaning of letters and words. Blocks, woodwork, and other building materials provide children with a kinesthetic experience and are a stimulus for language and for integrating print, such as signs and directions, in authentic contexts.

Learning Auditorily.   Hearing someone sing a song is different from trying to figure out the melody by reading the notes. Hearing the song sung is knowing it at the experiential level. Media can build on experiential knowledge. Media that can be used for listening and recording can contribute significantly to the literacy environment. Not only can children follow the print of commercially or teacher-prepared recordings, but they can tell stories and/or read the stories they write into a tape recorder. Children will often listen to a recording of their favorite book while following the text until they have the text memorized. Although some may not consider this reading, it is one way for children to learn and to develop a sense of the purpose and meaning of print.

Children who have watched *Sesame Street* will recognize jingles or songs associated with letters and words. Some children will use and imitate this type of learning in the classroom with audio recordings and letters. Recordings of traditional Spanish songs like *La marcha de las letras de Cri Cri* [The March of the Letters by Cri Cri] can be used to assist children in developing Spanish alphabet skills.

Having a variety of recorded poems, songs, and tongue twisters or a good anthology like *Días y días de poesía* [Days and Days of Poetry] (Ada, 1990) that invite children to imagine, fantasize, and experience a sense of wonderment will stimulate language and the use of literacy.

Learning Visually.   Looking at the display of noodles at the grocery store—linguini, fettuccine, rigatoni—and reading about them for the first time when you want to try a new recipe are two different ways of knowing about noodles. Visualization is important to the act of knowing. Children's growing independence in learning can be supported by providing access to visual materials. Furthermore, these materials can be used without assistance from the teacher. Materials that are clearly labeled with graphic representations of suggested uses provide occasions for ongoing literacy events.

Using color codes or shape codes as symbolic representations of categories in the environment will assist in calling children's attention to the interpretation of visual cues (e.g., all materials to be stored on a certain shelf have a yellow dot on

them). These symbolic representations can help create mental images that lend meaning to their environment. Labeling objects and areas (*mesa* [table], *biblioteca* [library]) in the class will also awaken and reinforce children's print awareness.

The use of easels, brushes, and paints, as well as other art media, is especially significant in the development of literacy. Young children will go from drawing to writing (Schwartz, 1988) and often integrate alphabetic and nonalphabetic symbols in their work. Drawing often serves as the stimulus for writing, and children enjoy adding illustrations to their texts as a means of providing content.

Learning with Technology. Identifying a muffler problem in a car is relatively easy because of the noise, but fixing the problem takes considerable skill. For young children, identifying letters is also considerably easier than writing them. The use of a computer with a word processing and graphics package adds a new dimension to the production and use of print. For children who do not have the coordination and muscle control to begin writing, the use of computers provides a tool for using written language. Children will "hunt and peck" the letters of their names, write signs and notes, and read their writing to the teacher and others. As children develop in their use of print, this technology gives them power over printing; they tend to write more and make more changes (edit) when using a computer (Daiute, 1983, 1986; Piper, 1983; Simon, 1984). Older children will benefit from the use of hypermedia (Bermudez & Palumbo, 1994) and interactive media, such as *Compton's CD-Rom Interactive Encyclopedia* (Compton's NewMedia, 1994), in which a flick of a mouse can locate visual and text information related to their thematic studies.

Assessing the Environment. Sufficient amounts and diversity of materials will foster the development of literacy skills through a variety of modes and experiences. The questions in Figure 8.1, adapted from Glazer and Searfoss (1988), can be used as a guide to the design or assessment of the classroom environment.

1. Are tables and chairs arranged for group and team work?
2. Is there a corner, nook, or cranny where students can enjoy a book quietly by themselves?
3. Are there shelf and surface areas for the display of materials for thematic units?
4. Are there open areas for dramatics, singing, or other physically active learning?
5. Is there an area for reading/displaying literature and trade books? Does this area have a rug, shelves, comfortable chairs, pillows?
6. Is there a space for kinesthetic materials (e.g., sand, puzzles, clay, blocks, woodworking, and games)?
7. Is there an area(s) with equipment for using and responding to language?
   a. Tape recorders, cassettes, and headphones
   b. Typewriters, computers, and word processing software
   c. Transparencies and overhead projector
   d. Still camera, videotape equipment, or 8mm or 16mm camera and projector
8. Are there areas for print displays (e.g., bulletin boards, calendars, and classroom charts)? Is the display of Spanish/English print equitable?
9. Are a variety of writing tools and paper accessible?
   a. Pencils, crayons, ballpoint pens, colored markers, chalk, and paints
   b. Lined/unlined paper, colored construction paper in various sizes, butcher paper, typing/computer paper, and colored tissue paper
10. Are materials for constructing and publishing available?
    a. Heavyweight paper (covered stock), bookmaking/masking/transparent adhesive tape, glue/rubber cement, needle, thread, yarn, and fabric
    b. Scissors, paper cutter, hole punch, stapler, and rulers
11. Is there chalkboard space designated for student writing?
12. Are there large sheets of paper on the walls for writing and composing?
13. Is there an easily accessible container (milk crate, file drawer, box) for student portfolios?
14. Is there a relatively private area for student/teacher conferencing?

Figure 8.1. Assessing the Integrated Biliteracy Environment

COMMUNITY RESOURCES

Spanish-language newspapers, magazines, radio, and television are now found in major metropolitan areas of the United States. Newspapers, magazines, bus schedules, and health pamphlets can be a source of print media for your classroom; radio and television can provide models of oral language for listening, studying, and analyzing. Many literacy activities can be built around the critical analysis of such things as advertisements, commercials, and programming. The personnel of news and entertainment media are also rich resources and are generally eager to assist by making classroom visits and presentations. Other Latino professionals in the community (doctors, attorneys, mechanics, small business owners) may also be willing to be guest speakers or have a class visit them on a field trip.

Parents as Resources

Parents are the first teachers of children and can be your strongest partners in developing literacy. Encourage parents to talk and read with their children, to ask children to express themselves through questions, and to include children in everyday home activities that can serve to expand their knowledge and experience.

INCIDENTAL TEACHING TECHNIQUES

Terrell H. Bell, in his book *Active Parent Concern* (1976), proposes that parents think of themselves as partners with the school in the responsibility of educating their children. Bell recognizes that the environment and routine experiences parents and children share provide many opportunities for teaching. This method is called *incidental teaching*. There are seven basic points to keep in mind.

2.   Remember that conversation teaches.

1.   Incidental teaching begins with active parents' concern for nurturing the minds of their children.

3.   Learn about what is on your child's mind.

4.   Know about the content of the school curriculum in which your child is currently engaged.

5.   Execute your incidental teaching plans every day as new experiences unfold.

6.   The skill of questioning is as important as listening when you use the incidental teaching method.

7.   Make each week a learning cycle.

Figure 8.2. Incidental Teaching Techniques

With parents, as with the children, your starting point is from their point of view. Ask parents what they do to help their children and this will give you an understanding of what they think of as "helping." Once you understand how they perceive of help, you can assist them in discovering new ways of helping their children. In a series of workshops in San Antonio, Texas, for example, Torres-Guzmán asked parents to illustrate "help" in mural form. Later, Torres-Guzmán included their drawings in the teaching of incidental teaching techniques (see Figure 8.2).

Parents and other community members are bearers of culture and sources of knowledge that classroom teachers often ignore (Moll & González, 1994). They can help you to think of appropriate solutions to problems that arise; they can provide contextual information on which you can build your themes and lessons; and they can help you elicit resources in the community. Vélez-Ibáñez (1988) classifies knowledge about mathematics, architecture, chemistry, physics, biology, and engineering with the repairing, planting, cooking, and other everyday life activities of a Latino community. These "funds of knowledge," as Vélez-Ibáñez calls them, can serve as intellectual resources for developing strategies for your literacy program.

Explicitly including parents in the process of developing literacy is important. In addition to eliciting and generating knowledge about their daily experiences, invite parents to your classroom. Our experience suggests that parental awareness of how teaching occurs gives them a greater appreciation of what goes into instruction. In the Pájaro Valley Project in California, Ada (1988) showed how to bring parents and children together in order to read, discuss, and write children's stories. By using the creative reading approach, she not only provided parents with the literacy skills necessary for helping their children in school learning, but helped the parents share common experiences through which they could speak and reflect critically on the events in their lives.

Public Libraries as Resources

Most public libraries in Latino neighborhoods will have a children's section of books in Spanish. If your neighborhood library branch does not have children's books in Spanish, make your need known to the librarian and have parents and other community members also request that the library purchase books in Spanish.

EVALUATING AND SELECTING LITERATURE

In evaluating and selecting literature for your classroom the primary criteria should be the students' interests and needs. Younger children love fantasy and here-and-now literature. Some children continue to love fantasy literature and develop an interest in science fiction, mystery, and mythology as they grow older; others develop strong interests in realistic fiction, biographies, and history. It is of basic importance for literature and trade books to have situations, themes, characters, and language that reflect the diverse circumstances of Latino children living in the United States. It is also an important enrichment for children to be exposed to the broader literature of the Spanish-speaking world. You will want to establish a set of criteria that is appropriate for the group of children you are teaching. In addition to student interest and need, there are more standard criteria you may want to consider, such as:

1. Does the piece have an important instructional or entertainment value?
2. Is the piece well written?
3. Is the piece free of race, gender, class, and other stereotypes?
4. Does the piece encourage an understanding of diverse cultures or human conditions?
5. Does the piece serve to inform, inspire, enlighten, or create wonderment?
6. Are the theme and reading difficulty appropriate?
7. Are the illustrations well done and appropriate to the text?

Professional groups of teachers have evaluated and made recommendations about the appropriateness and level of many titles available in Spanish in local libraries and teacher bookstores. Some state education agencies, county and regional offices of education, and teacher associations have also conducted evaluations of children's literature and made recommendations. For example, the California State Department of Education prints an annotated bibliography of selected titles in *Recommended Readings in Literature: Kindergarten through Grade Eight*. The International Reading Association's journal, *Lectura y Vida* [Reading and Life], reviews children's literature and is a good place to look for recent titles. *Lectura y Vida* also announces awards and prizes for the best of children's literature in Spanish. *The Reading Teacher* and *Language Arts* periodically review materials that are written bilingually, Spanish and English.

Bilingual education associations in most states and the National Association for Bilingual Education (NABE) are also places to look for guidance. The monthly newsletter *NABE News* runs a "Resources for Bilingual Educators" column that lists and describes new books and materials. Most of the state reading and bilingual education conferences include exhibits by publishers and distributors of children's literature in Spanish. Many of these publishers and distributors have received recommendations as to the grade level and subject matter of their books, most of which have been made by individual educators or teacher groups.

There are many publications from Latin America that can also guide you in the selection of a variety of materials, and Latin American countries are now placing greater importance on the development of children's literature. For example, Cuba began sponsoring the *Concurso Anual de La Edad de Oro* [Annual Contest of the Golden Age] prize in 1972 for best children's literature in the genres of poetry and the short story. In 1973, Puentes de Oyenard wrote a book entitled *Literatura infantil uruguaya* [Uruguayan Children's Literature] that received an award from *El Diario de México* [Mexico's Daily (newspaper)] in 1982. Following the 1975 Prague Conference of Writers of Children's Literature, an international conference on children's literature in Spanish was held in Mexico City.

Distributors of Children's Literature in Spanish

There are now many Spanish-language book distributors who offer a number of options and services. Many distributors will provide you with catalogs, some of which include critical evaluations of the children's selections. Another good source of information about vendors, distributors, and publishers of materials in Spanish is REFORMA (a Hispanic library and media organization), P.O. Box 9441, Washington, DC, 20016. The following is a brief list of distributors with selections of children's literature and trade books in Spanish:

Ateneo Booksellers
745 Crane Blvd.
Los Angeles, CA 90065

Bilingual Publications Co.
270 Lafayette St. Rm. 705
New York, NY 10012

Children's Book Press
6400 Hollis Street, Suite 4
Emeryville, CA 94608

Children's Press
5440 North Cumberland Ave.
Chicago, IL 60656

Donars Spanish Books
P.O. Box 24
Loveland, CO 80539-0024

Downtown Book Center, Inc.
247 SE 1st St.
Miami, FL 33131

Editorial Edil, Inc.
Box 23088, UPR Station
Rio Piedras, PR 00931

Hampton-Brown Books
P. O. Box 223220
Carmel, CA 93922

Hispanic Books Distributors
1870 W. Prince Rd., Suite 8
Tucson, AZ 85705

Lectorum Publications, Inc.
137 West 14 St.
New York, NY 10011

Mariuccia Iaconi Book Imports
1110 Mariposa
San Francisco, CA 94107

Perma-Bound
Vandalia Road
Jacksonville, IL 62650

Red Balloon
9819 IH10 West
San Antonio, Texas 78230

Santillana Publishing Co., Inc.
257 Union St.
Northvale, NJ 07647

Scholastic Inc.
730 Broadway
New York, NY 10003

Tortilla Press, Inc.
2731-C Vineyard Ave.
Oxnard, CA 93030

Technology and Computer Software in Spanish

Identifying technology and software resources requires keeping on the lookout for new products and services, which are constantly coming on the market. Many distributors carry some software in Spanish. Look for reviews and evaluations of software in the "Action for Equity" column in *The Computing Teacher*, the journal of the International Council for Computers in Education. Another source of information for software as well as new products and services is the "Technology and Language-minority Students" column in *NABE News* (monthly newsletter for the National Association for Bilingual Education). The National Clearinghouse for Bilingual Education in Washington DC (Tel: 800–321–NCBE) provides on-line resources for bilingual educators through Internet (a worldwide communication network). Many states provide accounts for teachers on their on-line networks where educational resources are shared, such as California On-line Resources for Education (CORE), New York State Educational Resources Network (NYSERNET), and Texas Education Network (TENET). The following companies have Spanish-language software available that could be added to the literacy environment:

DLM Educational Software
One DLM Park
Allen, TX 75002

MicroTac
525 Hawthorn St., Suite II
San Diego, CA 92101

Scholastic
P.O. Box 7502
2931 E. McCarty St.
Jefferson City, MO 65102

Sunburst Communications
39 Washington Ave.
Pleasantville, NY 10570

CHILDREN'S LITERATURE
FOR PRIMARY GRADES[1]

Picture and Predictable Books

Ada, A. F. 1989. *Sale el oso.* Illus. A. Myers. Carmel, CA: Hampton-Brown.
A bear goes out for a nighttime walk and finds one animal after another, all of whom he invites to join him. Big book format with lots of repetition.

Ada, A. F. 1989. *Los seis deseos de la jirafa.* Illus. D. Roy. Carmel, CA: Hampton-Brown.
When the giraffe complains that she does not like her own tail, the fish decides to grant her six wishes. After trying out an elephant tail, a monkey tail, and a few other tails, the giraffe decides that she really is better off with her own. Written in verse, big book format.

Ballesta, J. 1983. *Tommy y el elefante.* Barcelona: Editorial Lumen.
Tommy's best friend is an imaginary elephant. Life is wonderful for Tommy and his friend until Tommy's mother becomes concerned and takes Tommy to a psychologist. Now it's up to Tommy to protect his friendship, which he does by cleverly outwitting the psychologist.

Baum, W. 1977. *La expedición.* Caracas: Ekaré-Banco del Libro.
A wordless picture book about an admiral who discovers an island in the middle of the ocean. When he sights a beautiful temple atop the island, he proceeds to land with all his men and dismantle the temple to carry it back to his ship. He then discovers that his ship's engines and smokestacks are where the temple used to be. This book naturally lends itself to simple (or complex) discussions about conquest and colonialism, while even the youngest children will delight in the humor and simple justice of the plot.

Blocksma, M. 1986. *¡Manzano, manzano!* Trans. A. F. Ada. Illus. S. Cox. Chicago: Children's Press.
A story, told in verse, about an apple tree that generously gives away its apples to all who ask. When winter comes and all of its apples are gone, the apple tree becomes lonely for a true friend. A tiny worm offers to plant some apple seeds, and in the spring, the apple tree has a new sapling as friend and companion.

Blocksma, M. 1988. *Chirrinchinchina, ¿qué hay en la tina?* Trans. L. Kratky. Illus. S. Cox Kalthoff. Chicago: Children's Press.
A bathtime story about a boy and his dog. Father warns that the bathroom floor must stay dry, but that is easier said than done . . . This pattern book makes good use of repeated rhymes and simple language.

Broger, A. 1978. *Buenos días, querida Ballena.* Illus. G. Kalow. Barcelona: Editorial Juventud.
Enrique, a retired fisherman, has made friends with a whale whom he visits faithfully every six months. One season, when he fails to appear, the whale becomes very worried and decides to go visit him. It's a long journey upstream from the ocean to Enrique's little town on the river, but the whale's persistence overcomes all difficulties and the friends are reunited at last.

Cisneros, S. 1994. *Hairs: Pelitos.* Illus. T. Ybáñez. New York: Alfred A. Knopf, Inc.
A child describes how each person in the family has hair that looks and acts different, Papa's like a broom, Kiki's like fur, and Mama'a with the smell of warm bread. Written in Spanish and English and colorfully illustrated.

Claret, M. 1983. *El conejo de chocolate*. Barcelona: Editorial Juventud.
  Pedrito is a very mischievous little bunny rabbit. His father is a great artist who makes a living painting Easter eggs. One evening Pedrito has a major mishap with a kettle of chocolate that his mother is preparing for the family and inadvertently becomes the inspiration for his father's new line of chocolate Easter bunnies.

Dahan, A. 1988. *Hélico y el pájaro*. Trans. R. Torrents. Barcelona: Ediciones Destino.
  A young aviator finds a baby bird that has fallen from its nest. He feeds the bird, takes care of it, and teaches it to fly.

Kitamura, S. 1986. *Cuando los borregos no pueden dormir*. Madrid: Ediciones Altea.
  A young sheep cannot sleep. Before deciding to count all of his family members, he embarks on an adventurous nighttime journey in this whimsical counting book.

Lionni, L. 1969. *Nadarín*. Trans. A. M. Matute. Barcelona: Editorial Lumen.
  Nadarín (Swimmy) is a little fish who delights in exploring the wonders of the ocean. When a school of other tiny fish refuse to join him for fear of being preyed on by larger fish, Swimmy devises a plan. Ingenuity, cooperation, and mutual aid allow all the little fish to swim the oceans freely from then on.

Mora, P. 1994. *Listen to the desert: Oye al desierto*. Illus. F. X. Mora. New York: Houghton Mifflin Company.
  A Spanish and English poem that delightfully describes some of the onomatopoetic sounds of nature in a desert.

Mora, P. 1994. *The desert is my mother: El desierto es mi madre*. Illus. D. Lechón. Houston, TX: Arte Público Press.
  A young girl leads you through a poetic depiction of the desert as the provider of comfort, food, spirit, and life. In Spanish and English with pattern repetition.

Spier, P. 1987. *Gente*. Trans. by Ricardo Alezones. Caracas: Ediciones María di Mase.
  People, people everywhere—in a variety of shapes, sizes, colors, ethnicities, and nationalities. An excellent multicultural primer now available in Spanish.

Turin, A., & Bosnia, N. n.d. *Rosa Caramelo*. Trans. S. Ribeiro. Barcelona: Editorial Lumen.
  Once upon a time in the land of the elephants, there lived a herd in which all of the little girl elephants had soft, rosy pink skin, which they kept that way through a steady diet of flowers. Meanwhile, all of the little boy elephants ate whatever they pleased, rolled around in the mud, and roamed freely far beyond the girl elephants' fenced-in flower garden. But there was one little girl elephant whose skin would not turn pink no matter how many flowers she ate. When she decides one day to leave the fenced-in flower garden, things are never the same in elephant land again.

Folklore

Ada, A. F., & Olave, M. del P. de. 1979. *Aserrín, aserrán*. Loveland, CO: Donars Productions.
  Rounds, riddles, finger plays, lullabies, and more are included in this paperback edition.

Bravo-Villasante, C. 1978. *Adivina, adivinanza*. Madrid: Interduc/Schroedel.
  A hardback, comprehensive collection of children's folklore by a renowned specialist in this field. Illustrated with reproductions of Victorian paper cutouts.

de Paola, T. 1994. *La leyenda de la flor de nochebuena*. New York: G. P. Putnam's Sons.
  When Lucida is unable to finish her gift for the Baby Jesus in time for the Christmas procession, a miracle enables her to offer the beautiful flower we now call the poinsettia.

Kratky, L. J. 1989. *La gallinita, el gallo, y el frijól*. Illus. L. Yerkes. Carmel, CA: Hampton-Brown.

A traditional story about a hen who begs the river for some water in order to save her dear rooster. The river wants a flower in exchange for the water, the flower bush wants a string in exchange for the flower, the girl wants a comb in exchange for the string . . . Big book format.

La Fontaine, J. de. 1983. *El león y la zorra*. Trans. A. Gatell. Illus. M. Ginesta. Barcelona: La Galera.

A lazy lion decides that it is too much work to run down his prey and devises a plan whereby the animals come to him. However, a wily fox suspects foul play and puts an end to the lion's scheme for easy living. Told in modern language and accompanied by contemporary illustrations.

Puncel, M. 1987. *Estaba la pájara pinta y otras rimas infantiles*. Illus. R. Recio. Madrid: Ediciones Altea.

An illustrated selection of well-known children's rhymes and verses. Pocket sized, hardback edition.

Recio, R. (Illus.). 1987. *Mañana es domingo y otras rimas infantiles*. Madrid: Ediciones Altea.

A collection of humorous children's rhymes, fully illustrated. Pocket sized, hardback edition.

Valeri, M. E. 1974. *La liebre y la tortuga*. Trans. A. Lisson. Illus. by M. Rius. Barcelona: La Galera.

The traditional fable of the turtle and the hare is retold in contemporary language and set in modern Spain. The hare is so sure of his lead that he decides to spend the night with some relatives who live along the route, while the turtle steadily persists onward in order to claim the prize.

Narrative and Modern Fantasy

Alonso, F. 1978. *El hombrecillo de papel*. Valladolid: Editorial Miñón.

A little girl cuts a paper man out of a sheet of newspaper. The paper man is happy playing with the girl and her friends, but when he begins to tell the children stories, he realizes that all the stories he knows are stories of war, catastrophe, and human misery. He feels badly that he has saddened the children with his stories and decides to do something about it.

Balzola, A. 1983. *Los zapatos de Munia*. Barcelona: Ediciones Destino.

Munia becomes very worried when she notices that her shoes are getting too tight; she knows she hasn't stepped in any puddles. A conversation with Felipe, the friendly shoemaker, ends in delight as Munia realizes that her shoes haven't shrunk, it's she who has grown, and that her parents, instead of getting upset, will buy her a new pair.

Castañeda, O. S. 1993. *El tapiz de abuela*. Illus. C. O. Sánchez. New York: Lee & Low Books, Inc.

Esperanza's grandmother has a large birthmark on her face, and the local people do not buy her beautifully woven pieces because they fear she is a witch. For the feast day of the village, Esperanza helps her grandmother weave a special traditional Guatemalan tapestry and takes it to the market where the tapestry is a sensation.

de Beer, H. 1988. *¿A dónde vas, osito polar?* Trans. Humpty Dumpty. Barcelona: Editorial Lumen.

Little Polar Bear is sleeping next to Father Bear when the piece of ice he is on breaks off. When he wakes up, he finds himself floating out to sea, heading toward new lands, new adventures, and new friendships before eventually finding his way back to the North Pole.

de Paola, T. n.d. *Oliver Button es una nena.* Trans. F. Alonso. Valladolid: Editorial Miñón.
Oliver Button is mercilessly teased by the boys at school because he doesn't like to do the
things other boys do. Instead, he likes flowers, he likes to draw and cut out paper dolls,
and most of all, he loves to dance and sing while pretending he's a movie star. His parents finally decide to send him to dance class, and in the end, a local talent show provides
an opportunity for his classmates to gain a new appreciation of Oliver.

Esteban, A. 1986. *¿Dónde has estado, Aldo?* Text by R. Alcántara. Barcelona: Editorial
Juventud.
Aldo is a little boy who lives with his grandfather, a fisherman. Aldo is enchanted by the
lure of the far-off horizon and sets off one night on a special journey. Aided by a dolphin,
he saves an enchanted bird and helps rescue some baby sea turtles before his eventual re-
turn home.

Fox, M. 1988. *Guillermo Jorge Manuel José.* Illus. J. Vivas. Trans. G. Uribe. Caracas: Ekaré-
Banco del Libro.
A little boy lives next door to an old folks' home and makes friends with all of its resi-
dents, but he has one special friend in particular. When he overhears that she has begun
to lose her memory, he sets out to do what he can to help her. A very tender and touching story about bonds between children and elderly people.

Lionni, L. 1986. *Frederick.* Trans. A. M. Matute. Barcelona: Editorial Lumen.
A small family of mice work day and night preparing for winter, all except for Frederick,
who does not appear to be doing much of anything. Yet when winter comes, the mouse
family discovers, to their delight, the treasure chest of images, colors, and words that
Frederick the poet has gathered for them.

Schubert, I., & Schubert, D. 1988. *La Pequeña Zapatones.* Barcelona: Editorial Lumen.
When Maggie goes to brush her teeth one morning, she is surprised to find a tiny witch
with enormous feet hiding in the bathroom cabinet. Maggie gains the runaway witch's trust
by confiding that she, too, has something that she gets teased about—her large ears. Maggie
helps her new friend by decorating her shoes with brightly colored designs, and the little
witch returns the favor in a very special manner.

Sendak, M. 1988. *Donde viven los monstruos.* Madrid: Alfaguara.
Maurice Sendak's classic story about the young boy Max who, after being sent to bed
without supper for misbehaving, journeys to the land where monsters live. Max delights
in being king of the monsters until he starts to get lonely and returns home where, despite
his misbehavior, he knows he is always loved.

Velthuys, M. 1982. *El gentil dragón rojo.* Valladolid: Editorial Miñón.
What are the townspeople going to do with the dragon who has been devouring their grain
fields now that they have captured him? The general wants to turn him into an instrument
of war and the mayor wants to put him in a cage and charge admission to view him, but
the dragon is too peaceful and freedom-loving to go along with these plans. Finally, a scientist creates a solution: by breathing fire into the scientist's invention twice a day, the
dragon can generate heat and electricity for the whole town, keep his freedom, and be am-
ply rewarded with food for his efforts.

Viorst, J. 1989. *Alexander y el día terrible, horrible, espantoso, horroroso.* Illus. R. Cruz.
Trans. A. F. Ada. New York: Atheneum.
Alexander is having a terrible, horrible, awful day, which begins when he realizes that he
fell asleep with chewing gum in his mouth and now has chewing gum in his hair. It only
gets worse from there.

Williams, B. 1977. *El dolor de muelas de Alberto*. Trans. A. F. Ada. Illus. K. Chorao. New York: Dutton.

Albert the turtle has a toothache—a toothache so bad that he has to stay in bed. Unfortunately, no one in his family believes him. It takes a visit from Grandmother Turtle, who knows how to ask the right questions, before the mystery of Albert's toothache is solved.

Williams, L. 1979. *Un oso nuboso*. Illus. C. S. Vendrell. Trans. F. Caivano. Barcelona: Editorial Hymsa.

A boy befriends a bear made out of clouds and climbs up to the sky to visit him. However, the bear can only speak in rhyme, which proves to be too much for his human friend.

Poetry

Acevedo, M. 1988. *Llamo a la luna sol y es de diá*. México City: Editorial Trillas.

A selection of children's poetry divided into two sections: poetry to read and poetry to inspire other poems. Children are encouraged to send the poems that they write to the book's editor.

Aguirre, M. 1974. *Juegos y otros poemas*. Illus. T. Roggi. Havana: Gente Nueva.

Delightful wordplay and linguistic inventiveness characterize this work by one of the best children's poets in the Spanish language.

Darío, R. 1983. *Margarita*. Illus. M. Doppert. Caracas: Ekaré-Banco del Libro.

Rubén Darío's famous poem tells the story of a little princess who journeys up to the sky in order to pick a star for a brooch she has designed. The rhythm and beauty of Darío's language are complemented by full-page pen-and-ink illustrations.

Freyre de Matos, I. 1979. *ABC de Puerto Rico*. Illus. A. Matorell. Sharon, CT: Troutman Press.

The nature and culture of Puerto Rico are celebrated in this handsome book of poetry and vividly illustrated with original woodcuts.

Galarza, E. 1972. *Más poemas párvulos*. San José, CA: Editorial Almaden.

Inspired by Mother Goose, Ernesto Galarza has created these authentically Mexican poems to delight children of all ages.

Guillén, N. 1978. *Por el mar de las Antillas anda un barco de papel*. Managua: Editorial Nueva Nicaragua.

A collection of poems by renowned poet Nicolás Guillén. The selection includes some riddles and songs as well. The verses are lighthearted and humorous.

Plays

Armijo, C. 1980. *Guiñapo y pelaplátanos*. Valladolid: Editorial Miñón.

A woman, a policeman, and a marionette are the main characters in this play. Its plot revolves around the efforts of the policeman to apprehend the mischievous marionette and the woman's growing sympathy for the marionette's plight. Since the play has several scenes, different children can take turns playing the main characters.

de Paola, T. 1981. *Representación navideña*. Trans. M. T. Gabriel. Valladolid: Editorial Miñón.

The story of the first Christmas is told in beautiful and simple language and illustrated so as to suggest staging possibilities. The text is written in narrative form. Were students to enact the story, they could begin by adapting the text in order to create a script.

Informative Books

Ancono, G. 1994. *The piñata maker: El piñatero*. Orlando, FL: Harcourt Brace & Company. The Spanish and English text describes how Don Ricardo makes piñatas for the village birthday celebrations and fiestas. The photographs illustrate the traditional process and materials used in making piñatas.

Dultzin Dubin, S. 1981. *Sonidos y ritmos*. Illus. by L. Maciel. México City: Editorial Patria. Set in México and highlighted with bright and modern illustrations, this book explores the sounds and rhythms that exist all around us: animal sounds, natural sounds, musical rhythms, unpleasant noises. Also, the importance of music and dance in the lives of people everywhere is celebrated.

Frandsen, K. G. 1986. *Hoy fue mi primer día de escuela*. Trans. L. Kratky. Chicago: Children's Press.
A little boy tells us the story of how his day went on this very special occasion. Children will relive their own experiences and enjoy the humorous illustrations.

Greene, C. 1985. *Puedo ser jugador de béisbol*. Trans. L. Kratky. Chicago: Children's Press. A book detailing the life of professional baseball players, how baseball leagues are structured, and other information of interest to young baseball fans.

Jacob, E. 1984. *Las tortugas de mar*. Illus. F. Dávalos. México City: Conafe.
A beautifully illustrated book, written in clear and simple language, about the life cycle of sea turtles. Also included is an ancient Mexican legend about the sea turtle.

McKissack, P. 1988. *Ada la desordenada*. Trans. L. Kratky. Illus. R. Hackney. Chicago: Children's Press.
Ada's room is a mess: books, toys, and clothes all over the floor, cookie crumbs on the bed, paint stains on the wall. There's nothing left to do but clean it all up, and the end result is well worth the effort.

Mitgutsch, A. 1971. *De la arcilla al ladrillo*. Minneapolis: Carolrhoda Books.
The story of a clay brick is told: the clay is dug up out of the ground, mixed and molded, fired, and then used for building. The book is notepad sized, spiral bound, and fully illustrated.

Puncel, M. n.d. *El círculo y sus cosas*. Illus. A. Aragüez. Madrid: Ediciones Altea.
The circle's many adventures begin when it decides to jump off the traffic light. The circle goes through several incarnations (a ball, a wheel, a balloon, a birthday cake) before it decides that it really likes being a traffic light best of all.

Books in English

Ada, A. F. 1993. *The rooster who went to his uncle's wedding*. Illus. K. Kuchera. New York: G.P. Putnam's Sons.
A cumulative Latin American folktale in which the sun sets off a chain of events resulting in the cleaning of Rooster's beak in time for his uncle's wedding.

Aardema, V. 1979. *The riddle of the drum: A tale of Tizapán*. México. Illus. T. Chen. New York: Four Winds Press.
A folk tale from Jalisco, México, about a prince who is trying to win a beautiful princess's hand. In order to do so, he must first solve the riddle of the magic drum. Thanks to his faithful attendants, he is able to meet the challenge.

Griego, M. C., Bucks, B. L., Gilbert, S. S., & Kimball, L. H. 1987. *Tortillitas para mamá and other Spanish nursery rhymes*. Illus. B. Cooney. New York: Holt, Rinehart and Winston.

Beautifully illustrated by Barbara Cooney, this book is a compilation of Spanish nursery rhymes presented in both the original Spanish and in English translation. Some of the rhymes are also finger plays with instructions included.

Maury, I. 1976. *My mother the mail carrier*. Trans. N. E. Alemany. Illus. L. McCrady. Old Westbury, NY: Feminist Press.
A four-year-old girl describes her mother, a single working woman, their special relationship, and their life together in the city. Vibrant illustrations, Spanish and English text.

Politi, L. 1946. *Pedro, the angel of Olivera Street*. New York: Scribner.
Traditional Mexican Christmas celebrations are described in this charming story about a little boy who gets his wish when the piñata is broken open.

Politi, L. 1964. *Lito and the clown*. New York: Scribner.
Lito, a young Mexican boy, has lost his beloved kitten. When the circus comes to town, he is the only one who is not excited about it. Payaso, the tall clown who walks on stilts, offers to help him find his kitten.

Rosario, I. 1981. *Idalia's project ABC–Proyecto ABC: An urban alphabet book in English and Spanish*. New York: Holt, Rinehart and Winston.
An ABC book, in both Spanish and English, which describes life in an urban housing project in a realistic yet positive manner.

Serfozo, M. 1969. *Welcome, Roberto!* Chicago: Follett.
Roberto is welcomed to a kindergarten class where the boys and girls enjoy various activities. Illustrated with black and white multicultural photographs. Text in both English and Spanish.

Smith, M. L. M. 1984. *Grandmother's adobe dollhouse*. Illus. A. Blackstone. Santa Fe: New México Magazine.
Both the building traditions and the culture of the Southwest are depicted colorfully in this picture book for children.

Soto, G. 1993. *Too many tamales*. New York: G. P. Putnam's Sons.
Maria tries on her mother's wedding ring while helping make tamales for Christmas, kneads the dough, and remembers the ring only after it is missing from her finger and the tamales are cooked. Winner of the International Reading Association Teacher's Choice Award 1994.

Soto, G. 1992. *The skirt*. New York: Dell Publishing.
On Friday, Miata brought her folklórico skirt to show off at school and left it on the bus. The skirt belonged to Miata's mother when she was a child in México. The story tells of the situations, with which children will readily identify, that Miata and Ana get into trying to retrieve the skirt before the folklórico performance on Sunday.

Taha, K. T. 1986. *A gift for Tía Rosa*. Illus. D. deRosa. Minneapolis: Dillon Press.
A tender story about a little Hispanic girl's love for her great-aunt. When Tía Rosa dies, Carmela begins to overcome her sadness by learning to pass on the love that her aunt had always bestowed on her.

CHILDREN'S LITERATURE FOR INTERMEDIATE GRADES

Picture Books

Burningham, J. 1964. *Trubloff el ratón que quería tocar la balalaica*. Valladolid: Editorial Miñón.

Trubloff, a mouse, lives with his mouse family inside the woodwork of a European inn. Trubloff loves music, wants to be a musician, and one night gets his chance to run off with a traveling gypsy troupe. More adventures follow until Trubloff is at last both reunited with his family and successful at his chosen career.

Garza, C. L. 1990. *Family Pictures: Cuadros de familia.* San Francisco: Children's Book Press.

The author/artist uses traditional Mexican folk-art techniques to illustrate some traditional and unique scenes from her childhood in a Mexican American community in Texas. The text in Spanish and English describes the family and community life experiences.

Huisot. 1988. *Quiero una medalla.* Trans. J. Mila. Barcelona: (Premio Apelles Mestres, 1987) Ediciones Destino.

A wonderful "what if" book: a general decides to start a war because he has room for one more medal on his already abundantly festooned uniform. His army is met by an army of musicians whose unexpected sounds disconcert and disarm the general's army. Soon both sides are engaged in music making and the general decides to become a conductor instead.

Marzot, J., & Marzot, L. 1981. *Las liebres blancas.* Trans. A. Alos-Moner Vila. Barcelona: Editorial Lumen.

An artist has lost his inspiration and seeks refuge in the mountains. There he becomes intrigued by the multitude of fresh hare tracks in the snow all around him. Since the hares are also white, they remain invisible and the artist becomes obsessed with the idea of catching a glimpse of one. He begins to stalk them, gun in hand. Yet it is only after he learns to put down his gun and humbly begins to sketch the trees that surround him that he is finally able to be still enough to see the forest full of hares.

Ramírez, G. C. 1983. *El robo de las Aes.* Illus. Peli. Caracas: Ekaré-Banco del Libro.

A boy's love for his father leads him to steal all of the *A*s from the typesetter of the local church newspaper. He reasons that the priest will not be able to continue his politically motivated attacks on his father, who is backing a different candidate for president. Suspense, guilt, remorse, and forgiveness are all present in this thought-provoking story.

Turin, A., & Bosnia, N. 1976. *Una feliz catástrofe.* Barcelona: Editorial Lumen.

Before the catastrophe, the Mouse family lives in a very traditional manner. Father Mouse goes to work every day, Mother Mouse keeps house, and in the evenings Father tells proud stories of youthful adventures while Mother cleans up as quietly as possible. But when one of the water pipes breaks and floods the mouse hole while Father is away at work, it is Mother who organizes the family's rescue and leads the expeditions to find a new home. Life in the Mouse family is never quite the same again.

Tusquets, E. 1980. *La conejita Marcela.* Illus. W. Masip. Barcelona: Editorial Lumen.

Once upon a time, there was a land where all of the white rabbits lived upstream, ate the best food, and looked straight ahead while the black rabbits lived downstream, kept their gaze low, and never got angry even when stepped on by the white rabbits. One day a little black rabbit is born who does not fit in. When Marcela, the little outcast rabbit, runs away and finds a land where everything is backwards (the black rabbits lord over the white rabbits instead of the other way around), she realizes that this is not a solution either. She finds an outcast partner and goes on to create a true alternative of her own.

Folklore

Alegría, C. *Fábulas y leyendas americanas.* Illus. H. Elena. Madrid: Espasa-Calpé.

A collection of seventeen fables and legends from Latin America, the Andes, and the Amazon, by a writer famous for being the first to truly portray native South American sensibilities.

Behrens, J. 1985. ¡*Fiesta!* Trans. L. Kratky. Photography by S. Taylor. Chicago: Children's Press.
Bright photographs accompany the text and document the celebration of Cinco de Mayo, a major Mexican holiday commemorating the victory over the French in 1862. The photographs were taken at community and school festivities held in Los Angeles.

Bravo-Villasante, C. 1981. *China, china, capuchina, en esta mano está la china.* Illus. C. Andrada. Valladolid: Editorial Miñón.
A comprehensive collection of riddles, rhymes, tongue twisters, songs, and other folklore. Black and white illustrations.

Corona, P. 1978. *Pita, pita cedacero: Cuentos de nanas.* Illus. E. Pisarro. México City: Organización Editorial Novarro.
Five traditional Mexican stories, illustrated in full color: a little girl outwits a king, a young boy's elder brothers are jealous of him, a stubborn street sweeper's luck finally runs out, and more.

Elizagaray, A. M. 1988. *Fábulas del Caribe.* Illus. P. Gómez. Amecameca, México: Amaquemecan, Colección Los Nogales.
Told in simple, engaging, and accessible language, these traditional Caribbean fables, many of African origin, have not previously been available.

Feliciano Mendoza, E. 1979. *Sinfonía de Puerto Rico.* San Juan: Instituto de Cultura Puertorriqueña.
Diverse elements of the natural world of Puerto Rico are transformed into the protagonists of these legends and stories.

Kurusa, & Uribe, V. 1978. *El cocuyo y la mora.* Illus. A. Areco. Caracas: Ekaré-Banco del Libro.
A beautifully illustrated Venezuelan Indian legend that tells the story of how the lightning bug came to have its phosphorescent tail.

Mendoza, V. T. 1980. *Lírica infantil de México.* México City: Fondo de Cultura Económica.
A most useful songbook, as it presents the musical notations for each song's melody. Lullabies, Christmas songs, songs that accompany games, and songs that tell a story are all included.

Ramírez, E. 1984. *Adivinanzas indígenas: Cuentos y leyendas.* Illus. M. Javier. México City: Editorial Patria.
Short riddles, written in beautiful verse, each from one of the different indigenous traditions of México. Fully illustrated.

Rohmer, H. 1982. *The legend of food mountain: La montaña del alimento.* Trans. A. F. Ada & R. Zubizarreta. San Francisco: Children's Book Press.
A pre-Hispanic Mexican legend that tells the story of the origin of corn and why it is that to this day humans must pray for rain in order to obtain the food they need.

Rohmer, H. 1987. *La tierra de la madre escorpión: Una leyenda de los indios Miskitos de Nicaragua.* Trans. R. Zubizarreta & A. F. Ada. Illus. V. Stearns. San Francisco: Children's Book Press.
This Miskito Indian legend from Nicaragua tells the story of a husband and wife who are separated by death. The husband journeys to the land of the dead in order to remain beside his beloved wife and the pair are reunited at last.

Narrative and Modern Fantasy

Ada, A. F. 1989. *Encaje de piedra.* Illus. K. L. de Passalia. Buenos Aires: Editorial Guadalupe.
Set in the Middle Ages during the construction of a great cathedral, three children are involved in solving a mystery and apprehending some thieves.

Ada, A. F. 1993. *La moneda de oro*. Illus. N. Waldman. Madrid: Editorial Everest, S.A.
The story of a thief's transformation and change of heart as he follows a *curandera* [healer] throughout the countryside, originally with the intent of robbing her of all her gold.

Aguilera, C. 1982. *Citlalli en las estrellas*. México City: Novarro.
Set in preconquest México, the story is about a little girl who discovers her grandmother is a goddess that patrols the night.

Antoniorrobles. 1986. *Cuentos de las cosas que hablan*. Illus. J. R. Alonso. Madrid: Espasa-Calpe.
Twelve short stories by Antoniorrobles, who is widely recognized as being the first children's author to incorporate a humorous and magical yet decidedly surrealist element in his fiction.

Araujo, O. 1992. *Miguel Vicente pata caliente*. Caracas, Venezuela: Ediciones Ekaré.
Miguel Vicente is a poor shoeshine boy who dreams of traveling. One day a man gives him a book about Marco Polo, telling him it describes marvelous travels. Miguel does not know how to read but he imagines the people and sights contained in the book.

Carbadillo, E. n.d. *El pizarrón encantado*. Illus. M. Figueroa. México City: CIDCLI.
Adrian finds a magic chalkboard at his uncle's house and much mischief ensues as he begins using it to make changes in the everyday routine of the household. In the end, Adrian discovers that the chalkboard can also be used to influence more serious matters.

Cárdenas, M. 1982. *Celestino y el tren*. Illus. G. Cantú. México City: Novarro.
Pablo gets to go on a journey to the capital with his father, a pack driver. After much pleading, he also gets to take his beloved burro with him. The capital is full of adventures for Pablo and new things to learn. A beautifully illustrated work of historical fiction.

Delacre, L. 1993. *Vejigante masquerader*. New York: Scholastic.
Against all odds, a resourceful Ramon manages to get a costume together for carnival. Includes information for making your own *vejigante* [large bladder] mask.

de la Vara, A. 1982. *El tronaviaje*. Illus. F. Alexander. México City: Organización Editorial Novarro.
Set in the 1560s, this book tells the story of an eleven-year-old boy who decides to become a stowaway in order to accompany his uncle on a maritime expedition from México to the Phillipines.

Echeverría, P., & Echeverría, M. 1989. *Miwi*. Barcelona: Ediciones Destino. (Premio Apelles Mestres, 1988).
Miwi, the little koala bear, is taken from his beloved home in order to be the toy of a spoiled little girl. Yet he comes to realize that the little girl who treats him so badly is very sad and lonely herself. His anger turns to compassion, which frees them both.

Kurusa. 1981. *La calle es libre*. Illus. M. Doppert. Caracas: Ekaré-Banco del Libro.
A hillside on the outskirts of town becomes covered with houses and there are no open spaces left for the children to play in. The children decide they want an empty lot to be converted into a park and take their request downtown to city hall. It's not an easy struggle, but through the efforts of the whole community, the park is finally built. This book is based on a true story that took place in Caracas, Venezuela.

Martínez Gil, F. 1985. *El río de los castores*. Madrid: Noguera.
A young beaver sets forth on a great journey to discover the source of Great Brother, the river, who has become so ill and foul that many of the animals living alongside it are dying as well. His journey takes him to the heart of where Ma, the two-legged destroyer of all other life, lives.

Martí, J. 1972. *La edad de oro*. Buenos Aires: Editorial Nueva Senda S.R.L.

A classic by the great Cuban writer and leader José Martí, this book is a compilation of the four issues of the children's magazine of the same name that he published in New York in 1889, "for all the children of the Americas." The book consists of stories, biographies, poems, and informative articles, all of enduring value.

Matute, A. M. 1975. *El saltamontes verde*. Illus. C. Jaume. Barcelona: Editorial Lumen.

Two very moving stories. The first is about a boy who has lost his voice and travels the world over in search of it. The second story is about a miser to whom the whole town is indebted, and how he comes to have a change of heart.

Petterson, A. 1985. *El papalote y el nopal*. Illus. H. Ramirez. México City: CIDELI.

A kite flies high above everything until it is drenched by rain and sinks back to the earth. It lands on a solitary cactus, yet all the love and care the cactus bestows on the kite do not convince the kite to stay once it is dry again.

Puncel, M. 1983. *Abuelita Opalina*. Illus. M. Puncel. Madrid: Ediciones SM.

When Miss Laura asks the class to write a composition about one of their grandmothers, Isa has to make one up because she never knew her own. She borrows bits and pieces of her classmates' grandmothers in order to create her own imaginary grandma, but she has no idea of the trouble and misunderstanding that will ensue in this humorous and tender story.

Uribe, M. de la L. 1983. *La Señorita Amelia*. Illus. F. Krahn. Barcelona: Ediciones Destino. (Premio Apelles Mestre, 1982).

Miss Amelia is a tiny woman, so tiny that for the most part it is only children who can see her. She loves birds and the smell of fresh peaches. When she flies away, carried by her birds on a carpet made of leaves, the three children she has befriended will remember her as long as they live.

Valeri, M. E. 1982. *El pez de oro*. Trans. J. E. Pastor Canada. Illus. F. Risá. Barcelona: La Galera.

A new adaptation of an old Russian folktale about a magic fish that can grant wishes. Unfortunately, greed prevails over common sense and after a series of ever more extravagant wishes, the fisherman and his wife end up right back where they started.

White, E. B. 1988. *La telaraña de Carlota*. Trans. G. Solana. Illus. G. Williams. Barcelona: Noguera.

The classic children's story about the wise and loving spider who saves a young pig's life.

Poetry

Ada, A. F. 1987. *Una vez en el medio del mar*. Illus. U. Wensell. Madrid: Editorial Escuela Española.

This book of verses consists of four parts. It begins with short fantasies told in verse, which star different animal characters. It continues with a selection of counting verses, another selection of alphabet poems, and concludes with a selection of poems about dragons entitled "In Dragon Country." The poems are simple, humorous, and full of delight.

Carballo, F. M. (Ed.). 1962. *Los poetas*. México City: Fernández Editores, Colección Biblioteca Auriga.

A resource book for teachers containing a very select collection of the best of Hispanic poetry from Spain and the Americas. Footnotes are provided in the back to give some context and historical perspective on the poets that are included.

Ferrán, J. 1982. *Tarde del circo*. Illus. C. D'Ors. Valladolid: Editorial Miñón.
A series of inspired poems, each highlighting a different aspect of the circus, from the different circus animals to the performers to memories of circuses past.

Pelegrín, A. (Ed.). 1983. *Poesía española para niños*. Madrid: Taurus.
Grouped by subject matter, this collection offers a selection of the best of children's poetry from Spain.

Uribe, M. de la L. 1979. *Cuenta que te cuento*. Illus. F. Krahn. Barcelona: Editorial Juventud.
A collection of humorous stories told in delightful verse: a kingdom made entirely of paper, a tearful lady who is wooed by a gentleman who croaks like a frog, and a soldier who lives inside a melon.

Vega, B. de la. 1960. *Antología de la poesía infantil*. Buenos Aires: Editorial Kapelusz.
Although it was originally published in 1958, this is a useful anthology for teachers because it is grouped by age level and contains many classic poems.

Walsh, M. E. 1970. *Zoo loco*. Illus. Vilar. Buenos Aires: Editorial Sudamericana.
A collection of zany limericks, each written tongue in cheek and with a different animal as a theme. An excellent inspiration for a classroom writing project.

Walsh, M. E. 1977. *Tutú Marumbá*. Illus. Vilar. Buenos Aires: Editorial Sudamericana.
Whoever said poetry had to be serious? A series of humorous poems that are sure to tickle any child's funny bone.

Plays

Armijo, C. 1981. *Bam, bim, bom: Arriba el telón*. Illus. C. Andrada. Valladolid: Editorial Miñón.
Giants and dwarves playing tricks on each other, a king who wants two birthdays a year, an extraterrestrial fantasy . . . six short and humorous plays designed to be easily staged by children.

Fuertes, G. n.d. *Las tres reinas: Melchora, Gáspara, y Baltasara*. Illus. U. Wensell. Barcelona: Editorial Lumen.
Tradition is stood on its head as the three wise queens journey to visit the Prince of Peace instead of their husbands; the three wise men are all either off at war or the victims of it. Instructions for costumes and staging are included in the back of the book.

Giménez Pastor, M. l974. *¡Respetable público!* Illus. R. Fortín. Buenos Aires: Librería Huemul.
Six plays for puppets written by the well-known Argentine author Marta Giménez Pastor. Although the plays were written for professional puppeteers, they are simple enough that children will enjoy staging the plays themselves.

Menotti, G. C. 1963. *Amahl y los Reyes Magos*. Trans. A. Díaz-Plaja. Illus. J. M. Cuixart. Barcelona: Editorial Lumen.
This is a narrative version of the famous opera by Menotti about the little lame boy and his mother who host the Three Wise Men on their journey to visit the New King. Children can enjoy reading the story, then use it to create their own script and enact their own version of the play.

Vásquez Vigo, C. 1984. *Jugar al teatro*. Valladolid: Editorial Miñón.
Two short plays are included in this book, both using the technique of a play-within-a-play. The first play is about four children at home with chicken pox who are bored until they decide to create a performance. To their surprise, they receive some unexpected visitors. In the second play, three children use costumes in order to play a trick on a stingy and selfish old man who is making life miserable for them.

Informative Books

Abbado, C. 1986. *La casa de los sones*. Barcelona: Ediciones Destino.
  Written by a conductor, this book begins with an autobiographical account of how the author's love for music developed when he was a child. It then proceeds to describe the different families of instruments that make up an orchestra, the role of a conductor, and different genres of classical music.

Ancona, J. 1993. *Pablo recuerda la fiesta del día de los muertos*. New York: Lothrop, Lee & Shepard.
  During the three-day celebration of the Day of the Dead, Pablo and his family make elaborate preparations to honor the spirits of the dead.

Broekel, R. 1984. *Tus cinco sentidos*. Trans. L. Kratky. Chicago: Children's Press.
  Simple yet thoroughly scientific explanations of the five senses and how each of them operates.

Clark, M. L. 1984. *Dinosaurios*. Trans. L. Kratky. Chicago: Children's Press.
  An informative book on an ever popular subject among children.

Friskey, M. 1984. *Lanzaderas espaciales*. Trans. L. Kratky. Chicago: Children's Press.
  Space shuttles, space laboratories, and the world of new possibilities that they allow are explored in the text and abundantly illustrated through NASA photographs.

Gleiter, J., & Thompson, K. 1989. *Diego Rivera*. Trans. G. Contreras. Illus. Y. Miyake. Milwaukee: Raintree.
  An illustrated biography in Spanish and English of the famous Mexican muralist. Diego Rivera's social and political concerns are highlighted, as well as his artistic accomplishments.

Gleiter, J., & Thomson, K. 1989. *Miguel Hidalgo y de Costilla*. Trans. G. Contreras. Illus. R. Karpinski. Milwaukee: Raintree.
  The life story and historic deeds of the "Father of the Mexican Revolution" are told in both Spanish and English. Fully illustrated.

Jacobsen, K. 1985. *México*. Trans. L. Kratky. Chicago: Children's Press.
  Geography, culture, and history are all covered in this balanced presentation of México, illustrated with many colorful photographs.

Lewellen, J. 1984. *La luna, el sol, y las estrellas*. Trans. L. Kratky. Chicago: Children's Press.
  A scientific explanation of the wonders of the universe, illustrated with excellent photographs and diagrams. (Not meant, however, to be a substitute for the direct experience of gazing at a starry night.)

Books in English

Ada, A. F. 1993. *My name is María Isabel*. New York: Atheneum.
  Third-grader María Isabel, born in Puerto Rico and now living in the United States, wants badly to fit in at school, and the teacher's writing assignment "My Greatest Wish" gives her that opportunity.

Borton de Trevino, E. 1965. *I, Juan de Pareja*. New York: Farrar, Straus & Giroux. (Newberry Medal winner.)
  An engrossing historical novel in autobiographical form. Juan de Pareja, the son of an African woman and a Spanish man, is born as a slave. He eventually is given to the great Spanish painter Velásquez. Juan also becomes a painter and is at last granted his freedom,

while his relationship with Velásquez, which begins as master and slave, ends up becoming one of companionship, equality, and friendship.

Fisher, L. E. 1988. *Pyramid of the sun, pyramid of the moon*. New York: Macmillan.
A beautifully illustrated picture book for older readers that tells the story of ancient Toltec pyramids.

Franchere, R. 1970. *César Chávez*. Illus. E. Thollander. New York: Crowell.
A biography of the noted Chicano leader who was a disciple of Gandhi and King and the founder of the Farmworkers Union. Written in a direct, simple, and engaging style.

Gonzales, R. 1972. *I am Joaquín*. New York: Bantam Books.
An epic poem, published here in both English and Spanish, celebrating the Chicano people, their heritage and struggles, and the Chicano movement.

Mohr, N. 1986. *Going home*. New York: Dial Books for Young Readers.
Felita is a young Puerto Rican girl who has lived in New York all of her life and is going to visit her relatives in Puerto Rico for the first time. The challenges she encounters become opportunities for her to grow and develop her personal strength.

Mohr, N. 1989. *Nilda*. Houston: Arte Público Press.
Set in early 1940s New York, this is a story of a young Puerto Rican girl's coming of age. A sensitive portrayal of a young girl's feelings and inner life, and a vivid, realistic depiction of the social inequities and discrimination that Nilda, her family, and her community endure.

Mora, P. 1993. *Tomás and the library lady*. New York: Knopf.
Tomás and his family journey every year from Texas to the Midwest as migrant workers. Along the way he has an encounter with a library lady.

Rohmer, H. 1989. *Uncle Nacho's hat*. Emeryville, CA: Children's Book Press.
Uncle Nacho's niece, Ambrosia, gives him a new hat because his old one is tattered. Yet Uncle Nacho has such hilarious difficulties trying to get rid of the old hat that he forgets to enjoy his new one until his niece comes by again to remind him.

Salinas, L. O., & Faderman, L. (Eds.). 1973. *From the barrio: A Chicano anthology*. San Francisco: Canfield Press.
Essays, drama, poetry, and fiction are included in this anthology of Chicano writing. Not all of the selections included will be appropriate for children, yet the ones that are will make for engaging and motivating reading material.

Soto, G. 1992. *Neighborhood odes*. New York: Scholastic.
A collection of poems that tell of the daily sights, sounds, scenes, mysteries, and pleasures of the neighborhood.

CONTENT-AREA CHILDREN'S BOOKS

Science

Adler, D. 1987. *El mar y sus maravillas: Quiero conocer*. México: Sistemas Técnicos de Edición.
Others in Quiero Conocer series: *La vida de los animales; El agua y sus maravillas; Montañas y volcanes; Las islas y sus maravillas; El mundo del sonido; La vida de las plantas; El mundo de los árboles; Los ríos y sus maravillas; Migraciones animales*

Pacheco, M. A., & García Sánchez, J. L. 1974. *Soy una gota*. Madrid: Ediciones Altea. (K–1, Spanish, beautiful illustrations)
  Others in series *La Naturaleza: Soy el aire; Soy el fuego; Soy el sol; Soy un árbol; Soy un niño; Soy un pájaro; Soy un pez; Soy una fiera; Soy una roca*

Rius, M., & Parramón, J. M. 1987. *La vida bajo la tierra*. New York: Barron's.
  Other series and titles:
    Serie La Vida: *La vida bajo tierra; La vida en el mar; La vida en el aire; La vida sobre la tierra*
    Serie Las Cuatro Estaciones: *La primavera; El verano: El otoño; El invierno*
    Serie Los Cuatro Elementos: *La tierra; El aire; El fuego; El agua*
    Serie Un Día en . . .: *La montaña; El mar; El campo; La ciudad*
    Serie Los Cinco Sentidos: *La vista; El oído; El olfato; El gusto; El tacto*
    Serie La Familia: *Los niños; Los jóvenes; Los padres; Los abuelos*

Seymour, P. 1986. *Explorando el sistema solar: Un libro de Ciencia-Acción*. Buenos Aires: Editorial Atlántida.
  Others in series *Ciencia en acción: Descubriendo nuestro pasado; Los insectos en acción; Cómo funciona el tiempo*

Spamer, I. 1981. *El universo: El medio ambiente*. México, D. F.: Editorial Patria, S. A.
  Other series and titles in Colección Piñata:
    Serie El Medio Ambiente: *El agua; El mar; El universo*
    Serie La Flora: *Las frutas; El maíz*
    Serie Las Artes: *Sonidos y ritmos; Los títeres*
    Serie Las Materias Primas: *El barro; La lana; El papel; La seda; Tres colorantes prehispánicos; El azúcar; El chocolate*
    Serie La Vida Social: *El campo y la ciudad; El mercado*
    Serie Cuentos y Leyendas: *Adivinanzas indígenas*
    Serie Nuestro País: *La zona del silencio (México)*

Webster, V. R. 1986. *Experimentos Científicos: Así es mi mundo*. Chicago: Children's Press. (Translations)
  Others in *Así es mi mundo* series: *Dinosaurios; Experimentos atmosféricos; Experimentos científicos; La luna, el sol, y las estrellas; Lanzaderas espaciales; La policía; Los presidentes; México*

Social Studies

Aboites, L. 1983. *El campo y la ciudad*. México, D. F.: Editorial Patria.

Bebrens, J. 1984. *Puedo ser: Un astronauta*. Chicago: Children's Press.
  Others in series Puedo ser: *Conductor de camión; Jugador de béisbol*

Chlad, D. 1984. *Pueblo de seguridad*. Trans. L. Kratky. Chicago: Children's Press.
  Others in series: *Cuando cruzo la calle; Cuando hay un incendio, sal para afuera; Es divertido andar en bicicleta; Jugando en el patio de recreo; Los desconocidos; Viajando en autobús*

Fradin, D. B. 1987. *California en palabras y fotos*. Chicago: Children's Press.
  Others in series: *Texas en palabras y fotos*

García Sánchez, J. L. 1977. *Soy un banco*. Madrid: Ediciones Altea.
  Others in series Serie Roja: *Soy un circo; Soy un estadio; Soy una escuela; Soy un hospital; Soy un hotel; Soy un museo; Soy una estación; Soy un cine; Soy una tienda*

SUMMARY

The classroom environment created by the teacher and students will define how students interact with each other and with the assembled resources. When children are bombarded by print, attractive and interesting books, and a variety of media, their curiosity will lead them to explore the multiple ways of learning and using their reading and writing ability. Classrooms must be safe places, full of opportunities for children to experiment, to assume a range of roles, to make mistakes, to assess and try again, and to expand their repertoires. In assembling your classroom environment you will need to identify community and professional resources that will allow the students to integrate and expand on their linguistic and cultural resources.

ACTIVITIES

Journal Writing

1. Think about an environment that either relaxes or excites you. Reflect on the elements (color, lighting, sounds, furnishings, etc.) that contribute to these feelings.
2. Reread one of your favorite poems. Identify your feelings while reading the poem. Write about your feelings and the elements of the poem that contribute to these feelings.

Discussion Activities

1. Role play a parent/teacher visit or conference in which you are inviting the parents to share their knowledge about their children's preferred learning environment.
2. In small groups compare your observation assessment of biliteracy environments conducted in Field-Based Activity 1. In your discussion, contribute your personal responses to the climate of the classroom observed.

Field-Based Activities

1. Use the biliteracy environment checklist (Figure 8.1) to assess the environment, the levels of interaction (collaborative group work, whole class, individual student/teacher) and the types of learning that are facilitated by the environment.
2. Drive or walk around the neighborhood (three to four city blocks in all directions) of an elementary school and identify resources that might be available for teachers/students to invite and incorporate in their literacy studies.

NOTE

1. Rosalma Zubizarreta compiled the children's literature section in the first edition; the current changes are ours.

References

Ada, A. F. 1987. *A children's literature-based whole language approach to creative reading and writing*. Northvale, NJ: Santillana.

Ada, A. F. 1988. The Pajaro Valley experience: Working with Spanish-speaking parents to develop children's reading and writing skills in the home through the use of children's literature. In T. Skutnabb-Kangas & J. Cummins (Eds.), *Minority education: From shame to struggle*. Philadelphia: Multilingual Matters.

Ada, A. F. 1990. *A magical encounter: Spanish language literature in the classroom*. Compton, CA: Santillana.

Agar, M. H. 1980. *The professional stranger: An informal introduction to ethnography*. New York: Academic Press.

Allen, R. V. 1986. Developing contexts to support second language acquisition. *Language Arts, 63*(1), 61–66.

Alvarez, C. 1988. The social significance of code-switching in narrative performance. Ph.D diss., University of Pennsylvania, Philadelphia.

Anderson, A. B., & Teale, W. H. 1982. La lecto-escritura como práctica cultural. In E. Ferreiro & M. Gómez Palacio (Eds.), *Nuevas perspectivas sobre los procesos de lectura y escritura*. México, DF: Siglo Veintiuno Editores.

Anderson, A. B., Teale, W. H., & Estrada, E. 1980. Low-income children's preschool literacy experience: Some naturalistic observations. *The Quarterly Newsletter of the Laboratory of Comparative Human Cognition, 2*(3), 59–65.

Anderson, T., & Boyer, W. 1970. *Bilingual schooling in the United States*. Austin, TX: Southwest Educational Development Laboratory.

Anderson-Inman, L. 1987. The reading-writing connection: Classroom applications for the computer. *The Computing Teacher, 14*(6), 15–18.

Applebee, A. N., & Langer, J. A. 1984. Instructional scaffolding: Reading and writing as natural language activities. In J. M. Jenson (Ed.), *Composing and comprehending*. Urbana, IL: National Conference on Research in English.

Arias, M. B., & Casanova, U. 1993. *Bilingual education: Politics, practice, and research*. Chicago: The University of Chicago Press.

Askov, E., & Kamm, M. 1989. *Upgrading basic skills for the workplace*. University Park: Pennsylvania State University, Institute for the Study of Adult Literacy.

Au, K. H., 1995. Multicultural perspectives on literacy research. *Journal of Reading Behavior, 27*(1), 85–100.

Au, K. H., & Jordan, C. 1981. Teaching reading to Hawaiian children: Finding a culturally appropriate solution. In H. T. Trueba, G. P. Guthrie, & K. H. Au (Eds.), *Culture and the bilingual classroom*. Rowley, MA: Newbury House.

Baker, C., & Freebody, P. 1988. Talk around text: Construction of textual and teacher authority in classroom discourse. In S. de Castell, A. Luke, & C. Luke (Eds.), *Language, authority and criticism: Readings on the school textbook*. London: Falmer Press.

Barrera, R. B. 1978. Analysis and comparison of the first language and reading behavior of native Spanish-speaking Mexican-American children. Ph.D. diss., University of Texas, Austin.

Barrera, R. B. 1981. Reading in Spanish: Insights from children's miscues. In S. Hudelson (Ed.), *Learning to read in different languages*. Washington, DC: Center for Applied Linguistics.

Basso, K., & Anderson, N. 1973. A Western Apache writing system: The symbols of Silas John. *Science*, *180*(4090), 1013–1021.

Bean, F. D., & Tienda, M. 1987. *The Hispanic Population of the United States*. New York: Russell Sage Foundation.

Bellenger, L. 1979. *Los métodos de lectura*. Barcelona: Oikos-tau.

Belpré, P. 1969. *Santiago*. New York: Viking.

Bereiter, C. 1994. Constructivism, socioculturalism, and Popper's world 3. *Educational Researcher*, *23*, 21–23.

Berglund, R. L. 1989–1990. Convention sessions address whole language evaluation. *Reading Today*, *7*, 3.

Bergman, C. R. 1976. Interference vs. independent development in infant bilingualism. In G. D. Keller, R. V. Teschner, & S. Viera (Eds.), *Bilingualism in the bicentennial and beyond*. New York: Bilingual Press.

Berkey, R., Curtis, T., Minnick, F., Zietlow, K., Campbell, D., & Kirschner, B. W. 1990. Collaborating for reflective practice: Voices of teachers, administrators, and researchers. *Education and Urban Society*, *22*, 204–232.

Bermudez, A. B., & Palumbo, D. 1994. Bridging the gap between literacy and technology: Hypermedia as learning tool for limited-English-proficient students. *The Journal of Educational Issues of Language Minority Students*, *14*, 165–184.

Bissex, F. L. 1980. *Gnys at wrk: A child learns to write and read*. Cambridge: Harvard University Press.

Blocksma, M. 1986. *El oso más elegante*. Chicago: Children's Press.

Bloom, A. 1987. *The closing of the American mind: How higher education has failed democracy and impoverished the souls of today's students*. New York: Simon & Schuster.

Bloome, D. 1985. Reading as a social process. *Language Arts*, *62*, 134–142.

Borasi, R., Sheedy, J. R., & Siegel, M. 1990. The power of stories in learning mathematics. *Language Arts*, *67*(2), 174–189.

Brandt, D. L. 1983. Writer, context, and text. Ph.D. diss., Indiana University, Bloomington.

Bredo, E., Henry, M., & McDermott, R. P. 1990. The cultural organization of teaching and learning. *Harvard Educational Review*, *60*(2), 247–258.

Brown, J. S., Collins, A., & Duguid, P. 1989. Situated cognition and the culture of learning. *Educational Researcher*, *18*(1), 32–41.

Bruner, J. S. 1975a. Language as an instrument of thought. In A. Davies (Ed.), *Problems of language and learning*. London: Heinemann.

Bruner, J. S. 1975b. The ontogenesis of speech acts. *Journal of Child Language*, *2*, 1–19.

Bruner, J. S. 1978. The role of dialogue in language acquisition. In A. Sinclair, R. Javella, & W. Levelt (Eds), *The child's conception of language*. New York: Springer-Verlag.

Bruner, J. S. 1994. Life as narrative. In A. H. Dyson & C. Genishi, (Eds.), *The need for story:*

Cultural diversity in classroom and community. Urbana, IL: National Council of Teachers of English.

Burns, M. S., Haywood, H. C., & Delclos, V. R. 1987. Young children's problem solving strategies: An observational study. *Journal of Applied Developmental Psychology, 8,* 113–121.

Calkins, L. 1986. *The art of teaching writing*. Portsmouth, NH: Heinemann.

Canales, J. 1993. Innovative assessment in traditional settings. In J. V. Tinajero & A. F. Ada (Eds.), *The power of two languages: Literacy and biliteracy for Spanish-speaking students* (pp. 132–142). New York: Macmillan/McGraw-Hill.

Carpenter, T. P., Fennema, E., Peterson, P. L., Chiang, C. P., & Loef, M. 1989. Using knowledge of children's mathematical thinking in classroom teaching: An experimental study. *American Educational Research Journal, 26,* 499–531.

Carpenter, T. P., & Moser, J. M. 1983. The acquisition of addition and subtraction concepts. In R. Lesh & M. Landau (Eds.), *The acquisition of mathematics concepts and processes* (pp. 7–44). Orlando, FL.: Academic Press.

Carrasco, R. L. 1981. Expanded awareness of student performance: A case study in applied ethnographic monitoring in a bilingual classroom. In H. T. Trueba, G. P. Guthrie, & K. H. Au (Eds.), *Culture and the bilingual classroom: Studies in classroom ethnography*. Rowley, MA: Newbury House.

Carrasco, R. L. 1984. Collective engagement in the "segundo hogar": A microethnography of engagement in a bilingual first grade classroom. Ph.D diss., Harvard University, Cambridge, MA.

Carrasquillo, A., & Núñez, D. 1988. Computer-assisted metacognitive strategies and the reading comprehension skills of ESL elementary school students. *Research/Technical, 143,* 1–17.

Carrell, P. L., Pharis, B. G., & Liberto, J. C. 1988. Metacognitive strategy training for ESL reading. *TESOL Quarterly, 23*(4), 647–649.

Carrow, E. 1971. Comprehension of English and Spanish by pre-school Mexican-American children. *Modern Language Journal, 55,* 299–306.

Carrow, E. 1972. Auditory comprehension of English by monolingual and bilingual pre-school children. *Journal of Speech and Hearing Research, 15,* 407–457.

Cazden, C. B. 1983. Adult assistance to language development: Scaffolds, models, and direct instruction. In R. P. Parker & F. A. David (Eds.), *Developing literacy: Young children's use of language*. Newark, DE: International Reading Association.

Cazden, C. B. 1986. ESL teachers as language advocates for children. In P. Rigg & D. S. Enright (Eds.), *Children and ESL: Integrating perspectives*. Washington, DC: Teachers of English to Speakers of Other Languages.

Cazden, C. B. 1987. English for academic purposes: The student-talk register. *English Education, 19,* 31–43.

Cazden, C. B. 1988. *Classroom discourse: The language of teaching and learning*. Portsmouth, NH: Heinemann.

Cervantes, M. N. d. *La aventura de los leones*. Madrid: Editorial Everest, S.A.

Chamot, A., & O'Malley, M. 1987. The cognitive academic language learning approach: A bridge to the mainstream. *TESOL Quarterly, 21,* 227–250.

Chomsky, C. 1969. *The acquisition of syntax in children from 5–10*. Cambridge, MA: MIT Press.

Chomsky, C. 1971. Write first, read later. *Childhood Education, 47,* 296–299.

Chu, H. S. 1981. *Testing instruments for reading skills: English and Korean (grades 1–3)*. Technical report, George Mason University, Fairfax, VA.

Claret, M. 1986. *Los tres osos*. Barcelona: Editorial Juventud.

Claret, M. 1988. *Pedrito conejo, pintor.* Barcelona: Editorial Juventud.

Clay, M. 1975. *What did I write?* London: Heinemann.

Cobb, P., Yachel, E., & Wood, T. 1988. Curriculum and teacher development: Psychological and anthropological perspectives. In E. Fennema, T. P. Carpenter, & S. J. Lamon (Eds.), *Integrating research on teaching and learning mathematics: Papers from the first Wisconsin Symposium for Research on Teaching and Learning Mathematics.* Madison: University of Wisconsin, Wisconsin Center for Education Research.

Cognition and Technology Group at Vanderbilt. 1990. Anchored instruction and its relationship to situated cognition. *Educational Research, 19*(6), 2–10.

Cohen, E. G. 1987. *Designing groupwork: Strategies for the heterogeneous classroom.* New York: Teachers College Press.

Cohen, E. G., & De Avila, E. 1983. *Learning to think in math and science: Improving local education for minority children.* Final report to the Walter S. Johnson Foundation, Stanford University, Stanford, CA.

Cole, N. 1988. A realist's appraisal of the prospects for unifying instruction and assessment. In C. V. Bunderson (Ed.), *Assessment in the service of learning* (pp. 103–117). Princeton, NJ: Educational Testing Service.

Commins, N. L. 1989. Language and affect: Bilingual students at home and at school. *Language Arts, 66*(1), 29–43.

Commins, N. L., & Miramontes, O. B. 1989. Perceived and actual linguistic competence: A descriptive study of four low-achieving Hispanic bilingual students. *American Educational Research Journal, 26*(4), 443–472.

Compton's NewMedia, 1994. *Compton's Interactive Encyclopedia.* Calsbad, CA: Compton's Learning Company.

Conklin, H. 1949. Bamboo literacy in Mindora. *Pacific Discovery, 2,* 4–11.

Cook-Gumperz, J. 1986. Introduction: The social construction of literacy. In J. Cook-Gumperz (Ed.), *The social construction of literacy.* Cambridge: Cambridge University Press.

Couture, B. (Ed.). 1986. *Functional approaches to writing: Research perspectives.* London: Frances Pinter.

Cummins, J. 1979. Cognitive/academic language proficiency, linguistic interdependence, the optimum age question and some other matters. *Working Papers on Bilingualism, 19,* 121–129.

Cummins, J. 1981. The role of primary language development in promoting educational success for language minority students. In Office of Bilingual Bicultural Education (Eds.), *Schooling and language minority students: A theoretical framework.* Los Angeles: California State University, Evaluation, Dissemination, and Assessment Center.

Cummins, J. 1989. The sanitized curriculum: Education disempowerment in a nation at risk. In D. M. Johnson & D. H. Roen (Eds.), *Richness in writing: Empowering ESL students.* White Plains, NY: Longman.

Cunningham, P. M., Moore, S. A., Cunningham, J. W., & Moore, D. W. 1983. *Reading in elementary classrooms: Strategies and observations.* White Plains, NY: Longman.

Daiute, C. A. 1983. Writing, creativity, and change. *Childhood Education, 59,* 227–231.

Daiute, C. A. 1986. Physical and cognitive factors in revising: Insights from studies with computers. *Research in the Teaching of English, 20*(2) 141–159.

Davies, F. D. 1986. *Books in the school curriculum.* London: Educational Publishers Council and National Book League.

Dávila de Silva, A. 1983. The Spanish reading process and Spanish-speaking Mexican American children. In T. H. Escobedo (Ed.), *Early childhood bilingual education: A Hispanic perspective.* New York: Teachers College Press.

Davison, D., & Reyhner, K. 1992. Student generated story problems. *Arithmetic Teacher, 39,* 6–12.

De Avila, E. A., Duncan, S. E., & Navarrete, C. J. 1987. *Finding out/Descubrimiento. Teacher's Resource Guide.* Northvale, NJ: Santillana Publishing Co.

Delgado-Gaitán, C. 1987. Traditions and transitions in the learning process of Mexican children: An ethnographic view. In G. Spindler & L. Spindler (Eds.), *Interpretive ethnography of education: At home and abroad.* Hillsdale, NJ: Lawrence Erlbaum Associates.

Delgado-Gaitán, C. 1994. Sociocultural change through literacy: Toward the empowerment of families. In B. M. Ferdman, F. M. Weber, & A. G. Ramírez (Eds.), *Literacy across languages and cultures.* Albany: State University of New York Press.

Delpit, L. 1986. Skills and other dilemmas of a progressive black educator. *Harvard Educational Review, 56*(4), 379–385.

Díaz, S., Moll, L. C., & Mehan, H. 1986. Sociocultural resources in instruction: A context-specific approach. In *Beyond Language: Social and cultural factors in schooling language minority students.* Los Angeles: California State University, Evaluation, Dissemination and Assessment Center.

Donaldson, M. 1978. *Children's minds.* New York: Norton.

Downing, J. 1987. Comparative perspectives on world literacy. In D. Wagner (Ed.), *The future of literacy in a changing world.* Oxford: Pergamon Press.

Duffy, G. G., Roehler, L. R., & Herrmann, B. A. 1988. Modeling mental processes helps poor readers become strategic readers. *The Reading Teacher, 41*(8), 762–767.

Duin, A. 1987. Computer exercises to encourage rethinking and revision. *Computers and Composition, 4,* 66–105.

Durkin, D. 1966. *Children who read early.* New York: Teachers College Press.

Durkin, D. 1989. *Teaching them to read* (5th ed.). Boston: Allyn & Bacon.

Dyson, A. H. 1981. Oral language: The rooting system for learning to write. *Language Arts, 58,* 776–784.

Edelsky, C. 1978. Teaching oral language. *Language Arts, 55,* 291–296.

Edelsky, C. 1986. *Writing in a bilingual program: Había una vez.* Norwood, NJ: Ablex.

Ehlert, L. 1992. *Moon rope: Un lazo a la luna.* New York: Putnam.

Elías-Olivares, L. 1983. Preface. In L. Elías-Olivares (Ed.), *Spanish in the U.S. setting: Beyond the Southwest.* Rosalyn, VA: National Clearinghouse for Bilingual Education.

Elley, W., & Mangubhai, F. 1983. The impact of reading on second language readers. *Reading Research Quarterly, 19,* 53–67.

Emig, J. 1982. Literacy and freedom. Speech presented at the Conference on College Composition Annual Meeting, San Francisco.

Engle, P. J. 1975. Language medium in early school years for minority language groups. *Review of Educational Research, 45,* 283–325.

English-Language Arts Curriculum Framework and Criteria Committee. 1987. *English language arts framework for California public school kindergarten through grade twelve.* Sacramento: California State Department of Education.

Enright, D. S., & McCloskey, M. 1985. Yes talking!: Organizing the classroom to promote second language acquisition. *TESOL Quarterly, 19,* 431–453.

Erickson, F. 1971. The cycle of situational frames: A model for microethnography in urban anthropology. Paper presented at Midwest Anthropology Meeting, Detroit, MI.

Erickson, F. 1987. Transformation and school success: The politics and culture of educational achievement. *Anthropology & Education Quarterly, 18*(4), 335–356.

Erickson, F., & Shultz, J. 1981. When is a context? Some issues and methods in the analysis of social competence. In J. Green & C. Wallet (Eds.), *Ethnography and language in educational settings.* Norwood, NJ: Ablex.

Escamilla, K. 1994. The sociolinguistic environment of a bilingual school: A case study introduction. *Bilingual Research Journal, 18*(1&2), 21–48.

Escobedo, T. (Ed.). 1983. *Early childhood bilingual education: A Hispanic perspective*. New York: Teachers College Press.

Faltis, C. J. 1989. Code-switching and bilingual schooling: An examination of Jacobson's new concurrent approach. *Journal of Multilingual and Multicultural Development, 10*(2), 117–127.

Fantini, A. 1974. Language acquisition of a bilingual child: A sociolinguistic perspective. Ph.D. diss., University of Texas, Austin.

Farr, R. 1992. Putting it all together: Solving the reading assessment puzzle. *Reading Teacher, 46*, 26–37.

Feliciano Mendoza, E. 1983. Un cuento de elefantes. *Cajita de música* (pp. 25–26). Rio Piedras: Editorial de la Universidad de Puerto Rico.

Feliciano Mendoza, E. 1985. Desfile del circo. *Ilán-ilán* (pp. 25–26). Rio Piedras: Editorial de la Universidad de Puerto Rico.

Ferdman, B. M. 1990. Literacy and cultural identity. *Harvard Educational Review, 60*, 181–204.

Ferdman, B. M., Weber, R. M., & Ramírez, A. G. 1994. *Literacy across languages and cultures*. Albany: State University of New York Press.

Ferreiro, E. 1982. Los procesos constructivos de apropiación de la escritura. In E. Ferreiro & M. Gómez Palacio (Eds.), *Nuevas perspectivas sobre los procesos de lectura y escritura*. México City: Siglo Veintiuno Editores.

Ferreiro, E. 1989. The interplay between information and assimilation in beginning literacy. In W. Teale & E. Sulzby (Eds.), *Emergent literacy*. Norwood, NJ: Ablex.

Ferreiro, E. 1990. Literacy development: Psychogenesis. In Y. M. Goodman (Ed.), *How children construct literacy*. Newark, DE: International Reading Association.

Ferreiro, E., & Teberosky, A. 1982. *Los sistemas de escritura en el desarrollo del niño*. México, DF: Siglo Veintiuno Editores. (English translation, *Literacy before schooling*. Exeter, NH: Heinemann, 1982.)

Flood, J. 1986. The text, the student, and the teacher: Learning from exposition in middle schools. *Journal of Reading, 39*, 784–791.

Flores, B. 1981. Bilingual reading instructional practices: The three views of the reading process as they relate to the concept of language interference. *Journal of Teacher Education, 8*, 45–52.

Flores, B., & Garcia, E. A. 1984. A collaborative learning and teaching experience using journal writing. *Journal of the National Association for Bilingual Education, 8*(2), 67–83.

Flores, B., Garcia, E., Gonzales, S., Hidalgo, G., Kaczmarek, K., & Romero, T. 1985. *Bilingual holistic instructional strategies*. Chandler, AZ: Exito.

Freeman, Y. S. 1988. Métodos de lectura en español: ¿Reflejan nuestro conocimiento actual del proceso de lectura? *Lectura y Vida, 9*(3), 20–27.

Freire, P. 1970. *Pedagogy of the oppressed*. New York: Seabury Press.

Freire, P., & Macedo, D. 1987. *Literacy: Reading the world*. South Hadley, MA: Bergin & Garvey.

Galarza, E. 1971. *Barrio boy*. Notre Dame, IN: University of Notre Dame Press.

García, E. 1983a. *Early childhood bilingualism*. Albuquerque: University of New Mexico Press.

García, E. 1983b. Bilingual acquisition and bilingual instruction. In T. H. Escobedo (Ed.), *Early childhood bilingual education: A Hispanic perspective*. New York: Teachers College Press.

García, M. W., & Verville, K. 1994. Redesigning teaching and learning: The Arizona Student

Assessment Program. In S. W. Valencia, E. H. Hiebert, & P. P. Afflerbach (Eds.), *Authentic reading assessment: Practices and possibilities* (pp. 228–246). Newark, DE: International Reading Association.

Garfinkel, H. 1967. *Studies in ethnomethodology.* Englewood Cliffs, NJ: Prentice-Hall.

Genishi, C. 1976. Rules for code-switching in young Spanish-English speakers: An exploratory study of language socialization. Ph.D. diss., University of California, Berkeley.

Genishi, C., & Dyson, A. 1984. *Language assessment in the early years.* Norwood, NJ: Ablex.

Gibson, M. A. 1983. Home-school-community linkages: A study of educational opportunity for Punjabi youth. Washington, DC: National Institute of Education.

Gibson, M. A. 1987a. Punjabi immigrants in an American high school. In G. Spindler & E. Spindler (Eds.), *Interpersonal ethnography of education: At home and abroad* (pp. 281–310). Hillsdale, NJ: Lawrence Erlbaum.

Gibson, M. A. 1987b. The school performance of immigrant minorities: A comparative view. *Anthropology & Education Quarterly, 18,* 262–275.

Giroux, H. A. 1983. *Theory of resistance in education: A pedagogy for the opposition.* South Hadley, MA: Bergin & Garvey.

Glazer, S. M., & Searfoss, L. W. 1988. *Reading diagnosis and instruction: A C-A-L-M approach.* Englewood Cliffs, NJ: Prentice-Hall.

González-Edfelt, N. 1993. An introduction to computer assisted Spanish language learning. In B. J. Merino, H. T. Trueba, & F. A. Samaniego (Eds.), *Language and culture in learning. Washington, DC: The Falmer Press.*

Goodenough, W. 1964. Cultural anthropology and linguistics. In D. Hymes (Ed.), *Language in culture and society.* New York: Harper & Row.

Goodenough, W. 1971. *Culture, language and society.* Reading, MA: Addison-Wesley.

Goodman, K. S. 1969. Analysis of reading miscues: Applied psycholinguistics. *Reading Research Quarterly, 5,* 9–30.

Goodman, K. S. 1986. *What's whole in whole language?* Portsmouth, NH: Heinemann.

Goodman, K. S., Goodman, Y., & Flores, B. 1979. *Reading in the bilingual classroom: Literacy and biliteracy.* Rosslyn, VA: National Clearinghouse for Bilingual Education.

Goodman, Y. M., & Burke, C. L. 1972. *Reading miscue inventory: Procedure for diagnosis and evaluation.* New York: Macmillan.

Goodman, Y. M., Watson, D. J., & Burke, C. L., 1987. *Reading miscue inventory: Alternative procedures.* New York: Richard C. Owen.

Granowsky, A. 1986. *El tigre.* Lexington, MA: Schoolhouse Press.

Graves, D. H. 1978. Handwriting is for writing. *Language Arts, 55,* 352–363.

Graves, D. H. 1983. *Writing: Teachers and children at work.* Portsmouth, NH: Heinemann.

Greaney, V. 1986. Parental influences on reading. *The Reading Teacher, 39,* 813–818.

Grimm, 1980. *Caperucita Roja.* Barcelona: Editorial Lumen.

Grosjean, F. 1982. *Life with Two Languages: An Introduction to Bilingualism.* Cambridge, MA: Harvard University Press.

Gumperz, J. & Hernández-Chávez, E. 1975. Cognitive aspects of bilingual communication. In E. Hernández-Chávez, et al. (Eds.), *El lenguaje de los Chicanos.* Arlington, VA: Center for Applied Linguistics.

Guthrie, G. P., & Hall, W. S. 1981. Introduction. In H. T. Trueba, G. P. Guthrie, & K. H. Au (Eds.), *Culture and the bilingual classroom: Studies in classroom ethnography.* Rowley, MA: Newbury House.

Guthrie, J. T., Van Meter, P., & Mitchell, A. 1994. Performance assessments in reading and language arts. *The Reading Teacher, 48*(3), 266–271.

Hakuta, K. 1986. *Mirror of language: The debate on bilingualism.* New York: Basic Books.

Halliday, M. A. K. 1973. *Explorations in the functions of language.* London: Edward Arnold.

Halliday, M. A. K. 1988. Three aspects of children's language development: Learning language, learning through language, and learning about language. In C. Pinnell & M. M. Haussler (Eds.), *Impact of language research on curriculum*. Newark, DE: International Reading Association.

Halliday, M. A. K., & Hasan, R. 1985. *Language, context and text: Aspects of language in social-semiotic perspective*. Victoria, Australia: Deakin University.

Hamers, J. F., & Blanc, M. 1982. Towards a social-psychology model of bilingual development. *Journal of Language and Social Psychology, 1*, 29–49.

Haney, W. 1991. We must take care: Fitting assessments to functions. In V. Perone (Ed.), *Expanding student assessment* (pp. 142–163). Alexandria, VA: Association for Supervision and Curriculum Development.

Hansen, J. 1987. *When writers read*. Portsmouth, NH: Heinemann.

Harman, S. 1992. Snow White and the seven warnings: Threats to authentic evaluation. *The Reading Teacher, 46*(3) 250–252.

Harman, S., & Edelsky, C. 1989. The risks of whole language literacy: Alienation and connection. *Language Arts, 66*(4), 392–405.

Harris, V. J. 1992. *Teaching multicultural literature*. Norwood, MA: Christopher-Gordon.

Harste, J. C., Woodward, V., & Burke, C. L. 1984. *Language stories and literacy lessons*. Portsmouth, NH: Heinemann.

Heald-Taylor, B. G. 1984. Scribble in first grade writing. *The Reading Teacher, 38*, 4–8.

Heath, S. B. 1982. Protean shapes in literacy events: Ever-shifting oral and literate traditions. In C. Tannen (Ed.), *Spoken and written language: Exploring orality and literacy*. Norwood, NJ: Ablex.

Heath, S. B. 1983. *Ways with words: Language, life, and work in communities and classrooms*. Cambridge: Cambridge University Press.

Heath, S. B. 1986. Sociocultural contexts of language development. In Office of Bilingual Bicultural Education (Eds.), *Beyond language: Social and cultural factors in schooling language minority students*. Los Angeles: Evaluation, Dissemination, and Assessment Center.

Hedegaard, M. 1988. Teaching and the development of school children's theoretical relation to the world. *Activity Theory, 1*, 36–42.

Henk, W. A. 1981. Effects of modified deletion strategies and scoring procedures on cloze test performance. *Journal of Reading Behavior, 13*, 347–357.

Hennings, D. G. 1984. A writing approach to reading comprehension-schema theory in action. In J. M. Jensen (Ed.), *Composing and Comprehending*. Urbana, IL: ERIC Clearinghouse on Reading and Communication Skills.

Hiebert, F. H. (Ed.). 1991. *Literacy for a diverse society: Perspectives, practices, and policies*. New York: Teachers College Press.

Hirsch, E. D. 1986. *Cultural Literacy*. Boston: Houghton Mifflin.

Hornberger, N. H. 1989. Continua of biliteracy. *Review of Educational Research, 59*(3), 271–296.

Hornberger, N. H. 1990. Creating successful learning contexts for bilingual literacy. *Teachers College Record, 92*(2), 212–229.

Hornberger, N. H. 1992. Biliteracy contexts, continua, and contrasts: Policy and curriculum for Cambodian and Puerto Rican students in Philadelphia. *Education and Urban Society, 24*, 196–211.

Hudelson, S. 1981. An investigation of the oral reading behaviors of native Spanish speakers reading in Spanish. In S. Hudelson (Ed.), *Linguistics and literacy: Learning to read in different languages*. Washington, DC: Center for Applied Linguistics.

Hudelson, S. 1987. The role of native language literacy in the education of language minority children. *Language Arts, 64*(8), 221–247.

Hudelson, S. 1989. A tale of two children: Individual differences in ESL children's writing. In D. M. Johnson & D. H. Roen (Eds), *Richness in writing: Empowering ESL students.* White Plains, NY: Longman.

Hudelson-Lopez, S. J. 1975. The use of context by native Spanish-speaking Mexican-American children when they read in Spanish. Ph.D. diss. University of Texas, Austin.

Huerta, A. 1977. The acquisition of bilingualism: A code switching approach. *Working Papers in Sociolinguistics, 39,* Austin, TX: Southwest Education Development Lab.

Huerta-Macías, A. 1983. Childhood Bilingualism: To switch or not to switch? In T. H. Escobedo (Ed.), *Early childhood bilingual education: A Hispanic perspective.* New York: Teachers College Press.

Hymes, D. H. 1972a. Models of the interactions of language and social life. In J. J. Gumperz & D. H. Hymes (Eds.), *Directions in sociolinguistics: The ethnography of communication.* New York: Holt, Rinehart and Winston.

Hymes, D. H. 1972b. Speech and language: On the origins and foundations of inequality among speakers. In J. J. Gumperz & D. H. Hymes (Eds.), *Directions in sociolinguistics: The ethnography of communication.* New York: Holt, Rinehart and Winston.

International Reading Association & National Council of Teachers of English. 1994. *Standards for the assessment of reading and writing.* Newark, DE: International Reading Association.

Jacobson, R. 1982. The role of the vernacular in transitional bilingual education. In B. Hartford, A. Valdman, & C. R. Foster (Eds.), *Issues in international bilingual education: The role of the vernacular.* New York: Plenum.

Jacobson, R. 1990. Allocating two languages as a key feature of a bilingual methodology. In R. Jacobson & C. Faltis (Eds.), *Language distribution issues in bilingual schooling.* Clevedon, PA: Multilingual Matters.

Janosch, 1984. *Historias de conejos.* Madrid: Alfaguara.

Jiadog, Z. 1983. *Una corona para el hermano elefante.* Beijing, China: Editorial Zhaohua.

Jiménez, R. T. 1994. Understanding and promoting the reading comprehension of bilingual students. *Bilingual Research Journal, 18*(1&2), 99–120.

Jiménez, R. T., García, G. E., & Pearson, R. D. 1995. Three children, two languages, and strategic reading: Case studies in bilingual/monolingual reading. *American Educational Research Journal, 32*(1), 67–97.

Johnson, D. D., & Pearson, P. D. 1978. *Teaching reading vocabulary.* New York: Holt, Rinehart and Winston.

Kagan, S. 1985. *Cooperative learning resources for teachers.* Riverside: University of California, Riverside, Printing and Repro-graphics.

Kagan, S. 1986. Cooperative learning and sociocultural factors in schooling. In *Beyond language: Social and cultural factors in schooling language minority students.* Los Angeles: California State University, Evaluation, Dissemination and Assessment Center.

Kaisen, J. 1987. SSR/booktime: Kindergarten and 1st grade sustained reading. *The Reading Teacher, 40,* 532–536.

Karmiloff-Smith, A. 1979. *A functional approach to child language.* Cambridge, Eng.: Cambridge University Press.

Kitagawa, M. M. 1989. Letting ourselves be taught. In D. M. Johnson & D. H. Roen (Eds.), *Richness in writing: Empowering ESL students.* White Plains, NY: Longman.

Kjolseth, R. 1973. Bilingual education programs in the United States: For assimilation or pluralism? In P. R. Turner (Ed.), *Bilingualism in the Southwest.* Tucson: University of Arizona Press.

Krashen, S. 1982. *Principles and practice in second language acquisition.* Oxford; New York: Pergamon.

Krashen, S. 1985a. *The input hypothesis: Issues and implications*. White Plains, NY: Longman.

Krashen, S. 1985b. *Inquiries and insights: Essays on second language teaching, bilingual education and literacy*. Hayward, CA: Alemany Press.

Krashen, S., & Biber, D. 1988. *On course: Bilingual education's success in California*. Sacramento: California Association for Bilingual Education.

Ladson-Billings, G. 1994. *The dreamkeepers: Successful teachers of African American children*. San Francisco: Jossey-Bass Publishers.

Lambert, W. E., & Taylor, D. M. 1987. Language minorities in the United States: Conflicts around assimilation and proposed modes of accommodation. In W. A. Van Horne & T. V. Tonnesen (Eds.), *Ethnicity and language*. Milwaukee: University of Wisconsin System Institute on Race and Ethnicity.

Lampert, M. 1988. Connecting mathematical teaching and learning. In E. Fennema, T. P. Carpenter, & S. J. Lamon (Eds.), *Integrating research on teaching and learning mathematics: Papers from the first Wisconsin symposium for research on teaching and learning mathematics*. Madison: University of Wisconsin, Wisconsin Center for Education Research.

Langer, J. A., Bartolome, L., Vasquez, O., & Lucas, T. 1990. Meaning construction in school literacy tasks: A study of bilingual students. *American Educational Research Journal*, *27*(3), 427–471.

Lansdown, B., Blackwood, P. E., & Brandwein, P. F. 1971. *Teaching elementary science through investigation and colloquium*. New York: Harcourt Brace Jovanovich.

Lave, J., & Wenger, E. 1991. *Situated learning: Legitimate peripheral participation*. Cambridge, England: Cambridge University Press.

Legaretta, D. 1979. The effects of program models on language acquisition by Spanish speaking children. *TESOL Quarterly 13*, 521–576.

Liberman, A. M., Cooper, F. S., Shankweiler, D. P., & Studdert-Kennedy, M. 1967. Perception of the speech code. *Psychological Review*, *74*, 431–461.

Lindholm, K. J. 1992. Two-way bilingual/immersion education: Theory, conceptual issues, and pedagogical implications. In R. V. Padilla & A. H. Benavides (Eds.), *Critical Perspectives on Bilingual Education Research*. Tempe, AZ: Bilingual Press/Editorial Bilingüe.

Lindholm, K., & Padilla, A. 1978. Child bilingualism: Report on language mixing, switching and translations. *Linguistics*, *211*, 12–44.

Linn, R. L. 1994. Performance assessment: Policy promises and technical measurement standards. *Educational Researcher. 23*(9), 4–14.

Long, M., & Porter, P. 1984. Group work, interlanguage talk and classroom second language acquisition. Paper presented at TESOL, Houston, TX.

Lundsteen, S. W. 1976. *Children can learn to communicate: Language arts through creative problem-solving*. Englewood Cliffs, NJ: Prentice-Hall.

Mace-Matluck, B. J. 1982. *Literacy instruction in bilingual settings: A synthesis of current research*. Los Alamitos, CA: National Center for Bilingual Research.

Mackey, W. F., & Orstein, J. 1977. *The bilingual education movement: Essays on progress*. El Paso: Texas Western Press.

Matute-Bianchi, M. E. 1980. What is bicultural about bilingual/bicultural education? *The Urban Review*, *12*, 91–108.

McCollum, P. 1991. Cross-cultural perspectives on classroom discourse and literacy. In E. H. Hiebert (Ed.), *Literacy for a diverse society: Perspectives, practices, and policies*. New York: Teachers College Press.

McDermott, R. P. 1977. The ethnography of speaking and reading. In R. W. Shuy (Ed.), *Linguistic theory: What can it say about reading*. Newark, DE: International Reading Association.

McDermott, R. P., & Gospodinoff, K. 1981. Social contexts for ethnic borders and school failure. In H. T. Trueba, G. P. Guthrie, & K. H. Au (Eds.), *Culture and the bilingual classroom: Studies in classroom ethnography*. Rowley, MA: Newbury House.

McDermott, R. P., & Roth, D. R. 1979. The social organization of behavior: Interactional approaches. *Annual Reviews of Anthropology, 7*, 321–345.

McGroarty, M. 1989. The benefits of cooperative learning arrangements in second language instruction. *National Association for Bilingual Education Journal, 13*(2), 127–143.

McLaren, P. 1989. *Life in schools*. White Plains, NY: Longman.

Medina, M., & Garza, J. de la. 1989. Initial language proficiency and bilingual reading achievement in a transitional bilingual educational program. *National Association for Bilingual Education Journal, 13*(2), 113–125.

Mehan, H. 1979. *Learning lessons*. Cambridge, MA: Harvard University Press.

Menchu, R. 1985. *I, Rigoberta Menchu: An Indian woman in Guatemala,* London: Vers.

Milk, R. 1980. Variation in language use patterns across different group settings in two bilingual second grade classrooms. Ph.D. diss., Stanford University, Stanford, CA.

Milk, R. 1981. The issue of language separation in bilingual methodology. In E. Garcia & B. Flores (Eds.), *Language and literacy research in bilingual education*. Tempe: Arizona State University Press.

Milk, R. 1993. Bilingual education and English as a second language: The elementary school. In M. B. Arias & U. Casanova (Eds.), *Bilingual education: Politics, practice, and research*. Chicago: University of Chicago Press.

Mohatt, G., & Erickson, F. 1981. Cultural differences in teaching styles in an Odawa school: A sociolinguistic approach. In H. Trueba, U. Guthrie, & K. Au (Eds.), *Culture and the bilingual classroom: Studies in classroom ethnography*. Rowley, MA: Newbury House.

Moll, L. C. 1989. Teaching second language students: A Vygotskian perspective. In D. M. Johnson & D. H. Roen (Eds.), *Richness in writing: Empowering ESL students*. White Plains, NY: Longman.

Moll, L. C., & Díaz, S. 1985. Ethnographic pedagogy: Promoting effective bilingual instruction. In E. E. García & R. V. Padilla (Eds.), *Advances in bilingual education research*. Tucson: University of Arizona Press.

Moll, L. C., & Díaz, S. 1987. Change as the goal of educational research. *Anthropology & Education Quarterly, 18*, 300–311.

Moll, L., Díaz, S., Estrada, E., & Lopes, L. M. 1992. Making contexts: The social construction of lessons in two languages. In S. Arvizu & M. Saravia-Shore (Eds.), *Cross-cultural and communicative competencies*. New York: Garland Publishing.

Moll, L. C., & González, N. 1994. Lessons from research with language minority children. *Journal of Reading Behavior, 26*(4), 439–456.

Moore, D. W. 1986. A case for naturalistic assessment of reading comprehension. In E. K. Dishner, T. W. Bean, J. E. Readence, & D. W. Moore (Eds.), *Reading in the content areas: Improving classroom instruction* (2nd ed.). Dubuque, IA: Kendall/Hunt.

Moore, D. W., & Readence, J. E. 1986. Approaches to content area reading instruction. In E. K. Dishner, T. W. Bean, J. E. Readence, & D. W. Moore (Eds.), *Reading in the content areas: Improving classroom instruction* (2nd ed.). Dubuque, IA: Kendall/Hunt.

Morrison, R. 1987. Elementary snapshots. *Language Arts, 66*(3), 238–245.

Morrissey, M. 1989. When "shut up" is a sign of growth. In K. S. Goodman, Y. M. Goodman, & W. J. Hood (Eds.), *The whole language evaluation book*. Portsmouth, NH: Heinemann.

Nathenson-Mejía, S. 1989. Writing in a second language: Negotiating meaning through invented spelling. *Language Arts, 66*(5), 516–526.

Newman, D. 1994. Sciencing for young children. *Young Children, 27*(4), 15–29.

Newmann, F. M. & Wehlage, G. G. 1993. Five standards of authentic instruction. *Educational Leadership, 50*, 8–12.

Nieto, S. 1992. *Affirming diversity: The sociopolitical context of multicultural education.* White Plains, NY: Longman.

Nieto, S. 1994. What are our children capable of knowing? *The Educational Forum, 58,* 434–440.

Office of Educational Research. 1986. *What works.* Washington, DC: U.S. Department of Education.

O'Dell, S. 1964. *La isla de los delfines azules.* Barcelona: Noguera.

Ogbu, J. 1974. *The next generation: An ethnography of education in an urban neighborhood.* New York: Academic Press.

Ogbu, J. U. 1987a. Variability in minority responses to schooling: Nonimmigrants vs. immigrants. In G. Spindler & L. Spindler (Eds.), *Interpretive ethnography of education: At home and abroad.* Hillsdale, NJ: Lawrence Erlbaum.

Ogbu, J. U. 1987b. Variability in minority school performance: A problem in search of an explanation. *Anthropology & Education Quarterly, 18,* 312–334.

Ogbu, J. U., & Matute-Bianchi, M. E. 1986. Understanding sociocultural factors: Knowledge, identity, and school adjustment. In Office of Bilingual Bicultural Education (Eds.), *Beyond language: Social & cultural factors in schooling language minority students.* Los Angeles: California State University, Evaluation, Dissemination, and Assessment Center.

Olmedo-Williams, I. 1983. Spanish-English bilingual children as peer teachers. In L. Elías-Olivares (Ed.), *Spanish in the U.S. setting.* Rosslyn, VA: InterAmerica Research Associates.

Osorio, M. 1985. *Mariposa dorada.* Morristown, NJ: Silver Burdett.

Ovando, C. J., & Collier, V. P. 1985. *Bilingual and ESL classrooms: Teaching in multicultural contexts.* New York: McGraw-Hill.

Padilla, A. M., & Liebman, E. 1975. Language acquisition in the bilingual child. *The Bilingual Review/La Revista Bilingüe, 2,* 34–55.

Paz Impuana, 1988. *El conejo y el mapurite.* Caracas: Ekaré-Banco del Libro.

Pearson, P. D., & Valencia, S. 1989. Assessment, accountability, and professional prerogative. In J. Readence & R. S. Baldwin (Eds.), *Research in literacy: Merging perspectives.* Thirty-sixth yearbook of the National Reading Conference (pp. 3–16). Chicago: National Reading Conference.

Pedraza, P. n.d. Ethnographic observations of language use in *El Barrio.* Unpublished manuscript.

Peña, S. C., & Verner, Z. 1981. Developing reading skills in Spanish: Research, materials and practice. *Hispania, 64,* 425–432.

Peñalosa, F. 1981. *Introduction to the sociology of language.* Rowley, MA: Newbury House.

Pérez, B. 1987. Instructional technology and the education of Hispanics. *Intercultural Development Research Association Newsletter.* San Antonio, TX: Intercultural Development Research Association.

Pérez, B. 1993. The bilingual teacher (Spanish/English) and literacy instruction. *Teacher Education Quarterly, 20*(3), 43–53.

Pérez, B. 1994a. Spanish literacy development: A descriptive study of four bilingual whole language classrooms. *Journal of Reading Behavior, 26*(1), 75–94.

Pérez, B. 1994b. Biliteracy development in Latino communities. In R. Rodríguez, N. J. Ramos, & J. A. Ruiz-Escalante (Eds.), *Compendium of readings in bilingual education: Issues and Practices* (pp. 119–123). San Antonio, TX: Texas Association for Bilingual Education.

Peyton, J. K., & Mackinson-Smyth, J. 1989. Writing and talking about writing: Computer networking with elementary students. In D. M. Johnson & D. H. Roen (Eds.), *Richness in writing: Empowering ESL students.* New York: Longman.

Pfaff, C. 1979. Constraints on language mixing. *Language, 55,* 291–328.

Pham, L. 1994. Infant dual language acquisition revisited. *The Journal of Educational Issues of Language Minority Students, 14,* 185–210.

Philips, S. 1972. Participant structures and communicative competence: Warm Springs Indian children in community and classroom. In C. B. Cazden, V. P. John, & D. Hymes, (Eds.), *Functions of language in the classroom*. New York: Teachers College Press.

Philips, S. 1982. *The invisible culture: Communication in classroom and community on the Warm Springs Reservation*. White Plains, NY: Longman.

Piaget, J. 1957. *Logic and psychology*. New York: Basic Books. [Trans. by Marjorie Gabi.] New York: Humanities Press.

Piaget, J. 1959. *The language and thought of the child*. London: Routledge & Kegan Paul.

Pica, T., & Doughty, C. 1985. Input and interaction in the communicative language classroom: A comparison of teacher-fronted and group activities. In S. Gass & C. Madden (Eds.), *Input in second language acquisition*. Rowley, MA: Newbury House.

Piper, K. 1983. Word processing in the classroom: Using microcomputer-delivered sentence combining exercises with elementary students. Paper presented at National Educational Computing Conference, Baltimore, MD.

Poplack, S. 1979. *Sometimes I'll start a sentence in Spanish Y TERMINO EN ESPAÑOL: Toward a typology of code-switching*. Center for Puerto Rican Studies Working Papers, no. 4. New York: Center for Puerto Rican Studies, City University of New York.

Porter, P. 1986. How learners talk to each other: Input and interaction in task-centered discussions. In R. Day (Ed.), *Talking to learn: Conversation in second language acquisition*. Rowley, MA: Newbury House.

Pratt, M. 1977. *Toward a speech act theory of literary discourse*. Bloomington: Indiana University Press.

Purcell-Gates, V. 1995. *Other people's words: The cycle of low literacy*. Cambridge, MA: Harvard University Press.

Ramírez, A. G. 1985. *Bilingualism through schooling: Cross-cultural education for minority and majority students*. Albany: State University of New York Press.

Ramírez, J. D. 1991. *Final report: Longitudinal study of structured English immersion strategy, early-exit and late-exit transitional bilingual education programs for language minority children*. Washington, DC: Office of Bilingual Education.

Ramírez, J. D. 1992. Executive Summary. *Bilingual Research Journal*, *16*(1&2), 1–62.

Rankin, E. F. 1970. How flexibly do we read? *Journal of Reading Behavior*, *3*, 34–38.

Rayner, K., & Pollatsek, A. 1989. *The psychology of reading*. Englewood Cliffs, NJ: Prentice-Hall.

Readence, J. E., Bean, T. W., & Baldwin, R. S. 1985. *Content area reading: An integrated approach* (2nd ed.). Dubuque, IA: Kendall Hunt.

Reyes, M. de la L. 1992. Challenging venerable assumptions: Literacy for linguistically diverse students. *Harvard Educational Review*, *62*, 472–446.

Reyes, M. de la L., Laliberty, E. A., & Orbanosky, J. M. 1993. Emerging biliteracy and cross-cultural sensitivity in a language arts classroom. *Language Arts*, *70*(8), 659–668.

Richard-Amato, P. A. (Ed.), 1988. *Making it happen: Interaction in the second language classroom*. White Plains, NY: Longman.

Rigg, P. 1986. Reading in ESL: Learning from kids. In P. Rigg & D. S. Enright (Eds.), *Children and ESL: Integrating perspectives*. Washington, DC: Teachers of English to Speakers of Other Languages.

Rivero Oramas, R. 1981. *La piedra del Zamuro: Un cuento del tío Nicolás*. Caracas: Ekaré.

Robles Boza, E. 1984. *Chispa de luz*. Mexico City: Trillas.

Rockwell, E. 1982. Los usos escolares de la lengua escrita. In E. Ferreiro & M. Gómez Palacio (Eds.), *Nuevas perspectivas sobre los procesos de lectura y escritura*. México City: Siglo Veintiuno Editores.

Rodríguez, M. V. (in progress). Opportunities for literacy in an urban Dominican community. Ph.D. diss., Teachers College, Columbia University.

Rood, R. N. 1973. *Cómo y por qué de los insectos*. Barcelona: Editorial Molino.

Rosaldo, R. 1989. *Culture and Truth: The remaking of social analysis*. Boston: Beacon Press.

Rosenblatt, L. M. 1978. *The reader, the text, the poem.* Carbondale: Southern Illinois University Press.

Saint Expuéry, A. de. 1989. *El Principito.* New York: Harcourt Brace Jovanovich.

Salinger, T., & Chittenden, E. 1994. Analysis of an early literacy portfolio: Consequences for instruction. *Language Arts, 71*, 446–452.

Samuels, S. J., & Dahl, P. R. 1975. Establishing appropriate purpose for reading and its effect on flexibility of reading rate. *Journal of Educational Psychology, 67*, 38–43.

Saville, M. R., & Troike, R. C. 1971. *A handbook of bilingual education.* Washington, DC: Teachers of English to Speakers of Other Languages.

Sayers, D. 1989. Bilingual sister classes in computer writing networks. In D. M. Johnson & D. H. Roen (Eds.), *Richness in writing: Empowering ESL students.* White Plains, NY: Longman.

Scardamalia, M., Bereiter, C., & Lamon, M. 1994. CSILE: Trying to bring students into world 3. In K. McGilley (Ed.), *Classroom lessons: Integrating cognitive theory and classroom practice* (pp. 201–228). Cambridge, MA: MIT Press.

Schwartz, J. I. 1988. *Encouraging early literacy: An integrated approach to reading and writing in N–3.* Portsmouth, NH: Heinemann.

Scieszke, 1991. *La verdadera historia de los tres cerditos.* New York: Viking Press.

Secada, W. G., & Carey, D. A. 1990. Teaching mathematics with understanding to limited English proficient students. Urban Diversity Series No. 101. *ERIC Clearinghouse on Urban Education.* New York: Institute on Urban and Minority Education, Teachers College, Columbia University.

Serrano de Moreno, S. 1989. El docente y la evaluación de la lecto-escritura. *Lectura y Vida, 10*(3), 16–19.

Seymour, P. 1986. *Explorando el sistema solar: Un libro de ciencia-acción.* Buenos Aires: Editorial Atlántica.

Shanahan, T., Mulhern, M., & Rodriguez-Brown, F. 1995. Project Flame: Lessons learned from a family literacy program for linguistic minority families. *The Reading Teacher, 48*(7), 586–593.

Silva, A. D. 1979. Oral reading behavior of Spanish-speaking children taught by a meaning-based program. Ph. D. diss., University of Texas, Austin.

Silva, A. D. 1983. The Spanish reading process of Spanish-speaking Mexican-American children. In T. Escobedo (Ed.), *Early childhood bilingual education: A Hispanic perspective.* New York: Teachers College.

Simon, J. 1984. Teaching writing on a word processor: Relationships of self-management and locus of control. Ph.D. diss., Boston University, Boston, MA.

Simonson, R., & Walker, S. 1988. *Multi-cultural literacy: Opening the American mind.* Saint Paul, MN: Graywolf Press.

Simpson, M. L. 1987. Alternative formats for evaluating content area vocabulary understanding. *Journal of Reading, 31*, 20–27.

Siu-Runyan, Y. 1991. Holistic assessment in intermediate classes: Techniques for informing our teaching. In B. Harp (Ed.), *Assessment and evaluation in whole language programs* (pp. 109–136). Norwood, MA: Christopher-Gordon.

Slavin, R. 1983. When does cooperative learning increase student achievement? *Psychological Bulletin, 94*(3), 429–445.

Slavin, R. E. 1989. Comprehensive cooperative learning models for heterogeneous classrooms. *Pointer, 33*, 12–19.

Smith, C. B. 1989. Shared learning promotes critical reading. *The Reading Teacher, 43*(1), 76–77.

Smith, F. 1986. *Understanding reading*. Hillsdale, NJ: Lawrence Erlbaum.

Stigler, J. W. 1990. *Mathematical knowledge of Japanese, Chinese, and American elementary school children*. Reston, VA: National Council of Teachers of Mathematics.

Stoodt, B., & Balboa, E. 1979. Integrating study skills instruction with content. *Reading World, 18*, 247–252.

Street, B. V. 1984. *Literacy in theory and practice*. Cambridge: Cambridge University Press.

Suárez-Orozco, M. M. 1987. Towards a psychosocial understanding of Hispanic adaptation to American schooling. In H. T. Trueba (Ed.), *Success or failure?: Learning and the language minority student*. Rowley, MA: Newbury House.

Suárez-Orozco, M. M. 1989. *Central American refugees and U.S. high schools: A psychosocial study of motivation and achievement*. Stanford, CA: Stanford University Press.

Sund, R. B., Adams, D. K., Hackett, J. K., & Moyer, R. H. 1987. *Enfasis en la ciencia*. Columbus, OH: Merrill.

Swain, M., & Wesche, M. 1975. Linguistic interaction: Case study of a bilingual child. *Language Science, 37*, 17–22.

Teale, W. H. 1982. Toward a theory of how children learn to read and write naturally. *Language Arts, 59*, 555–570.

Teale, W. H., & Sulzby, E. 1986. Introduction: Emergent literacy as a perspective for examining how young children become writers and readers. In W. H. Teale & E. Sulzby (Eds.), *Emergent literacy*. Norwood, NJ: Ablex.

Teberosky, A. 1982. Construcción de escritura a través de la interacción grupal. In E. Ferreiro & M. Gómez Palacio (Eds.), *Nuevas perspectivas sobre los procesos de lectura y escritura*. México City: Siglo Veintiuno Editores.

Teberosky, A. 1990. Nuevas investigaciones sobre la adquisición de la lengua escrita. *Lectura y Vida, 11*(2), 23–27.

Tharp, R., & Gallimore, R. 1988. *Rousing minds to life: Teaching learning and schooling in social context*. New York: Cambridge University Press.

Thonis, E. W. 1976. *Literacy for America's Spanish-speaking children*. Newark, DE: International Reading Association.

Tiedt, I. M., et al. 1989. *Reading/thinking/writing: A holistic language and literacy program for the K–8 classroom*. Boston: Allyn & Bacon.

Tolchinsky Landsmann, L. & Levin, I. 1987. Writing in four to six year olds: Representation of semantic and phonetic similarities and differences. *Journal of Child Language, 14*, 127–144.

Torres-Guzmán, M. E. 1989. *El Puente/Teachers College research collaborative: Final report*. Washington, DC: Hispanic Policy Development Project.

Torres-Guzmán, M. E. 1990. *Voy a leer escribiendo* in the context of bilingual/bicultural education. *Computers in the Schools, 7*, 145–171.

Torres-Guzmán, M. E. 1992. Stories of hope in the midst of despair: Culturally responsive education for Latino students in an alternative high school in New York city. In M. Saravia-Shore and S. F. Arvizu (Eds.), *Cross-cultural literacy: Ethnographies of communication in multiethnic classrooms*. New York: Garland Publishing.

Torres-Guzmán, M. E. 1994. Language minorities: Moving from the periphery to the center. *The Educational Forum, 58*, 409–420.

Torres Quintero, T. 1973. *Guía del método onomatopéyico*. México City: Editorial Patria.

UNESCO. 1953. The use of vernacular languages in education. In J. A. Fishman (Ed.) (1968), *Readings in the sociology of language* (pp. 688–719). The Hague: Mouton & Co. N.V.

Urzúa, C. 1980. A language learning environment for all children. *Language Arts, 57*(1), 38–44.

Valadez, C. M. 1981. Identity, power and writing skills: The case of the Hispanic bilingual student. In M. F. Whiteman (Ed.), *Writing: The nature, development, and teaching of written communication*. Hillsdale, NJ: Lawrence Erlbaum.

Valdés-Fallis, G. 1976a. Code-switching in bilingual Chicano poetry. *Hispania, 59,* 869–886.

Valdés-Fallis, G. 1976b. Social interaction and code-switching: A case study of Spanish-English alternation. In G. D. Keller, R. Teschner, & S. Viera (Eds.), *Bilingualism in the bicentenial and beyond*. Jamaica, NY: Bilingual Press.

Valdés-Fallis, G. 1978. *Code-switching and the classroom teacher*. Arlington, VA: Center for Applied Linguistics.

Valdez-Pierce, L. 1987. Cooperative learning: Integrating language and content-area instruction, based on finding out descubrimiento (FO/D). *Teacher Resource Guide Series*. Washington, DC: National Clearinghouse for Bilingual Education.

Valeri, M. E., & Ruis, M. *El león y el ratón*. Barcelona: La Galera.

Vélez-Ibáñez, C. G. 1988. Networks of exchange among Mexicans in the U.S. and México: Local level mediating responses to national and international transformations. *Urban Anthropology and Studies of Cultural Systems and World Economic Development, 17,* 27–52.

Vogt, L. A., Jordan, C., & Tharp, R. G. 1987. Explaining school failure, producing school success: Two cases. *Anthropology & Education Quarterly, 18,* 276–286.

Vygotsky, L. S. 1978. *Mind in society*. Cambridge, MA: Harvard University Press.

Vygotsky, L. S. 1986. *Thought and language*. (Rev. ed.) A. Kozulin (Ed.). Cambridge, MA: MIT Press.

Vygotsky, L. S. 1988. Interaction between learning and development. In P. A. Richard-Amato (Ed.), *Making it happen: Interaction in the second language classroom*. White Plains, NY: Longman.

Webster, V. R. 1986. *Experimentos científicos*. Chicago: Children's Press.

Weir, R. 1966. Some questions on the child's learning of phonology. In F. Smith & G. E. Miller (Eds.), *The genesis of language: A psycholinguistic approach*. Cambridge, MA: MIT Press.

Weiss, B. 1994. California's new English-language arts assessment. In S. W. Valencia, E. H. Hiebert, & P. P. Afflerbach (Eds.), *Authentic reading assessment: Practices and possibilities* (pp. 197–217). Newark, DE: International Reading Association.

Wolf, D. P. 1989. Portfolio assessment: Sampling student work. *Educational Leadership, 46,* 35–40.

Wolf, R. E. 1978. Using subject-matter areas to raise reading achievement scores. *Reading Improvement, 15,* 242–245.

Wong-Fillmore, L. 1985. When does teacher talk work as input? In S. Gass & C. Madden (Eds.), *Input in second language acquisition*. Rowley, MA: Newbury House.

Wong-Fillmore, L. 1986. Research currents: Equity or excellence? *Language Arts, 63,* 474–481.

Wong-Fillmore, L., & Valadez, C. 1985. Teaching bilingual learners. In M. C. Wittrock (Ed.), *Handbook of research on teaching* (3rd ed.). New York: Macmillan.

Zentella, A. C. 1984. *Ta' bien*, You could answer me *en cualquier idioma*: Puerto Rican codeswitching in bilingual classrooms. In Duran, R. P. (Ed.), *Latino language and communicative behavior*, second printing (pp. 109–131). Norwood, NJ: Ablex.

Index

Academic performance
    classroom culture and, 10–13
    native language literacy instruction and, 45
    variations in, 9, 10
Accommodation, as component of psychological
    adaptation, 27
Ada, A. F., 104, 112, 191
Alphabetic principle
    explanation of, 35, 43
    writing assessment of students using, 173, 174
Alphabet reading method, 49–50
Anchored instruction, 126, 128
Anderson, A. B., 54–55
Anderson, T., 32
Assessment
    of classroom environment, 188
    naturalistic, 178–179
    by observation, 37, 178–181
    overview of, 160–161
    portfolio, 163–167
    purpose of, 161–163
    of reading, 167–173
    of writing, 173–178
Assimilation, 27
Assimilationist model, 46
Attendance charts, 68, 69
Au, K. H., 14–16, 89
Auditory learning, 187
Authentic literacy events, 66–67
Author studies, 112

Barrera, R. B., 167, 168
Basal reading programs, 88–89
Bellenger, L., 49
Belpre, P., 112
Berglund, R. L., 180
Biber, D., 45
Bilingual children
    cognitive functioning in, 29–30
    language development in home environment
        of, 22–26
    studies in reading instruction for, 15
Bilingual communication strategies, 172

Bilingual education
    characteristics of, 45–46
    literacy goals of, 46
    types of programs used in, 46
Biliteracy. *See also* Literacy
    classroom as context for, 55–59
    explanation of, 54
    integrated approach to, 67
    scaffolding and, 172
Bloom, A., 6
Bloome, D., 55
Books
    predictable, 85, 86, 92
    self- and class-composed, 80–83
    trade, 84–86
Bruner, J. S., 26
Burke, C. L., 57, 167

Carey, D. A., 130
Caribbean Spanish speakers, 44
Carrasco, R. L., 161
Castelike minorities, 10
Cause-effect text structure, 138–139
Chomsky, N., 45
Cisneros, S., 112
Class-composed books, 80–83
Classroom
    as context for biliteracy, 54–59
    promotion of cultural diversity in, 9, 16
    routines used as lessons in, 68–70
Classroom culture
    academic performance and, 10–13
    community resources used to transform,
        13–16
Classroom discourse
    assessment of, 173
    type of, 56
Classroom environment
    assessment of, 188
    multisensory, 186–188
    relationship between literacy and, 184–188
Cloze procedure, 169–170
Codes, awareness of, 24–26